"Ted DesMaisons brings decades of experience as a student, teacher and philosopher to bear in this book. He charts new territory in blending improv and mindfulness. There is a lightness to this approach, but **make no mistake: this book offers profound life advice.**"

> --Patricia Ryan Madson, author of *Improv Wisdom*

"**This is the stuff of transformation.** I found mindfulness and creativity heroism here and my work as a teacher, husband and father are more grounded for it. If you want a gentle path toward nurturing your soul, Ted DesMaisons understands how to bring both inspiration and calm to the human experience."

> --RG Richards, Theatre and Dance Chair, Philips Exeter Academy

"**What a valuable resource for any teacher or mindfulness practitioner!** Ted masterfully takes us to the enthralling and alluring place where mindfulness and improv meet. Along the way we learn a variety of lessons - including how to skillfully relate to failure, how to tap into the creativity of the present, and —maybe most importantly—how to have more fun in our life and practice!"

> --Doug Worthen, Director of Mindfulness Programs, Middlesex School

"Ted's **insight, humor, and humility** makes his application of improv principles both powerful and compelling. We're in the midst of an improvisation renaissance and *Playful Mindfulness* **brings the art form even further into everyday life.**"

> --Rebecca Stockley, Co-Founder BATS Improv, Applied Improvisation Practitioner

"When coaches, holistic practitioners and entrepreneurs want to attract millions of dollars' worth of clients, **quality connection matters more than anything else.** *Playful Mindfulness* helps you build an unmistakable presence that makes that kind of connection easy, spontaneous and, yes, playful. **Ted's work offers a breath of fresh air!**"

> --Sharla Jacobs, CEO and Co-Founder, Thrive Academy

"**A joyful journey indeed!** Inspired by his podcast with Lisa Rowland, Ted DesMaisons invites you to get passionately and positively present in your life. Like a good friend taking you on a pleasant walk, this book demonstrates the opportunities and advantages of curiosity and provides a simple, clear way to use both improvisation and mindfulness to **become more forgiving— with yourself and with others.**"

> --Dan O'Connor, Co-Founder and Producing Artistic Director, Impro Theatre, Los Angeles

"To call this exploration of mindfulness and improvisation—the value of each and their intersection—**nuanced and sophisticated** might make it sound dry or inaccessible. To call it **simple and actionable** might give the impression it is pedestrian. To point out that Ted has written with a **light and playful spirit** might miss the profound thoughtfulness with which he moves both fields forward and offers value for newcomers and experienced practitioners alike. But don't be misled: *Playful Mindfulness* does contain that much goodness. Are you interested in enriching your daily experience of life? If yes, this is **a must-have addition to your library.**"

> --Kat Koppett, President and Eponymous Founder of Koppett & Company, author of *Training to Imagine*

"After *Playful Mindfulness*, I'm **calmer, more confident and more content.** What negative people say has less impact on my self-esteem and happiness. I worry less—and dance more!"

> Joke van der Hurst, Stanford Continuing Studies student

"This book is **a treasure trove of practical, nuanced, and actionable insight**. Ted shows us how to learn and embody qualities like curiosity, courage, gratitude, and a growth mindset—and he's included a rich glossary of improv games and exercises. I highly recommend *Playful Mindfulness* for educators and facilitators and it's got such **great life skills for people of all ages!**"

> --Jessica Morey, Executive Director of Inward Bound Mindfulness Education

"*Playful Mindfulness* **allows me to be my true self**. I don't have to worry about what others think and can just be in the moment."

> --Ben Larson, Stanford Continuing Studies student

"If you're curious about improvisation and mindfulness, and if you're ready to romp through their many intersections, then pick up this book. **It's a deep dive into an insight-filled ocean. Immerse yourself and emerge enriched!**"

> --Paul Z Jackson, Co-founder and long-time president of the Applied Improvisation Network and author of *Easy, Impro Learning* and *58½ Ways To Improvise In Training*

"*Playful Mindfulness* has helped me become more confident and more aligned with who I am. **My perspective has changed** in so many ways: things are no longer black or white or grey. **The world is colorful!**"

> --Jennifer Liu, Stanford Continuing Studies student

"As a world expert in healing addiction for more than 30 years, I know the key to long-term recovery is **connecting to joy, a sense of peace with the world and an enduring sense of play.** Ted has nailed it. Even if he weren't my son, I'd be telling everyone about this resource."

> --Dr. Kathleen DesMaisons, PhD, author *Potatoes Not Prozac*

# PLAYFUL
# MINDFULNESS

*A joyful journey to everyday
confidence, calm, and connection*

Ted DesMaisons, MBA, MTh

For Dan-
May the magic
in each moment
unfold with ease!
Ted D.

Based on the "Monster Baby" podcast

ANIMA Learning
Daly City, CA 94015
www.animalearning.com

First Edition: March 2019

Printed in the United States of America

ISBN: 978-1-950373-01-7

Library of Congress Control Number: 2019901345

Cover design by Jelena Mirkovic, www.jelenamirkovic.com
Cover image by istock/damedeeso
Author photos by Lindsay Miller, Wildly Visible Photography

*To the spirit of curiosity and kindness*

*which animates all things*

This book will help you **discover the wide-ranging benefits** of combining

- **Mindfulness** (simply put, the art of staying present, curious, and kind) and
- Improvisation (making life up courageously as you go along).

Put the two traditions together and life becomes **a joyful journey,** one that naturally leads to greater **confidence, calm, and connection.**

Thanks for coming along!

# table of contents

prologue: *an orientation to the adventure* ........................ i

part one: *laying the groundwork* ............................... 1

   **1.**     a word about words .................................... 3

   **2.**     take a circus bow ..................................... 25

part two: *playing with paradox* .......................... 47

   **3.**     impulse or pause? ..................................... 49

   **4.**     you then me, me then you ...................... 67

   **5.**     want without need .................................. 83

part three: *a new mindset emerging* ................ 105

   **6.**     the power of positivity ......................... 107

   **7.**     chaos theory .......................................... 127

   **8.**     meta-tation .............................................. 137

   **9.**     ch-ch-ch-changes ................................... 153

   **10.**     got presence? ........................................ 167

part four: *four more qualities  (and one last paradox)* ... 185

   **11.**     adventure time! .................................... 187

   **12.**     isn't that curious? ................................ 203

   **13.**     attitude of gratitude ........................... 217

   **14.**     a cup of courage .................................. 231

   **15.**     it's not about you ................................ 245

epilogue: *wrapping up the journey* ................ 259

glossary of games ........................................... 263

    1-2-3 or Clap-Snap-Stomp ..................... 264

    Advance-Color-Emotion ......................... 266

Ball ............................................................... 268

Camera Game .............................................. 269

Clover.............................................................271

I Am A Tree .................................................. 273

I Am Playing 'I Am A Tree'...............................274

Line-at-a-Time Drawing (or Muse or Deity)......................275

Metamorphic Circle.......................................276

Positivity/Negativity Spectrum .............................278

Sound Ball.....................................................279

Three Things ................................................ 281

Three-Words-at-a-Time Poems .............................283

What Comes Next?...................................... 284

Word-at-a-Time Exercises .............................285

bibliography...................................................287

acknowledgments ......................................... 291

about the author..............................................297

# prologue
## an orientation to the adventure

Our little Improv Wisdom retreat group had formed a circle outside the yurt at Green Gulch Farm Zen Center, just north of San Francisco. The sun shone through the redwoods that towered above us, gently dappling the deck with patterns that danced in the wind. The morning fog had lifted just before lunch, but the air remained cool and crisp. Even before we started, the setting seemed a magical location to play the "Camera Game."

I stepped forward and got a volunteer to demonstrate the exercise. Armando would play my 'camera' and I would serve as 'photographer.' When Armando closed his eyes, I guided him slowly and gently by the shoulders, leading him into position to capture a 'snapshot' that I thought might delight him. A tilt of the head here, a bend at the waist there: everything aligned before I'd click the 'shutter' by lightly pinching his earlobe to indicate he should open his eyes and take in the image. Just a few quick moments—maybe two, maybe three seconds—and then I'd let go of his earlobe and his eyes would close. After giving a few more instructions to the group—*Take good care of your precious photographic equipment. Only speak if you're giving instructions for safety. Feel free to get creative with panoramas or other unusual framings*—I sent our participants off as pairs into the surrounding woods.

After each person had taken five "pictures" and played photographer for another five, the group returned to report on their experience. As I had hoped, everybody liked the game.[1]

"I appreciated how my photographer's steady hand on my shoulder kept me safe even though I felt vulnerable," reported one person.

"I loved the way each image came alive. I never really look at these details that way," offered another.

"The delight of surprise kept surprising me," added a third. "I can remember each image so vividly."

Rewarding as these comments were to hear, this exercise had generated these types of insight before so I took them in stride.

It was Armando who took us to a whole new level. "This exercise reminds me of God," he asserted.

*Wow*, I thought to myself. I hadn't considered this angle, but Armando continued. "It's like God is the photographer and we're the camera. God composes amazing things for us to see. Each morning when we wake up, God pinches our earlobe and we open our eyes. Then we get to see the whole day. At the end of the day, God lets go of our earlobe and we close our eyes. We choose whether or not we've enjoyed the 'photo' God showed us."

You may or may not consider yourself religious. You may or may not believe in God. But Armando's powerful image holds either way. Every day represents an opportunity, a gift given by whatever forces continue conspiring in our creation. Each moment offers a glimpse of opportunity, another chance for choosing openness and connection. Whatever the timeline, you're presented with all manner of "photographs": will you choose to see them, to *really* see

---

[1] For complete directions to the "Camera Game," please see the Glossary of Games at the back of the book.

them—and then to engage *with* them? What wonders become possible if you do?

This book is for you if you want to greet each day with a Camera Game sense of wonder, anticipation and engagement—if you want to play with each moment that arises. Maybe you want to approach and connect with people you're attracted to. Or speak up in a meeting when you have an insight that needs sharing. Maybe it's time to go on that adventure or take a step toward your dreams. Only you will discover the full range of possibilities.

Whether you're a leader or teacher, parent or partner, performer or wallflower, this book is designed to help you act with a buoyant boldness—and to simultaneously make space for others. If you struggle with anxiety or long for confidence, it offers practical steps for finding relief and building bravery. If you feel locked into a schedule or routine, it will open a new sense of possibility. If you place too much focus on yourself and your own needs, it will show you how to turn your attention to others around you. And if you're just about to step into a transition—leaving or starting a job, letting go of a relationship, making a move across country—this book will ease your stress and set you up for greater fulfillment, whatever comes next.

If you were the type who needed academic evidence for these claims, I could point to the growing raft of studies that show how the practice of mindfulness—staying present with curiosity and kindness—brings a host of benefits: reduced anxiety, depression, aggression, and reactivity. Increased clarity, calm, compassion, and courage. Higher test scores. Better relationships. The list goes on long enough that I might start to sound like a snake oil salesman. *Trust me. Mindfulness makes EVERYTHING better.* Thing is, it kind of actually does.

To emphasize the extra benefits of making that mindfulness *playful*, I could cite testimony from the thousands of companies, schools, teams, and individuals of all sorts who draw on improvisation's ability to refine attention, build confidence, ignite collaboration, improve storytelling, and boost charisma. Improvisation and play change lives from the inside out—and they do it more quickly than more muted approaches alone.

There's plenty of data. And we could reference it all. But I'd rather you dive in to investigate these worlds for yourself. Better to come to your own conclusions, to draw on your own experience.

So, consider this an invitation to adventure. To a new way of seeing and being. To a new you—or maybe more accurately, to a fuller, more expressive you. The nimble, creative, connected you that's been lying dormant beneath the surface. That raw, energetic, ready-to-meet-the-day you that's been chomping at the bit. Maybe this part feels young, unprepared, clumsy or even dangerous but you still sense its power. Perhaps you have developed well-entrenched habits or tensions that make such vitality seem a long way away. And maybe societal or familial forces around you have worked to keep this vibrant part tightly hemmed in. I'm here to show you how to find, feed, and befriend this side of you so it becomes a great ally. You deserve an eagerness for the opportunities that lie before you.

Whether you've received this book as a gift, you're reading it while standing in an old-school independent bookstore, browsing it online, swiping through it on an e-reader, or listening out loud, you've gotten it in your hands or in your ears somehow. Now you have an opportunity: to ask questions, experiment boldly, and reconnect with the joyful gift of being alive. Now you have a new roadmap—not to any destination in particular, but instead to wherever **you** are. This present moment. Here. Now.

In preparation to serve as your guide, I've been exploring the worlds of mindfulness and improvisation for over 30 years now. I first started practicing meditation as a teenager and soaked up learning from many spiritual traditions: Christianity (Catholic and Protestant), Native American and other Earth-centered traditions, Buddhism, Quakerism, Hinduism, poetry, astrology, and more. Continuing that long-time interest in meaning and mystery, I studied to be an interfaith minister, taught religious studies and philosophy at a New England boarding school and trained to become a formal mindfulness instructor with Jon Kabat-Zinn, Saki Santorelli, and a host of other brilliant teachers at the UMASS Center for Mindfulness and the UK-based Mindfulness in Schools Project.

Improvisation entered my life during my first year at Stanford University. On the invitation of a friend and co-worker, Scott Allen, I signed up for a dorm-based intro class and had a total blast. I immediately sought out the official drama department course with Patricia Ryan Madson—the woman who would become a great mentor and the author of *Improv Wisdom*—and ended up serving as her teaching assistant several times. When I returned to Stanford for graduate school four years later, I took more improv classes and joined the newly-formed Stanford Improvisors. After earning a second graduate degree, this time at Harvard Divinity School, I taught and performed whenever I could. Not until a two-week professional development trip to the Loose Moose Theater in Calgary, Alberta, though, did my love for the art form fan to a full flame again. Eventually, I moved across the country from New England to San Francisco so I could join the burgeoning improv scene there. I'm deeply grateful for all I've learned since I did so.

What I've discovered in the worlds of both mindfulness and improvisation has forever changed the way I live my life. The two disciplines show us how to get more engaged in whatever's actually happening, coming to full awareness with humble curiosity. Each asks us to cultivate the skill of quality presence—and to do so in different and complementary ways. Over the last few years, I've co-led retreats that combine the two realms. I've done presentations for corporate teams, doctor cohorts, senior citizens, and high school assemblies. I've performed with mindful improv troupes and improvised with meditators. With my colleague Lisa Rowland, I've co-hosted and produced the Monster Baby podcast from which this book is drawn.[2] Every chance I get to combine these traditions brings me great joy.

Why so much passion? Because I've seen the combination benefit countless others, too. They experience more freedom. More ease. More joy. More adventure. In short, more life and more YES.

That leads us to this book. You'll notice the "joyous journey" chooses a conversational style. Please though, don't be misled: an intentional structure lies behind and beneath that more casual tone. In each chapter, you'll get insights and practices drawn from mindfulness and improvisation. Most chapters include a game or exercise you can try out with friends and family who also want to laugh and grow. In addition, every chapter identifies a challenging tension or paradox to explore as part of your growing practice.

I'll do my best to keep the pace moving along...and there's a lot here to chew on. If you ever feel stressed by all the stretching and growing, feel free to take a breath or slow down. Each chapter's a dish best savored, not devoured. We're on a romp, not a regimen.

---

[2] The term "monster baby" refers to the part of ourselves I described earlier, the part that may seem dangerous or troublesome but, if well-cared for, can fuel our most powerful expression and most intimate connections. In other words, the monster baby's a way to visualize the irrepressible life force that moves through us all. For the podcast, "monster baby" also describes a provocative character in an improvisation scene when Lisa and I first met each other. If you'd like further details about the name's origin story, you can listen to Episode #1 of the podcast at www.monsterbabypodcast.com.

We'll start in Part One establishing some common terms—*just what do we mean by "mindfulness" and "improvisation"?*—and clearing out our old ways of thinking about failure and learning. Early on, Stanford social psychologist Carol Dweck's growth-mindset concept will prove a huge ally along our path.

We'll then move on to Part Two where we'll encounter some of the great questions raised by combining improv and mindfulness. *Is it better to follow your impulses or to pause before you act? How do you include other's voices without surrendering your own? What's the best way to balance your desire for improvement with an acceptance of things the way they are?* Each of these questions leads directly into valuable insight for a life well-lived.

In Part Three, we'll explore more of the wisdom that emerges from these practices: why starting with positive choices makes for better life "stories," how best to handle the chaos that often consumes our lives, how to find the peace of a wider perspective, and how to make sense of the march of change.

Part Four will help us consider four interrelated qualities that make life far more fun and a heck of a lot healthier: adventurousness, curiosity, gratitude, and courage. To close our romp out, after we've explored all these different avenues for improving your life, we'll consider one last paradox: how it's not all about you, anyway.

To strengthen your learning as you go, check out the "Gems for the Journey" review at the end of each chapter. Those sections will also reiterate that chapter's key paradox to keep playing with. For your best-of-the-best results, try out the inquiries in each "Going Deeper" section as you move through the book. The Glossary of Games at the end of the book, in particular, offers clear directions and insider tips for 15 games and exercises that will strengthen and deepen your understanding—in a playful way. Ultimately, it's doing the actual practices that really gets you to a life well-lived.

My sincere hope for you? By the time you reach the end of these pages, you will feel more acutely alive and more exquisitely connected to yourself, to those around you, and to the world at large. You'll see more, feel more, love more—and inspire others to do the same. There's delicious wisdom waiting for you in these pages, and I can't wait to start so you can see for yourself. Enough preamble, then—let's get to the journey!

# part one
## *laying the groundwork*

So, you've decided to join this playful adventure. Awesome. Let's make sure we've got the equipment you'll need.

*A willing heart?* Check.

*A desire for joy?* Got it.

*An open mind?* Mm-hmm.

Only two more things to confirm before we head into the wild. First, that we're super clear on our key terms, mindfulness and improvisation. Second, that we're not carrying any extra weight from worry about failure and mistakes.

Let's double-check those now so we're fully prepared to forge ahead.

# a word about words
## defining mindfulness and improvisation

WHEN LISA ROWLAND AND I RECORD EPISODES of the Monster Baby Podcast—"a curious romp through the worlds of mindfulness and improvisation"—we usually choose a theme for the episode, set up the mics, and sit down to chat. Sometimes we prepare a question or an insight (or two). More often, we improvise and see what emerges. We discover the conversation. And it's all in service to the question: *how can we get more present, more adventurous and more skillful with this thing we call life?* I hope to convey some of that same spontaneous spirit in this book.

That said, it also makes good sense to define our terms so we know what the heck we're talking about. If we're going to bridge the worlds of mindfulness and improvisation, it'll be good to know the foundation we're drilling that bridge's support towers into. What's the groundwork?

### one word, many meanings
Let's start with mindfulness. Due to its growing surge into the cultural zeitgeist, there are approximately 8 kajillion definitions out there.[1] Some consider mindfulness the formal practice of monks on a mountaintop: *the Tibetan guys with the funky yellow hats and the twenty-foot long trumpets, right?* Others consider a far less stringent qualifier, giving themselves credit for being 'mindful' when they

---

[1] Give or take a zillion or two.

allow an elderly lady to cross the street without revving their engine to scare her. Somewhere between those poles lies a humbler definition and a more accurate truth.

Many folks equate mindfulness with meditation but that only holds part of the story. While overlaps between the two certainly exist, meditation is more like the means and mindfulness the end. Meditation builds your capacity for mindfulness. It's a focused practice that builds a different way of seeing and being in every moment of your life.

At minimum, mindfulness involves a kind of mind-body awareness. It doesn't take much to realize that our thoughts and emotions connect inextricably to our physical experiences. Imagine standing on the edge of a tall cliff—go ahead, try it now—and you'll likely feel a twirl in your stomach or an increase in your heart rate. Or conjure up a trip to the dentist's office and notice if your breath shortens or your jaw tightens. Anticipate your dog's tail-wagging dash down the hallway when you arrive home and maybe a smile crosses your face, or you feel a warmth in your chest.[2] Part of mindfulness includes noticing such physical, mental and emotional tugs and pulls.

It also involves pausing, taking your foot off the accelerator to hang out in the present moment for a bit. You can take a breath, look around, and notice whatever's there without editorializing or forming an opinion. You can stay in an open, sensing mode rather

---

[2] Unless you're just not a dog person and it was your partner who insisted you get the dog but you really wish you hadn't because now you have to take it for a walk in the rain when you'd really rather crack open a cold beverage and put your feet up—in which case you might notice a different mind-body reaction. ☺

than a more judgmental thinking mode. You can observe your experience while also staying engaged in it.[3]

Some describe mindfulness simply as receptive listening. That could mean in a literal sense: "What sounds are coming from my surroundings and registering with my ears?" Or it could refer to a more figurative manner, as in choosing to sit and listen to the entirety of a given moment. "What's going on in my brain?" "Wow, I'm thinking about this now." Or "I'm a little cold." Or "I hear the traffic." Whatever it is, it involves listening and taking in the world. A bit like approaching the day with a friendly greeting: "OK, life, what's happening today?" And then really receiving the response as it comes, never rushing to judgment about it.

Most folks teaching secular mindfulness today lean on the work of Jon Kabat-Zinn, founder of the Center for Mindfulness at the University of Massachusetts and creator of Mindfulness-Based Stress Reduction (MBSR). He offers a more formal definition that I and many others find super-helpful:

*Mindfulness means paying attention on purpose to the present moment and things as they are with curiosity and kindness.*

Let's parse this out phrase by phrase.

### Paying attention...

We've all got a spotlight of attention, a beam of awareness that we can shine on objects and experiences in the outer world or on thoughts, feelings and sensations coming from our inner world. Most of us have little control over where that attention goes. The spotlight gets pulled from one shiny enticement to another, lurching toward whatever stimulus stirs our emotions or reactions. Over time

---

[3] We'll discuss these aspects of mindfulness more in Chapter 3, "Impulse or Pause: Moving from Judgment to Discernment" and Chapter 8, "Meta-tation: The Benefits of a Bigger Picture."

and with effort, though, we can learn to move that spotlight in a direction of our choosing. Maybe I put my awareness on my knee or my heart. Maybe I turn it to background sounds coming in, to a child's request, or to the news on the television. I can adjust the spotlight's focus as well, shifting from a close-up investigation to a wider panorama---or vice versa. Maybe I'm sensing the tip of my big toe. Maybe I'm sensing my body breathing as a whole.

Once you notice that you can choose where to place your attention, of course, you almost immediately start to notice how difficult it is to keep that attention focused. Many have used the analogy of a "puppy mind" that needs formal training: it won't sit still, it wants to sniff everything, it's clumsy and well-meaning, it can make horrific messes, and it brings back stuff that makes you go "hmm...."

When I teach mindfulness classes, I use a funny video of a dog-skills competition to illustrate this analogy. The first canine competitor, a sheep-herding type, waits eagerly at the starting line. Upon release, the dog has to walk through a gauntlet of distractions: food, play toys, chew toys, whatever interesting smells the course-setters can cook up. That first dog hesitates a moment, like it wants to turn to the food, but then pulls itself together, maintains its focus, and runs into its trainer's arms. The video then shows a well-trained German shepherd. When its human companion calls, that dog strides through the temptation like a champ, disciplined, determined, and undeterred. Lastly, the film shows a golden retriever. True to type, the dog gets released...and runs straight to the first chew toy. And then it runs over to a tennis ball and dives further into sniffing and smelling. Then it goes to the food, now completely lost to its handler. Chomp, chomp, chomp. The retriever can't make it through one third of the course.[4]

---

[4] See https://www.youtube.com/watch?v=5iTTNRE-njM to watch the video.

After my students pick themselves up off the floor from laughing so hard, we talk about how, without having trained our ability to maintain focus, our minds act like that golden retriever, lost in all the chaos and stimuli of the world, simply jumping from shiny toy to great-smelling treat.

In part, then, mindfulness practice represents that necessary puppy training. You invite that attention to come on back, sit, and stay. You choose an anchor for your spotlight—the breath, a sensory experience, thoughts, emotions—and then sustain your attention there. *Can you stay with a focus on your breath for ten seconds?* When the mind wanders off—which it most certainly will—you simply bring it back with patient, firm, kind repetition. *That's okay, just come on back now.* You ask the puppy to sit and reward it when it does. When it takes off again, you reward it for returning again. *Good job, mind! Let's do it again.*

### ...on purpose...

Mindfulness has a direction, an intentionality about it. It's not just letting the mind wander willy-nilly—though daydreaming has its value, for sure. It's about *choosing* what to focus on. In this sense, you're counteracting inertia or any tendency to scatter or go numb. You turn off your auto-pilot, reengage with full mental and emotional acuity, and behold the entirety of your experience: the pleasant, the unpleasant, *and* the neutral. Your motivations might be many: to reduce stress, to see more clearly, to respond more wisely, or to savor the "good" and work more skillfully with the "bad." Whatever the specifics, you elect to place your attention somewhere on purpose. You choose to live a fuller life, to become more fully human.

### ...to the present moment...

Most of us spend most of our time living in the past or in the future. Odds are, we're ruminating on regrets from our past or amping up anxiety about what's to come. Either pole can generate a snowball of momentum that bowls us over and knocks us off center. Suddenly, we can't find a grounded calm. Unease starts to rise and we get caught in a dizzying twirl of obligation, criticism and judgment. We're stuck and the cycle keeps magnifying.

Perhaps surprisingly, mindfulness suggests that we also let go of nostalgia—the longing for a long ago—and pull back from anticipation. Or more accurately, that we avoid getting stuck in their seductions. No matter your mental machinations, you ultimately live your life in this moment. The more you bring yourself to staying present with what's before you, the more you register it with all your senses—body, mind, and heart—and the more you can savor. Or, when facing challenges, the more you can learn. This way, you actually start to live your life rather than just thinking about it.

Either way, mindfulness invites you to pause. Take a breath. (Sure, go ahead. Take one now.) And return to the present moment. This is where your attention rests when you've got the full range of your natural powers: with your sensory awareness, your actual surroundings, and your current experience. This is where life is really happening.

### ...and things as they are...

Mindfulness asks you to take in "things as they are." Not how you wish they were, how they used to be, or how you hope they will be at some point. In the practice, you choose to stop fighting reality and to accept what is true. Often, this means acknowledging the fundamental truth of change, transition and loss. Things come and go. This, too, shall pass. Other times, it means coming to recognize your own blind spots, limitations and assumptions. The way you see or interpret the world may not align with what's actually there. So, you clean your lenses, sharpen your senses, and triangulate with like-minded investigators. What is true? What is real?

***... with curiosity and kindness.***

Lastly, whatever you find under the spotlight of your attention, mindfulness invites you to explore it with friendly interest. You catch whatever judgments you might normally make and transform them into kind-hearted inquiries. Rather than thinking "That sucks" or "They're insufferable," you might ask "What can I learn?" "What's interesting about this situation?" or "What's really going on for that person?" There's a compassion or generosity for life itself and for other people. You make space for uncertainty. You give the other person the benefit of the doubt.

Mindfulness invites you to extend such softness towards yourself as well. Maybe your newly developed focus starts to uncover unsavory qualities or pockmarks from your past, so you choose to meet that vulnerability with a spacious kindness. You recognize that you've done your best and you intend well. That generosity can of course extend into your mindfulness practice as well. As you continue to train the puppy mind, you avoid berating yourself when your mind wanders off and instead celebrate when your mind returns. Rather than fueling a sense of disappointment, you feed a seed of development. You celebrate the remembering.[5]

So, it's a concise definition but a big job—*paying attention on purpose to the present moment and things as they are with curiosity and kindness.* Simple, but not easy. Again, it's a muscle to build up. It's a practice to perfect, never-ending but always intending.

In that way, mindfulness practice takes real rigor. It's open to the world, but it's not passive or wimpy. It takes discipline to refine and hold your attention on the present moment, especially in a world

---

[5] The Pali term for mindfulness, *sati*, originally meant "to remember" or "to recollect." I often think of it as re-collecting—like bringing my thoughts back from their travels away from the present—or re-membering—like bringing my arms and legs, my actual members, back into connection with my body.

where so many forces conspire to keep you distracted or sedated. It requires a capacity for paradox—*how can I be both receptive and intentional? How do I engage my experience while also observing it?*—that we'll explore in great depth throughout this book. And it takes courage. You simply can't know ahead of time what demons or blessings will emerge from under the rocks you turn over. You'll notice more. You'll feel more. You'll be asked to take responsibility for what you find. Whether it's the suffering of the world or the beauty of the world, you're really vulnerable when you take in all of life's fullness. Not everyone has the guts for such an adventure.

For those who do set out on its path, however, mindfulness represents a homecoming.[6] In that spirit, perhaps, you've chosen this book: welcome back to you.

## mindfulness misconceptions

Now that we have a better sense of what mindfulness *is*, it might also help to consider what it's *not*. To start, mindfulness is not...

- *just attention*—Sometimes you'll hear folks talk about mindfulness as if it were solely a function of focused attention. Strip the practice of its religious connotations and deeper demands and use it as a performance enhancement tool. Training one's focus is a part of mindfulness, for sure. But promoted alone, such attention starts to resemble the harsh light of a bare bulb over an interrogation table. The warmer, more welcoming spotlight we're going for includes compassion and those elements of curiosity and kindness. The written Chinese character for mindfulness actually includes two other characters: the one for "heart" and the one for "present." That's more like it. Mindfulness as present-heartedness.

---

[6] Another paradox: we set out on a journey in order to return home.

- *yoga*—One could practice yoga in a mindful way—and many do—but some studios also transform the ancient, sacred practice into a modern-day, ego-laden, body-toning tool. Mindfulness practice might involve movement in synch with the breath, as yoga does. And it could promote physical stretching and strengthening as a byproduct, as yoga does. But the point of mindfulness remains a growing awareness of present-moment experience rather than a building of tightness in buns of steel. For sure, mindfulness won't demand you pick up any spandex gear.[7]

- *solely Buddhist*—Much of modern mindfulness draws directly from Buddhist wisdom, especially as expressed through teachers who have come to the West in the last half-century. It's important to recognize and honor that heritage—many men and women suffered through great oppression to pass those teachings along—and one can learn from a tradition without becoming an adherent. That said, many if not most mindfulness teachers in the U.S. these days do their work in a secular manner. No codified beliefs to take on. No strict rituals. Just the work (and play!) of coming back to the present moment again and again.

- *just silence*—There's great insight in silence and solitude, especially when shared with others. And mindfulness practice often brings us to a place of great stillness where words feel inappropriate. At the same time, one can also cultivate present-moment awareness through interaction, movement, art, music, dance…and improvisation! The possibilities are endless.

- *a fly-by-night fad*—Interest in mindfulness has taken off and some of its present popularity has a superficial

---

[7] Though, heck, if it's your thing, go right ahead.

quality to it—a more performance-oriented McMindfulness, as author Ron Purser has called it. *If our workers are more focused, they'll be more productive. If they handle stress more effectively, we can ask them to do more!* Deeper forces continue at work below such superficialities, though. Especially in our social media-obsessed culture, there's an honest yearning for the antidote of authentic connection and deeper presence. That's not going away anytime soon.

- *just relaxation*—Mindful practice often leads to a feeling of calm or physical release. But that endpoint comes more as a byproduct than as a targeted destination. When we turn attention to what's happening now, we may notice anxiety, disturbance, or upset and that can be OK. Seeing that, feeling it, and actively experiencing it may actually increase our sensations of distress in the short term. It will also likely give us greater spaciousness for handling and processing the disturbance over time.

- *emptying the mind*—Sometimes folks imagine they're only doing mindfulness "right" if nothing's happening in their brain, if their mind has gone quiet. That's a misunderstanding. It's not about emptying or stopping the mind. The mind has a mind of its own. It's more about changing your relationship *to* the mind, allowing it to do its thing and investigating that thing with kind curiosity. You don't resist the bad thoughts or cling to the good ones. You hang out by the side of the river and watch 'em go by. Thoughts and feelings arise and fall away. They arise and fall away. They arise and fall away. As with relaxation as a byproduct of mindfulness, our thoughts might quiet over time and we'll feel more "empty." Or the thoughts that come might start to offer clearer insights or more original connections. But they might not. And that's fine.

## defining improvisation

Although the word mindfulness can prove a bit slippery, the term "improvisation," thankfully, is much easier to describe.

Improvisation shows up in music or dance when performers find notes and gestures to express themselves. It can flow through the words of a freestyle rap. It can take the shape of invention or problem-solving, as with a master auto mechanic under the hood or a detective piecing together clues that unlock a stubborn criminal case. Wherever it shows up, it's a "free play of consciousness as it draws, writes, paints, and plays the raw material emerging from the unconscious."[8] It always involves a level of uncertainty and risk—we cannot know the full range of possible outcomes. Most often in this book, we'll speak about and learn from improvisation through the lens of spontaneous *theatre*.[9]

Of course, improvisation also plays out in the mundane moments and everyday arenas of our lives. No one's given a script for conversations or decisions we need to make.[10] Every time you open your mouth to speak, you select from a set of grammatical and vocabulary building blocks to piece together new constructions. There are rules of syntax, yes, but you play with those limits—and sometimes bust them open. You respond to what you hear and create again, always adjusting to the conditions laid before you. Even if you don't consider yourself an "improvisor," you still

---

[8] Stephen Nachmanovitch, *Free Play: The Power of Improvisation in Life and the Arts* (Jeremy Tarcher: New York, NY, 1990), p. 9.

[9] Throughout the book, I will use the British spelling (*theatre* vs. *theater*) for two reasons. One, my improvisation teachers used it. Two, and more importantly, it preserves a helpful distinction between the art form (actors, directors and stagehands all take part in creating *theatre*) and physical buildings (those productions happen in a *theater*).

[10] Except maybe at a call center or in the military where soldiers train well enough to maintain protocol under the duress of attack. Even in that case, though, the uncertainties of the battlefield will likely demand stepping off-page.

improvise any time you say anything. It's as familiar and as constant as breathing.

Almost as if it, too, were improvising, life keeps sending a steady stream of cues and possibilities. Moment to moment, they bubble up within and around us. Sometimes those signals come from the natural world. Other times from the human world. Sometimes they're accidental. Sometimes they're intentional. A comet shoots across the sky. A car alarm goes off. The cashier smiles at you. Your business partner enters the room wearing a bold shirt. An insight comes to mind. The faucet stops working. You burp. In life as in an improv show, anything that happens potentially invites a response and thus becomes an "offer": *Here. Here's something to work with. Want to play? Care to riff?* We take what we're given, mix-and-match, and come up with our best guess for what comes next. We make a choice, move forward, and start the whole process again.

Whether on-stage or off, sometimes we experience these choices unfolding before us with calm clarity. All our skill and attention converge into a finely focused sense of purpose. But these moments of heightened resourcefulness seem to come and go unpredictably. The muse arrives in her own time, right? Well, sort of. Though you can't *control* or *command* the muse that inspires improvisation, you *can* make a more skillful invitation. You can cultivate the conditions that make her arrival more likely. Our work here is to find those flashes of flow and stretch them out, lengthening and strengthening them until they become indistinguishable from the other moments that populate our lives. You remove obstacles to the flow until you become the flow. That's improvisation.

For moving forward then, let's define the term this way:

**Improvisation is the art of present-moment creation in relationship to the many offers coming from one's inner life and from immediately surrounding people and circumstances.**

On that further reflection, it's clear that we all—you and I included—improvise. The question is: can we and will we do so in an unconscious way or in a skillful way, one that honors our deepest longings for play, for expression, for recognition and connection?

> **more words about words:**
> **'improvisation' vs. 'improv/impro' vs. 'applied improvisation'**
>
> Most folks who hear the word "improv" (or "impro" in the UK) think of comedy, either stand-up routines at a brick-walled night club or made-up short-form skits, a la the hilarious TV show "Whose Line Is It Anyway?" The word often conjures simultaneous delight—*Oh, those guys are great!*—and terror— *Don't put me on stage; I could never do that!* Either reaction can distance you from the simple wisdom of your own creativity.
>
> As an art form, improvisational theatre includes far more than just jokes and gags. It also includes dramatic and sensitive portrayals that run the entire range of human experience. You might witness a short scene that explores the heart-wrench of lost love, a silent register of political protest, or a three-act stage play that explores betrayal and family ties.
>
> *Applied improvisation* carries the insights of spontaneous theater, music and dance into non-performance settings like business, health care, education, law, medicine, personal growth and the like.
>
> In this book, if I use the term "Improv," I'm almost always using it as shorthand for the longer, more deeply nuanced term "improvisational theatre."

### aligned in spirit

One of the great delights of improvisation (and improvisational theatre more specifically) is that it dovetails so beautifully with the principles and practices of mindfulness. Each supports and enriches the other. Consider, for example, the ways in which improvisation aligns with each component of Jon Kabat-Zinn's mindfulness definition that we parsed earlier.

### *improv and paying attention...*

Improvisational theatre provides an unusual opportunity to pay precise attention. In any moment, there's so much going on and you don't know what exactly you're looking for. When building a scene, you might look into a juicy relationship that emerges... or you might find yourself co-creating a more superficial encounter. You and your stagemates might find "the game" within a scene, a pattern or riff that provides reliable humor and opportunity for storytelling, or you might discover a quieter, more natural slice-of-life scene unfolding. You might need to define and refine the imaginary physical environment you're in and you might need to let that environment go. The possibilities are endless so you can't fine-tune too much. You simply have to stay open.

Some might counter with, "Well, improv isn't so special. You've got to pay really close attention if you are walking down a potentially dangerous street in New York." While that may be true, if you're a Big Apple native, you also have a sense of the kinds of risks to watch for. To keep yourself safe, you don't need to notice the text on the building, the height of the moon in the sky, or the color of the shoes on the guy walking past you. Those won't signal potential danger. Said another way, in most endeavors where you need to pay attention, you know what you need to pay attention for. You don't keep as many channels open.

In improv, there's far more to register: the space on the stage, your improv partner, what they're saying, what they're doing, what they're making up, the environment they're creating, the tone of their voice, the emotional quality behind it, how they're related to you, the information they're giving you, how they're responding, and so on. And all this is happening at the same time, waterfalls of information gushing forth. In *that* kind of moment, the text on the building, the moon in the sky or the blue suede shoes passing by may actually represent the precise detail you need. Each could be the detail that takes the scene from the ordinary to the sublime.

In this way, improvisation can become a gorgeous form of listening. You don't go onto an improv stage with a set agenda saying *I know exactly what I'll do up there!* Instead, you show up totally open so you notice the stimulus you get from your partner, even a stimulus they didn't intend to send you: a glance, a tilt of their posture, an extra-rapid blink.[11] It matters less what offer they make than it does which offer you choose to pick up on. Listen. Receive. What do you notice?

Again, training the puppy mind helps immensely. In a simple mindfulness practice, you might return your attention to the anchor of your breath. With improv, you return your focus to the unfolding scene. Instead of wandering off with distracting or self-critical thoughts—"I'm not doing a good job," "the audience doesn't like me," or "this other improvisor is *so* annoying"—you stay ready to take in what's actually happening whether it's external, like an event, or internal, like an emotion or a body sensation. If there's a feeling arising, it could inform the scene as well.

### improv on purpose...

Earlier, you read about mindfulness practice as a conscious, intentional choice to develop full presence and resourceful response-ability. Improvisation gives us an embodied opportunity to notice and investigate those same intentions in live action. *Just what the heck are we doing here?*

---

[11] Notice that your "partner" here could be a specific person but could also be the theater itself or the audience—they're sending visual and auditory suggestions too!

Many of the instructors at BATS Improv[12] in San Francisco begin warm-ups with an active game called: "Ball." The rules of Ball resemble those of volleyball—just without a court, a net, or any sense of opposing teams.[13] In this case, the group works as one unit to keep a soft, inflatable fabric ball up in the air, everyone counting aloud each time the ball gets hit. As in volleyball, no player can hit the ball twice in a row. If that happens or if the ball hits the floor, the group pauses, resets the count to one and starts back up.[14]

Sometimes, especially with newer performers, folks will play Ball just by going through the motions. A half-hearted gesture here. A delayed reaction there. In other words, there's no intention to actually show up and play well. In those cases, the instructors will usually ask participants to make a conscious shift: "Look. It's not enough that you're in the room. Showing up means something more. It means actually being here with all of who you are. Decide to show up. Decide to be good at the game. Don't goof off and half-ass it. Don't just check a box to say you've done it. Try really playing." Soon, eyes widen, hands ready and weight shifts to the balls of the feet. Sound picks up and folks start flying across the space to make remarkable saves. The ball stays up. The count goes higher. And the group comes together. The game of Ball demonstrates clearly that a shift happens when we really commit.

That kind of sustained intention helps when you're waiting in the wings too, especially in a long-form improv show where a story might last a full 90 minutes. In that situation, players can't afford to take a break—they're still responsible for what's happening onstage. Thinking *Whew, I did my thing, I'm off now!* leads to all sorts

---

[12] Formerly Bay Area Theatresports, one of the oldest, most beloved, and most influential improvisational theatre groups in the country.

[13] OK, so maybe it's not as much like volleyball as I originally thought. Stick with me.

[14] See the Glossary of Games at the back of the book for more complete instructions on how to play Ball.

of catastrophes later. Each player has to decide over and over again to be there, to come back. They *choose* to stay present for themselves, for their stagemates and for the larger overall story. And that's a perfect parallel for how you might choose to stay present for the emerging story of your life as well.

### improv in the present moment...

Skillful improvisation rests on a curious balance point between the past and the future. It works best when players can incorporate and re-incorporate what has come before. What has happened *does* inform where things might go. And it helps to have a sense of potential destinations. But you cannot abandon the current moment for the story you were imagining. The story has evolved as it has moved along. If players get too worried about either the past or the future, they're no longer present with what's actually happening.

The best improvisors have developed this part of their brain to work like random access memory in a computer. They've built up an ability for that working memory to hold names, the comparative location of imaginary objects in space ("space objects"), character traits and the like, and still reserve processing power for what's unfolding. *Tuck that previous information away and retrieve it when needed but stay present with this, now.* A new improvisor might melt down under the weight of that much demand. They can hold onto plot or character or names, but not all three. It takes time to develop a bandwidth to take it all in, but it's possible, both on stage and in life. You *can* train the puppy.

### improv relating to things as they are...

On the first day of any beginning improv class worth its salt, students learn the critical importance of letting go of what they think *will* happen or *should* happen. Instead, they learn to respond to what actually *is* happening. If I think we're doing a science fiction piece and I imagine myself in a spaceship where my hands are playing with a(n imaginary) databank of ship controls, and you come in and decide that the controls are in fact mailboxes, I've got to switch my hands immediately to stuffing mailboxes. That's responding to things as they are. Your declaring them mailboxes made them so. I have to adjust.

Because they're immersed in it all the time, improvisors get good at that kind of instant redefinition pretty quickly. *Great, we're in the Old West now? Cool, I've got my spurs and chaps on.* Or *Oh, I thought I was your Mom. Turns out I'm your professor? Got it.* The players discover the reality of the scene together and go with it.

Staying flexible in that way gets tougher in a long-form story where the arc of the storyline has a much longer time to create expectations and attachments. It may seem obvious to one player exactly where the story is going, so much so that they can't see any other option. They just figure everybody else is on the same page and can see the same next narrative extension they're imagining. When another player comes into that scene with a different direction, it can be really tough to let go. Often, rather than adjusting to the new "what is," the original improvisor starts thinking, "OK, how can I incorporate that into *my* storyline? How can I *make* that make sense? How can I fix this from going off the rails?" Well, maybe the rails now head in a different direction that you didn't foresee. Maybe the rails make a new reality. Making that shift from "How do I fix this?" to "This doesn't need to be fixed. This is now the new story" takes enormous discipline and generosity.

Again, you can apply this insight from the worlds of mindfulness and improvisation to the cozier confines of your daily life. You can look at your life and see that it might not match the story you *thought* you'd be living. *I thought I'd be married by now. I imagined I'd be more successful. I thought I'd know what I want to do with my life.* Ultimately, of course, holding on to what you *thought* would or should or could be true won't help you make the best next step. Life is what it is now. Once you acknowledge what's actually going on, you get more resourceful. And then you're better prepared to discover what might unfold.

### improv as curiosity and kindness...

Some improv styles and traditions don't emphasize curiosity and kindness so much. They're more about hustle and flash, finding the funny and going for it with force and dedication. Relationships are secondary, so the laughs might come at someone else's expense. And the players are trying to invent or create the scene rather than discover it.

That said, I learned improvisation as a shared discovery. *What's here? We don't know. Let's find it together.* At the top of the priority list? Be good to each other and make each other look good. Sharing a stage with folks who share such values becomes a true delight. We step into the mystery and play. Sometimes the discovery works. Sometimes it doesn't. But it never feels like a bomb went off, more like a rocket never launched. You're in an uncertain space together with another human being, unearthing a creation together. *I'll take the next step. You take the one after that. Ok, good, here we go.* It's just glorious to be out on that ledge, dangling over an abyss and knowing you've got each other's backs. You may have no clue what you'll discover in your bizarre scene, but you've got your partner. You serve as each other's safety net. It's all good.

### improv demands rigor...

Like mindfulness, skillful improvisation asks you to give your best. Working at the top of your intelligence and creative abilities demands you stay "in shape" with spontaneity, listening, flexibility, and boldness. It means challenging patterns that start to become entrenched—*Am I regularly playing the same types of characters? Do I always fall into a lead or a support role? Do I default into introducing supernatural elements?*—so that you stay fresh. It also asks you to walk the line between the freedom of unleashing your creativity and tending to your concerns for social justice and interpersonal sensitivity. When you cross the line with your stagemates or with an audience, you need the courage and discipline to step up and heal those hurts. Improvisation creates art in the moment, but it's more than "winging it" with sloppy laziness. Done well, it's a committed practice.

In that sense, improv supports maintaining the same openness and discipline in regular life. *Where do I fall into automatic routines? What reactions seem to always show up? What's my default pick-me-up, calm-me-down, or get-me-home approach?* There's always more injustice to unearth and disassemble—do you have the discipline to put in the work to do so?

## improvisation misconceptions

As I mentioned in the earlier sidebar about the difference between "improv" and "improvisation," a few misunderstandings linger about the art form. While we're getting our foundation terms straight, let's clear those up too.

Skillful improvisation is not...

- *just paying attention*—An improvisor can offer her full attention and listen keenly, but if she does so without a spirit of generosity and playfulness, she'll come off as cold, robotic or mercenary.

- *just spontaneity*—True, free access to spontaneity helps, but effective storytelling requires more than stream-of-consciousness output. The best scenes emphasize the subtleties and landscapes of emotional connection. We see relationships grow. We see characters change in relationship—to themselves, to others, to their environments.

- *only the superficial*—In the same way that mindfulness can open us up to the full range of our experience in the world, so too can improv show us the depth, poignancy, and fragility of being alive. When players tap fully into the moment, they bring their audiences right in there with them. Everyone feels the feels.

- *just comedy*—as we've mentioned before, improvisation works best when the laughter comes as a byproduct of the discovery rather than as the focus of a show. A straight-up comedy show can offer sweet and memorable moments, for sure. As with candy, though, its sweetness won't offer enough heft to sustain us in the long term. We want more.

- *just a fad*—Improv has been having a moment recently as more folks recognize its value. Some say its appeal will fade as quickly as it has blossomed. But the skills of improvisation—openness, collaboration, creativity—remain fundamental to real-world relationships and enterprises. Connected presence, resourceful responsiveness, and effective partnership will always have value.

## ready to romp

All righty. This chapter has served as our pre-adventure preparation. We've sorted our gear and checked our equipment. We've got our mindfulness and improvisation provisions on board. We've decided what extra weight we could leave behind. Our next step before fully setting out? Considering an absolutely crucial and critical topic: your relationship to failure.

# Chapter 1
## A Word About Words: *Defining Mindfulness and Improvisation*

### GEMS from the JOURNEY

- *Mindfulness includes mind-body awareness, learning to reside in the present moment, and pausing to replace reactivity with artful response.*

- *Mindfulness means paying attention on purpose to the present moment and things as they are with curiosity and kindness.*

- *Improvisation means creating in the present moment in relationship to the many "offers" we get from our inner and outer worlds.*

- *"Improv" (or improvisational theatre) can include humor and laughs but doesn't have to. Also, one can apply its principles and insights without ever getting on stage to perform.*

### PARADOX

- *Both mindfulness and improvisation can be super easy— Just pause and take a breath. Just say what shows up. At the same time, they both demand real rigor. We've built up lots of default patterns to challenge and doing so takes time and effort. Though you can never do either perfectly, you can do either or both as a practice that provides tangible, joyful benefit.*

### GOING DEEPER

- *Keep the definitions for mindfulness and improvisation in your mind as you go through your week. Can you identify where you tend to place your attention and what primary attitude accompanies that attention? What happens when you pick up on the "offers" that start to come your way, either from friends and family or from life as a whole?*

# take a circus bow
## changing your relationship to failure

NOW THAT YOU UNDERSTAND THE TOOLS WE'LL BE USING—mindfulness, improvisation, and the rigor of dedicated practice—you'll need to address the mindset you're coming in with. In other words, if you already think you can't *possibly* embrace a sense of adventure—or meditate or improvise—then you'll likely create that very reality. A self-fulfilling prophecy. *Look, Ma—I'm right! When I tell myself I can't do it, I can't do it!*

Of course, trying to get a glimpse of your own mindset is like inviting a camera to see its own lens. Or asking a fish to see the water it swims in. It's tough to gain perspective on something you're embedded in. That said, the task is not impossible. Once you learn to **see** your mindset, you can start to **choose** your mindset. That choice will have a profound impact on your ability to learn and grow, your willingness to get back up after getting knocked down, and your readiness to collaborate with those around you.

### just what is a mindset?
In brief, a mindset serves as a mental filter. It's a set of beliefs that determines your behaviors, outlooks, and attitudes. It's an array of assumptions about what's possible and what's real. Think of it like a colored lens between the world as you perceive it and as it really exists. If you wear a pair of green-tinted glasses, everything you see will take on that hue. Likewise, everyone who sees you through them will think *you* have a green hue yourself. Parts of the world

may, in fact, be green, as may you—but it's hard to know for certain when anyone looks through that filter. By the end of *Playful Mindfulness*, I hope you will have at least tried on—if not adopted—the mindset of a mindful improvisor. It makes life way more fun.

As part of that, one of the most crucial filters to investigate is how you think about failure and mistakes. How many of us are afraid to mess up all the time? Maybe you notice it more when you're taking an apparently big risk—like stepping on stage in front of other people to make stuff up on the spot!—or maybe you find a similar fear in small moments—like when you want to do meditation "right." You try it a couple times, imagine you're not getting the hang of it and then abandon ship. *Oh, I tried mindfulness. I did it twice for five minutes and it didn't work. I couldn't keep my mind steady. Or I was thinking a lot.* You're afraid of looking bad and getting shunned, so you tense up—and make it more likely that you'll actually fail.

Or maybe the fear of failure keeps you from ever starting new projects. You pass on the dance class because you don't trust your clumsy feet. You'd never try out for the musical because some jerk in high school said you couldn't sing. Or you imagine your mind could "never" work the way an improvisor's does. I had wanted to play guitar from the time I was a little kid, entranced by my summer camp counselors who led fireside sing-alongs. But I didn't have the stomach for being bad, so I resisted starting. The obvious result from that choice: I didn't get the joy of music-making, at least not for another 13 years when I finally found a new reservoir of resolve and picked up a friend's six-string. I wish I'd had a different mindset early on.

## mindfulness as teacher: just do it

Mindfulness practice helps to heal this hesitation. You consciously and willingly turn your spotlight of attention to the here and now. You come back to center from any nostalgia or regret lodged in the past *and* from any anticipation or anxiety about the future. Rather than judging what you find, you stay open and curious, poking around for new insights or emergent patterns. That includes any information coming from within. *Huh. What does this body sensation have to say today? What's **this** feeling all about? What do these thoughts tell me?* And you do all that with an eye toward what really is true, not what you wish to be true or what used to be true. Unblinded by assumptions or preconceptions, what's actually going on now? The best part of this kind of practice? You're not looking for any particular outcome. You're staying with the process.

In other words, it's not about doing mindfulness or meditation well. It's about doing it or not doing it at all. Failing isn't even part of the equation. Of course, the quality of your experience as you practice may change over time. You may get "better" at it, in that you feel more skillful, more resilient, or more equanimous. But even if you get stuck in the relentless cackling and howling of the monkey mind, when you sit down to feel your breath for just two minutes, you're still doing the practice. Any time you notice your attention to breath has gone and you bring it back, you're victorious. If you're trying, you're succeeding.

Moreover, "formal" meditation practice need not be so formal. Maybe your practice looks like a longer, more diligent stretch of sitting for 30 or 40 minutes, but maybe it's just 5 or 10 minutes in the office chair. Can you pause from the thinking mode—evaluating, planning, reviewing, judging, sorting, and configuring—and just reside in a sensing mode of noticing what's happening in the body, with the senses, and maybe with the thoughts or the feelings? Can you do that independently from your likes and dislikes? Rather than judging that your mind has gone off somewhere, can you calmly note, *Ah, yes, my mind has wandered again*? It wanders off again, you bring it back again. That's the practice. That's just doing it, formal or informal.

## improvisation as teacher: the circus bow

One way to counteract the fear of failure is to simply get yourself back into the fray. You can also prepare yourself for greater resilience by rewriting your expectations of what will happen if—and when—you fail. The Circus Bow, one of the greatest options in the improvisor's toolkit, proves particularly helpful for interrupting the habitual demons of self-doubt and self-judgment.

Usually, when we hesitate or make mistakes, we cringe to some degree. Expecting punishment or pain from the outside, we scrunch up our eyes, curl our shoulders, tighten our breath, and clench our fists in a "failure flinch." Or, maybe we roll our eyes hoping that if we proactively punish ourselves for our ineptitude, we can deflect criticism from others. Sometimes we flinch for just a fleeting moment. Other times, the posture and its aftereffects hang around for longer. In either case, the visible recoil or apology only emphasizes the error, signaling to those around us that we're worthy of their judgment.

Back in the mid-1980's, knowing that such responses got in the way of unfettered, honest improvisational scene work, Seattle-based improvisors Edward Sampson and Matt Smith came up with an antidote called the Circus Bow. They had seen big-top tumblers, trapeze artists, and clowns who popped up with a smile and an arms-flung-wide bow after stumbling. So Sampson and Smith suggested that their improv students embrace their moments of "failure" by stepping proudly forward, flinging their arms in the air, and pronouncing a full-throated, goofy-smiled. "I failed! Woo hoo!"

This move simultaneously takes responsibility for the error—the player recognizes he did, in fact, "mess up"—and lightens the mood, making more space for creativity. Rather than spiraling downward or inward, he chooses to respond with good cheer, celebrating the boldness that led to the failure. *I'm learning! I'm growing!* Over time, the spirit of the gesture becomes so ingrained that the impulse to cringe fades away almost completely. And the physical release delivers a jolt of joyous energy that has its own power. Whether you didn't get the rules right, you made a mistake, or you just didn't fulfill the task in the way that you intended, you shout, "Ta-Da!!! Woo Hoo!!"

As with mindfulness practice, the Circus Bow also develops a skill—that of bringing attention back to the present moment—that improvisors desperately need. When a circus clown stumbles, she won't wallow in the mistake. Instead, she'll wave her arms triumphantly and move with authority into a deep and magnificent bow, first in one direction, then the other. The mistake has shaken her awake. She resets her focus outward, and in so doing, gains new life. The show must go on.

I first learned a variation, the "Ta-Da!" bow, from Patricia Ryan Madson, my improv teacher and mentor at Stanford University. In her version, each player in the group practices the technique before it is ever needed, bowing after a confident "Ta-Da!" and receiving raucous applause from other troupe members. Then, having developed the muscle memory as a group, you could break out the practice—and the support that comes with it—whenever you need it.

As Ryan Madson details in her gem of a book, *Improv Wisdom*, the Circus or Ta-Da! Bow can also help in arenas outside the theater or circus—like when she was by herself in front of a crowd of thousands at Stanford's Frost Amphitheater. In 1992, she had accepted an invitation to read the words of Jane Stanford, one of the school's founders, at the august occasion of the inauguration of new university president, Dr. Gerhard Casper.

Ryan Madson tells the story:

*I wore the traditional cap, gown, and academic hood under the bright California sun. The day was radiant and warm. According to the program, my reading followed a stately musical tribute to President Casper, composed for the occasion and performed by the Stanford orchestra, who were on stage behind the academic cadre. The conductor launched the stirring piece, guiding the musicians skillfully. As the music came to an end and a small silence ensued, I rose and walked to the podium, placed my book on the stand, took a full breath and declaimed: "And now, the words of Jane Stanford..." And, at that moment, the horns and violins commenced the final movement of the piece.*

*Wrong cue.*

*Oh, dear.*

Understandably, Ryan Madson froze. She knew she needed to return to her seat and wait out the music and applause, but... the horror! In that moment of mortification, though, she also felt a "little tingle like angel's wings bubbling up through my shoulders, as if I were lifting my arms in a Ta-Da Bow." She held her head high, turned, and returned to her seat with dignity. When the music ended and the applause died down, she approached the podium again and resettled, this time beginning "And *now*, the words of Jane Stanford." The audience rustled with a soft laughter, recognizing the humanness and the humor of the moment, allowing everyone— including Ryan Madson—to return to the more formal message. Even though she had only *thought about* the Bow, her history with it and the support she'd had from others gave her the means to stay present and turn her attention to what needed to come next. As she writes, "I did not let the miscue become the event, just one moment of it."[1]

---

[1] Patricia Ryan Madson, *Improv Wisdom: Don't Prepare, Just Show Up* (Random House: New York, 2005), pp. 107-108. Quotation used by permission.

## get over it!

Unlike many moments of our lives, in the chaos of an unfolding scene on stage there's no time to brood over little hiccups or missteps. If forgetting a character's name gets your self-judgment juices flowing—*Dammit, I messed up! I'll never be a good improvisor!*—you're no longer listening to what's happening in this moment. And you won't be ready for what comes next. The scene on stage requires you to find a bit of self-compassion and let it go.

At some point, what's required is even more than that. It's not the most important that you're kind to yourself—though that does matter—it's that you need to get over yourself. In other words, as we'll explore in more detail in a later chapter, it's not about you.[2] If you're berating or shaming yourself, you're no longer available to your partners. Your teammates need *you*, not your self-punishment. Your pity party is not only uncomfortable for you, it's unproductive for everybody else. So snap out of it, friend.

This is not to say that mistakes don't happen. Like, maybe you did forget a character's name in a scene. The appropriate response is to say internally, *It's fine. Let's keep playing.* Again, on stage—as in life—you're dealing with what's in front of you *now*. That you failed at something two seconds ago is not relevant to continuing to perform now. Eventually, when it comes time to go back to the mistake, you can then approach it with mindful curiosity and kindness rather than with a jagged or judgmental edge. You can make an open-ended inquiry rather than slapping a FAILURE label on it.

Of course, all this holds true in life as well as on stage. If you're in a meeting at work and you realize you've got the wrong set of slides for a presentation, hyperventilating with extended self-flagellation won't help you and your team determine the wisest next step. If you

---

[2] See Chapter 15, "It's Not About You: Finding the Ease of Wider Concern."

spill a pot of spaghetti, a blame game won't get food into your kids' bellies any faster. A Circus Bow—fully enacted or simply imagined—can release the tension and help you get on with whatever step comes next. That way, you can still contribute.

## the importance of community mindset

You can make much of this adjustment on your own. Once you know the Circus Bow, you won't ever forget it. That said, having friends and colleagues working from a similar mindset amplifies the effect. In some ways, your ability to fully change your relationship to failure actually *depends* on your community. You know you're going to fail at some point. To reach your fullest and best, you need to mess up in a context that won't send you back into your shell. Could you arm yourself with a tolerance for being berated rather than hoping for a supportive response? Sure you could. Even better though: remove yourself from such toxic environs altogether and instead choose communities that forgive and transform mistakes.[3]

The more you hang out with people who do this for each other, the more resilient you become. You try, you fail, you recover. You try again and maybe you fail again or maybe you succeed. Knowing your pals have your back, you're willing to get back up on the horse. You can make a mistake and still belong to the group.

Greater resilience also leads to improved results. When you're with people who make space for all of you, including your mistakes, their spacious, inclusive attitude becomes fertilizer for the ground of your imagination, sunlight for your plants of possibility. That your

---

[3] It's funny. Creating and contributing to such a community can seem generous: Oh, look at how accepting and loving those people are to each other. But it also makes sense from a self-serving perspective! If I make space for your failure, I can start to trust that you'll make space for mine. We need not gather an altruistic circle of saints before forming a mutual benefit society.

efforts—and mistakes or failures—will be celebrated and not ridiculed encourages broader and deeper thinking. You get bolder. Your ideas get better.

Admittedly, recognizing this truth might lead to some painful separations. Maybe you leave an improv troupe or a spiritual community. Maybe you find a new job. Or maybe you let go of a relationship or drift away from toxic family connections. When you start to see just how much you're shaped by your community, such choices leap to the fore. In the end, you have to decide which pain (staying with the naysayers) holds you back and which pain (cutting off ties with them) leads you to a new birth.

### right association

The Buddha also suggested that the friends and acquaintances that surround you really matter. As part of his fundamental teaching, he described an Eightfold Path for ending suffering and reaching enlightenment. That path includes practices like Right Speech, Right Action, Right Livelihood, and Right Concentration. Before you even get to that Eightfold Path, though, he suggests starting with Right Association. If you spend time with people who treat you unkindly or hector you for your failures, your spiritual growth will suffer. They may not be bad people, but they won't help your development. Conversely, if you find yourself among folks who support you, encourage you, and stick with you as you take bolder and bolder steps, you might want to hang with them more. Ultimately, the question comes down to, "Are you swimming in a pool of 'yes' or a pool of 'no'?" And then, the follow-up: "Which of those do you want?"

## the 'taxonomy of failure'

By now, it's probably becoming clear how changing your thinking *about* failure, whether on your own or in community, shifts your reaction to failures when they happen. You're lighter with yourself and others, and you can stay present to what needs to be done.

Another shift you can make is to change *what you define as failure in the first place.* Usually, we think of a failure as not following through on an intention, not reaching a goal in a particular instance. Or maybe we mean trying something out and having it not work. Or that someone has somehow caused harm, suffering or hassle. Our "mis-takes" have somehow missed the mark—a miscalculation, a misunderstanding, a misperception, a misattribution.[4] You have made an error of some sort. In any of these cases, you can acknowledge the facts of a mistake—*I didn't accomplish what I intended to accomplish*—without diving reflexively into the failure flinch. Maybe you can even find an alternative interpretation of those facts, one that leads you to more productive action or more empowered choices going forward.[5]

For example, here's a list of six ways to reframe mistakes and so-called "failures." I call it the Taxonomy of Failure.

- *A Matter of Inconsequence: A small or unimportant "failure."* When you're used to being hard on yourself, you can generate self-judgment for the tiniest of stimuli. Maybe you stumble going up a set of stairs. Or you make a wrong turn that costs us an extra minute of travel time.

---

[4] The Hebrew word for "sin" means, literally, "To miss the mark."
[5] I once played on a volleyball team where everyone apologized after every mistake they made. When the chorus of "Sorry"s became too much, we decided to can it. *Look, you know you didn't mean it. Don't worry about it. Let's focus on the next play.* The impulse to apologize soon turned into a humorous admission of responsibility: *That shot was not what I intended. I would have liked to serve that ball over the net rather than into it.* Not surprisingly, the added lightness helped us refocus on the next play.

Though such mistakes don't matter in the grand scheme, you still get harsh with yourself. The inner critic rages on. Knowing what you know now, however, you can change that response and defang the flinch. Such errors are small. *Woo hoo!* Let 'em stay small.

- *The Winds of Chance: You misperceive it or it's actually not even a failure.* Sometimes your "mis-take" is in thinking you made a mistake at all. This would include the time you thrashed around on the way to the airport because you'd forgotten your passport—and then realized you had tucked it away in a side pocket of your backpack. Or when you pulled your hair out because you'd lost your sunglasses only to find out they were already on your head. Or, more achingly, a relationship ended not because you'd done anything wrong but because the other person decided to leave. We can launch ourselves into a self-judgmental storyline like the best of authors, but it makes sense to at least pause first to confirm that we've actually messed up.

  Other times, we punish ourselves for mistakes that don't even belong to us. You're late to a meeting because an accident on the highway backed up traffic for miles and you had no way to exit. You miss a conversation because someone stole your smartphone. You have to cancel a date because you've gotten sick enough that you can't stand up. While each of these scenarios include disappointment and letting others down, you can't really say they're *your fault*. Sometimes stuff just happens.

- *The Stepping Stone: An iteration on a path to success.* Too many of us have what Stanford social psychologist Carol Dweck calls a fixed mindset (as opposed to a growth mindset). The concept of a fixed mindset holds that intelligence, talent and ability don't change—they're fastened immutably in place. What gifts you have, you're given at birth. People with this mindset spend a great deal of time trying to demonstrate their abilities, building self-image by shaping what others think of them. Because they spend so much time and energy trying to *look* good, they carry a constant fear of getting called out as impostors, as not good enough. For folks living in this frame, failure demonstrates a lack of ability and should thus be avoided at all costs. Likewise, challenge only increases the possibility of negative exposure—so it, too, should be avoided.

In contrast, a growth mindset suggests that we can build our intelligence, talent, and abilities through application and adjustment. You work your way into new capabilities by trying stuff out. Where folks with a fixed mindset see life as a test where you have to *prove* yourself, those with a growth mindset see life as a journey where you get to *improve* yourself. With the latter, rather than provoking panic, challenge creates excitement and eagerness for learning.

In a growth mindset, our so-called failures instead become opportunities for feedback, an invitation for a next iteration. You expect—and welcome—mistakes along the path of learning because they give you the chance to move the needle forward. You fall down. You get back up. You try again. As with design thinkers who lightly put forward multiple prototypes along the path to product release, you know that almost every offering can serve as a less-rough draft of what came before. You constantly learn and grow. More information. More insight. [6]

---

[6] Grid on next page adapted from Carol Dweck, *Mindset: The New Psychology of Success* (Ballantine Books: New York, 2006).

| For those with a.... | |
|---|---|
| **Fixed Mindset** | **Growth Mindset** |
| *Intelligence is...* | *immutable; given by genetics, chance, or God* | *mutable and can be developed, improved, and expanded.* |
| *Life is...* | *a test where we have to PROVE ourselves.* | *a journey where we get to IMPROVE ourselves.* |
| *The primary concern is...* | *managing others' impressions.* | *exploring one's own curiosity.* |
| *Failure...* | *demonstrates a lack of ability, unworthiness.* | *presents an opportunity for feedback.* |
| *Challenge...* | *generates fear.* | *creates excitement, eagerness for learning.* |
| *Effort...* | *shouldn't be needed.* | *is THE key to improving ourselves.* |
| *Others' success...* | *diminishes, exposes, or shames.* | *lifts up, offers a chance to learn and grow from greatness.* |
| *The end result is...* | *an early plateau, never reaching one's potential.* | *ever higher levels of achievement and a greater sense of personal agency.* |

- *The Mystery: It's too soon to tell.* Maybe what you perceive as a mistake or failure now will eventually represent a gift or a blessing. You don't get a job you applied for but that leaves you free to take up an unexpected opportunity to travel. You scratch an LP record but meet a new love at the audiophile store when you're buying a replacement. Your business flops but your bankruptcy lawyer connects you with a future investor who changes your life. Were any of those actually "failures"?

The oft-cited Taoist tale of the old farmer speaks to just this dynamic:

> An old farmer is approached by a neighbor who offers condolences for an unexpected loss: "Oh, I heard your horse ran off. I'm so sorry to hear that. What a tragedy!" The farmer slowly smiles and simply replies, "We shall see."
>
> A few days later, the horse returns with a group of other wild horses it has befriended. Again the neighbor stops by, this time to celebrate: "What a great thing! You now have all these new horses! The universe is generous!" And again, the farmer replies "We shall see."
>
> The next day, as he's trying to tame one of the horses, the farmer's son gets thrown and breaks his arm. The neighbor shows up with some flowers, lamenting "Oh, it's so awful your son got hurt!" Once more, the farmer looks at him and says, "We shall see."
>
> Two days later, the emperor's royal guard come by the farm to forcibly enlist any able-bodied young men to fight in their new war. Because the farmer's son has a broken arm, they pass him by. So the neighbor comes by to rejoice: "How wonderful that your son was not taken away, as mine was." Once more, the farmer responds as he has all along: "We shall see."

The story could continue endlessly in like fashion. Whether events in the farmer's life turn out good or bad—success or failure—always remains to be seen. Likewise, when you appear to make a mistake, maybe your evaluative lens is off or your mirror needs polishing. You can't know without more perspective. It's simply too soon to tell.

- *The Disguised Gift: A mistake that makes things even better.* As you practice such reframes over time, mistakes morph even further. What you had once considered cringe-worthy errors soon become helpful invitations to adventure. *How can you incorporate or justify the 'mistake'? What unexpected or delightful place does it catapult you to? What's now possible that wasn't before?* American singer-songwriter David Wilcox's tune, "Leave It Like It Is," offers a perfect example of this technique. In the song, a jar of paint spills in the kitchen—a bona fide, top-notch, USDA Grade-A mistake in most people's book. Like a fine improvisor, though, the homeowner looks for the possibility in the moment ("Good God, look at that pattern!") and transforms the first-glance failure into a signature feature of her home. After she paints a frame around the spill and puts up gallery lighting to highlight the 'work,' visitors ask "Who's the artist?" and declare "My, what a beautiful home!" [7]

Improvisors are trained for just this kind of creative reframe. No matter what happens on stage, it *has* happened. There's no do-over. So the eyes, ears and other creative faculties tune into using that reality to discover a greater possibility. And the audience will want to come along for the ride. Honestly, performers often strive for a show without errors, but those watching don't. At an improv show, they *want* to see the players stumble and then watch them recover good-naturedly. If the audience wants predictable perfection, they'll take in a well-scripted play. They see the charm of the art. They know there's a perfection in imperfection.

---

[7] David Wilcox, "Leave it Like it Is," from *How Did You Find Me Here*, A & M Records, 1989. Go to https://youtu.be/S7mkdHQX-NE?t=2m56s to hear the song.

One time, I performed with Lisa Rowland (my "Monster Baby" podcast partner) in a two-person production at Phillips Exeter Academy. We started a scene as two long-time friends chatting in a garden. Shortly into the scene, Lisa's hidden microphone apparatus (we were both wearing lapel mics to help our voices carry throughout the large space) dropped loudly onto the floor. We easily could have apologized to our audience, potentially even with a sheepish Failure Flinch posture: "Oh, sorry, just give us a minute. Oh, so sorry." Or we could have distracted ourselves and lost track of what was happening between the characters. Fortunately, in a rare moment of inspiration, I thought to say in character: "Wait a minute. Are you spying on me???" The audience laughed and we relaxed. The microphone then became a centerpiece to the unfolding scene, the key that unlocked a tale of espionage and intrigue. The mistake became a gift.

The Japanese aesthetic of *wabi-sabi* also speaks to the way that mistakes can become gifts. Roughly translated, the word means "flawed beauty," especially the kind of beauty that emerges over time. Here, the unevenness in the curve of a bowl or the chip on a sculpture becomes a signature mark of distinction. What was a problem becomes precious.

*Wabi-sabi* can apply to concrete things; it can also apply to relationships. The quirks, silly patterns and annoying habits of the other actually become the very qualities that make them special. For example, I once had a partner who used vitamins and supplements obsessively (in my then-eyes). Each Sunday, she would lay out a specific pattern of pills for every morning, noon, and night of the week, dropping lozenges and tablets into a carefully organized portable container. This had always seemed over the top to me: how could she spend so much time and money on these dang supplements? When she and I separated, however, I found myself missing her ritual of precision. The whole sequence had seemed a bit odd, but, I realized, it was one of the sweet qualities that made her *her*. The apparent imperfection was actually beautiful.

Individuals and groups who actively and eagerly look for the opportunity and unique beauty in mistakes create a safety net that inspires healthy risk-taking and genuine innovation. Improv troupes, workplace teams, and intimate relationships can all reap the same benefit. If even our mistakes can create magic, what do we have to fear?

- *The Let Down: An actual failure with real-world consequences.* Sometimes there's no such thing as reframing a failure. There's no iterative process at work. There's no noble intention or silver lining behind the cloud of disappointment. Maybe it's just carelessness or negligence, but you've messed up and real people have suffered as a result of your actions. That's not the time for a cavalier Circus Bow that tries to brush away any potential resentments: "Oh, hey guys. Sorry I'm late for our presentation. I was out drinking last night. Woo hoo!" No, no, no. Real mistakes are a time for apologies and making amends. In other words, do what you need to do to make up for your hurtful behavior.

  Note that even in the case of a flat-out blown assignment or unquestionable mess-up, however, beating yourself up never helps. It's possible to take responsibility for the error without drowning yourself in toxic self-talk or draping yourself in that visible, pre-emptive shroud of shame.

Instead, you can bring an attitude of curiosity and kindness to the situation and to yourself. Breathe. Explore. Investigate. Look for lessons to learn. You can even keep an eye out for an unexpected positive possibility to emerge. But do so humbly and with a respect for the turbulence you've caused. You bring the mistake into the light. You own it. You sit in the vulnerability of the feelings, yours and theirs. And you begin the process of healing and reconciliation. *I'm sincerely sorry. This is totally my fault. I will do my best to make up for the damage I've done.*

## finding and freeing our full humanness

Wherever a so-called failure falls within the taxonomy above—and certainly we could generate more categories—you can know this: shifting your mindset about it from self-blame to inquiry and integration will help. A more compassionate response to messing up keeps you present and available for what's needed next. Practicing such kindness on small mistakes also develops your mindfulness muscles for when the true doozies hit. In that sense, every "Woo hoo!" you do falls like a drop of water, washing away the judgment that might normally stick. You cleanse. You cleanse. You cleanse some more. Eventually that clear-hearted water seeps into deeper levels where you uncover more existential shame—*Crap, I don't think I've lived my life the way I want to live it! What am I worth?*— and now you have a wider and deeper reservoir of resilience to draw on. *What if I took the same compassionate and forgiving approach I've been practicing all along and applied it to this bigger struggle?*

Ultimately, the decision to shift your relationship to failure leads you to become more present, more resilient, more fully human. Yes, you want to reward and reinforce learning from a mistake and taking positive risks. And yes, finding unexpected benefits after the fact trains you to see that what you originally considered an error may not actually be one. You need not go into flinch mode when you've seen evidence that something good can come out of what just happened. Added to that—and maybe more essentially—you're cultivating the value and power of a joyful recovery. As Matt Smith affirmed, "The Failure Bow isn't designed to reward or focus on the failure. It's designed to reward the *willingness to be transparent, the capacity to remain available in the present moment, and the ability to get back on the horse without residing in shame."* [emphasis mine]

So much of the pain of our so-called failures comes from our resistance to them or our identification with them. You can expend enormous amounts of energy trying to change the reality of a mistake or hiding it from yourself or the people around you. And you can try to hide your shame about them as well. But pretending doesn't change the fact of what's going on. There's something marvelous and magical about putting it all out in the open and not fighting to make it different. In this new mindset, it becomes OK to acknowledge, "I totally screwed up. I did a bad thing." Or "I feel ashamed of who I am right now." Or "I don't feel like a worthy inhabiter of space." You can feel your feelings without having them overwhelm you. "I failed" need not metastasize to "I'm a failure."

These choices you make affect others as well. When you find the courage to take forgiving responsibility for your actions and feelings, you give others permission to do the same. Your being real rings like a meditation bell whose vibrations start to shake loose the limitations in others. Now, such 360-degree openness might prove scary for those who have never seen—or refuse to see—their own shame. Your authenticity running free might freak out those who have locked theirs away. That said, for those yearning for a more integrated wholeness, there's nothing more refreshing or electrifying. Somebody speaking their truth and not shying away from it? *Thank God. If they're being themselves, I guess I get to be myself.*

Early on here, you're recognizing that improvisation and mindfulness connect us to real tenderness. In improvisation, you'll likely laugh with delight at some point. In meditation, you may encounter moments of peace or bliss. And…you'll almost certainly find places of pain and poignancy as well. When you're fully present, people will see your "stuff." Ultimately, though, you opt for vulnerability because you can't connect authentically without showing and sharing the full range of your experience. The humor *and* the challenge. The success *and* the failure. The seeing *and* the being seen. All of you is welcome. Including your so-called mistakes.

## Chapter 2
### Take a Circus Bow: *Changing Your Relationship to Failure*

### GEMS from the JOURNEY

- *Your mindset about life and learning acts like a filter that affects everything you see and experience. Changing your mindset about failure has a profound impact on your willingness to learn, grow, and take on joyous adventures.*

- *Mindfulness practice offers a great chance to keep coming back, again and again, after so-called "failure."*

- *The "Circus Bow" enables you to meet mistakes with boldness, openness and playful vulnerability, moving you out of the "failure flinch" and into a posture of success and celebration.*

- *Finding a circle of friends who share this new relationship to failure will make a huge difference in your ongoing success.*

- *The Taxonomy of Failure shows us that most of what we usually call "failure" is probably better described as inconsequential or unlucky, a stepping stone on the way to larger success, a mystery that has yet to be fully revealed, or a disguised gift that improves things.*

- *Even when you've made a real mistake with painful consequences, it never helps to beat yourself up for it. Take stock of what happened. Clean up the mess. Apologize and move on.*

**PARADOX**

- Something that goes wrong can also serve as the seed of real opportunity.

**GOING DEEPER**

- Once you understand the idea of mindsets, you can start to examine your own—and that in itself starts to build a more resilient and curious mindset. Watch your thoughts and feelings about failure as you prepare for a challenge, for example, and jot down a few notes in response. What do you say to yourself beforehand? What do you feel in your body? Where in your body do you feel it?

- For further contemplation, observe how you respond after a letdown. Do you celebrate the risk you took or seek out the growth in the experience (eventually, at least)? Or does your inner critic rise to the fore? Or do you do both? What happens if you try a Circus Bow instead— ideally, the full-throated, open-armed version but, at minimum, a little finger raise and a quiet "Woo hoo"?

- Notice how you respond to others when they fail. What judgments arise in you? What spaciousness emerges? Are you drawn to connect or withdraw based on that person's mistake or shortcoming? How might you support that person to make an elegant recovery?

- Try out the "1-2-3" exercise described in the Glossary of Games at the end of the book.

# part two
## *playing with paradox*

Normally, you wouldn't go looking for gold in a wetland. Better to stay on predictable ground so you keep your solid footing. But this is no ordinary romp. It's a curious one.

For that reason, now that you've got your bearings, we're going to head straight into some swampy territory: the world of paradox. If you consider life's contradictory truths on your own, you might feel you're sinking into quicksand.

> *We're divinely unique **and** we're specks of dust in an infinite universe.*
> *Humans can be courageously kind **and** they can be callously cruel.*
> *Transformation can happen in a moment **and** real change takes time.*

Where's our handhold in all this ambiguity? Surely, *something* must be true, right? What the muck?

Thankfully, it's actually possible to *play* within such seeming contradictions rather than getting swallowed by them.

> *Should we go with our gut **or** pause for a moment? Yes.*
> *Is it better to act boldly **or** to defer generously? Absolutely.*
> *Should we assert our aspirations **or** accept what is? Precisely.*

In this section, mindfulness and improvisation will help you embrace such questions, get a bit muddy, and emerge on the other side with greater wisdom and vitality. Trust me, there's truth in paradox.

Grab your swamp boots and let's jump in!

# impulse or pause?
## moving from judgment to discernment

MINDFULNESS AND IMPROVISATION BLEND BRILLIANTLY to help you stay calm in the face of chaos and buoyant in stormy emotional times. There's at least one place where the two worlds diverge and perhaps even conflict, though: whether to stop or go in any given moment. In other words, do you do best when you pause for reflection or when you follow your impulses? Red light or green light?

### the mindful pause
An everyday mindfulness practice includes at least three crucial elements, two of which we've already mentioned. The first, paying attention or training your awareness, builds a disciplined focus so you can sustain whatever effort you're making. The second involves cultivating curiosity and kindness for every experience you have. When you observe and act from even just those two places, insight and opportunity open up in a more relaxed, joyful, and integrated way. The third element will take you even further: learning to pause when triggered by the stimuli of life's events.

For most of us, something occurs and we react immediately. X happens and we do Y. Say a driver cuts in front of you. Instantly, your blood boils and you scream at the guy. A text chimes on your phone and you check it immediately, regardless of what conversation or task you're engaged in. You hear a political argument from someone with a different worldview and feel a surge of derision and disbelief that the other person could be so ignorant. In each of these cases, you don't *think* about how to respond. Your reaction shows up instantly and automatically.

Such reactivity can occur under more pleasant circumstances as well. You eat a salty, crunchy potato chip and automatically reach for another. Your teenager turns on his megawatt smile, so you give him the keys to the family car for the night. You get good news and grab your phone to post a notice on social media. Again, the stimulus prompts a reaction without the intervention of conscious thought.

Either way, we're all getting pulled by things we like or don't like. The things we like, we move towards. The things we don't like, we move away from—or build walls against. The stimuli might be small, but our reactions still come strong and fast. It's almost as if we have puppet strings attached to our physical, mental and emotional limbs. We're just herky-jerked into a typical reaction. (Don't take this assertion personally—it happens to every living being.)

Mindfulness says, "OK, notice that original stimulus." X happens. Now, before it automatically triggers another reaction, what if you insert a simple pause between X and Y? Take a breath. And maybe another. Now, in the space of that pause—*bwhoop! bwhoop! bwhoop!*—other options show up.[1] When that driver cuts in front of you, maybe you feel glad that at least you avoided an accident. Or you imagine that he's got a good reason for needing to get where he's going fast. Or you realize that in the big picture, it doesn't matter so much and you could just let it go. Your original reaction—the screaming and cussing—remains available. But now you've got other options as well, ones that might better serve you and your health. Slowing down creates spaciousness. Spaciousness

---

[1] That was meant to be the sound of a thought bubble popping up, in case it got lost in translation. Those listening along to the audio book will get the full experience.

generates feelings of generosity. And in your generosity, you're more able to promote peace and wise action. You can take control of your response-ability.

## the improv impulse

In contrast to the mindful option of pausing to think, improvisation often—and maybe even most of the time—encourages us to remove our self-limiting filters and go with whatever suggestion comes through. Improv wants raw, unfiltered creativity. We celebrate the immediate, often non-verbal impulse and where it can lead. We seek the rat-a-tat-tat passion that gets us out of our minds and vaults us into a scene or story. In many ways, the spontaneity of improvisational theatre compares with letting a pent-up dog off-leash.

Of course, there's a risk involved—no matter how well the dog has been trained, you're really not sure what's going to happen. Even if your dog *tends* to stay nearby on its romp, you always have the uneasy sense you'll end up having to chase her through the woods or into some snowbank late at night. She might snarf down a child's sandwich. She might poop on a neighbor's lawn. Such uncertainty shows up during an improv show too. Even with well-trained improvisors, you never know what will happen. An entire scene or show could crash or go off the rails at any moment.[2]

Acknowledging the risk, you do gain palpable energy by taking your dog off-leash. All the surge that had previously pulled against the collar rockets off into open space. The dog wants to sniff and search and discover new sights and smells. The entire world suddenly comes alive. As the dog's caretaker, you get to see your pooch's strength, beauty and speed, all of which normally stay under wraps. You also improve your own health and happiness, getting to enjoy your pet's companionship without needing the hassle and tension

---

[2] To be fair, I have never seen an improvisor poop on a neighbor's lawn.

of constant control. The dog's joy becomes your own, especially knowing that, once home, your pet will likely drop into a satisfied sleep.

So it is when you allow your impulses freer rein. Your creative mind, which normally stays restricted, gets to run around in open space. You feel the same lift of curiosity and energy as you discover unexpected possibilities and rewards. Movements and ideas gain a quicksilver fluidity and flexibility. You make connections where you'd previously found dead ends. And you find a relaxed, easy joy that leads to a greater satisfaction at day's end.

This is why beginning improv classes emphasize spontaneity right from the start. With a free flow, scenes find range. Stories come alive. Play gets better. Unfortunately, most of us have learned tragically well—from parents, from school, from the workplace, from society—to keep a tight censor's leash on our ideas. As a result, we remain disappointingly uninspired. To get into that more joyful space, we have to release the restriction we discussed last chapter: the fear of failure or embarrassment.

Keith Johnstone, one of the fathers of modern improv, suggests in his classic introductory textbook *Impro* that three main inhibitions keep us from expressing our natural creativity. First, we don't want to look like psychos! If we seem sane, predictable and safe, other people will trust us, like us, and want to hang out with us.[3] Improv students need explicit permission to express the "craziness" they carry inside—that we all carry inside in some way or another—so they're free from having to prevent its release. That doesn't mean they need to share it openly all the time, but to allow that it exists and know that it's OK.

---

[3] Of course, in that case, we could ask if the "us" they know is actually *us* but that's a fuller exploration for another time and place.

Johnstone also asserts that we hold ourselves back for fear of appearing obscene. *What if my creativity leads me to overt or perverted sexual suggestion? What if my impulses suggest violence or cruelty? What if my prejudices and –isms get exposed?* Indeed, what if? We don't know to what extent these forces might be innate or conditioned. Either way, they do live within us and our fullest creativity involves making some peace with that fact. As Swiss psychologist Carl Jung suggested, the shadow, that hidden and unwanted part of ourselves, becomes most dangerous when denied or caged. In the light of day, we can integrate or even befriend it. Again, Johnstone suggests, the instructor's attitude makes a huge difference: "It does help if improvisation teachers are not puritanical and can allow the students to behave as *they* want to behave.... If it isn't possible to let students speak and act with the same freedom they have outside the school, then it might be better not to teach them drama at all."[4]

Lastly, Johnstone argues, we restrain our "first thoughts" because we want to avoid seeming unoriginal. We'd rather strive for the clever, the witty, the strategic. Ironically, in Johnstone's view, such forced effort produces just the opposite: "Striving after originality takes you far away from your true self and makes your work mediocre."[5]

To some degree, such concerns about opening to the unconscious have value. Psychotics can be dangerous. Obscenity or oppressive comments can create discomfort or cause harm. Lack of creative range can prove boring. Fair enough. It's interesting to note, however, that our concern about these possibilities less often stems from the concern that we will *be* that way but that we will be *seen*

---

[4] Keith Johnstone, *Impro: Improvisation and the Theatre* (Methuen: New York, 1981), p. 87.
[5] Johnstone, *Impro*, p. 88.

that way. In other words, we're being driven by our fears about others' approval and acceptance.

Either way, in the creative arena, such self-judgment isn't helpful. In fact, it's toxic. As with emotions, we can't do selective blocking. If we shut down or wall off one stream, we limit them all. If I'm unwilling to feel fear or grief or rage, I'm unable to experience joy and love. If I seal off the seemingly psychotic, obscene, or unoriginal in me, I lose access to the creative and the inspired.

A fascinating study of jazz musical improvisation by Dr. Charles Limb at the University of California, San Francisco in 2008 demonstrated evidence of this dynamic. When he had jazz pianists improvise while in the sights of an MRI (using a custom-constructed plastic keyboard so no metal would get sucked into the machine), he found the parts of the brain linked to self-expression—the medial prefrontal cortex or "default network"—lit up to a greater degree. Simultaneously, the part of the brain connected to self-inhibition and control—the dorsolateral prefrontal cortex—quieted down and almost went to sleep entirely. With self-judgment defanged, the musician could find the creative flow needed to improvise.[6]

This is why a good improv teacher provides resolute, unflinching protection of a welcoming space. It's how her students loosen self-restriction. Especially in classes and rehearsals—the equivalent of a fenced dog park—this effort means establishing safe allowance for whatever comes through. When working with spontaneity, I, as a teacher, say out loud, "If something offensive or unpleasant comes out, I will take ownership of the repercussions. It's not on you." The

---

[6] Sandee LaMotte, CNN, "Jazz Improv and your brain: the key to creativity?", Updated 7:58 pm ET, Sunday April 29, 2018.
https://www.cnn.com/2018/04/29/health/brain-on-jazz-improvisation-improv/index.html

more vibrant, pulsating ideas can emerge and sniff around, getting to interact with other ideas in that safely bounded arena.

In short, when you move from a status quo disposition of rejecting or controlling your ideas—yanking them back into place so they stay in line—to one of celebrating and interacting with them, you start to move from a default "no" to a presumed "yes."[7] You loosen your desire for safety and welcome the possibility of adventure, allowing ideas to run with greater freedom and fluidity than we could have imagined possible. Want the joy of creativity? Take off the collar of self-criticism. Unleash the hounds.

## wisdom in the body

Along those lines, improv teachers often recommend that we trust our body over our brain. The body can have an idea—can know what's needed—before the brain offers its approval or runs the idea through its current likelihood-of-failure or how-will-I-look algorithm. You'll see this happen often when a group first learns an improv standard like I Am a Tree.[8] In the game, players, in no preassigned order, take turns jumping into the middle of a circle and contributing to the unfolding image (the game gets its name from the first entrant who always declares "I am a tree!"). Almost inevitably, a subtle dance of hesitation emerges. Someone takes a breath and shifts their weight forward—it's clear their body wants them to step in. And then, just as quickly, they pull themselves back. Their weight retreats onto their heels and they stop, still glued to the outside rim. When I teach improv, I'm always eager for that moment because it gives a chance to offer a crucial exhortation: "If you notice your body leaning in like that, follow it. Something deeper than your brain knows it's time to enter! Trust that you'll have something when you get to the middle."

---

[7] We'll say more about this in Chapter 11, "Adventure Time! Seeking the Joy of New Experience."

[8] See "I Am a Tree" in the Glossary of Games at the back of the book.

Again, this kind of gut-based, heart-based, rhythm-based impulse lives inside the body, not exclusively in the head. It's not "I have a great idea." An impulse is different from an idea. It's also different from an intuition, which may have a more spiritual or mystical connotation. Our brain may not trust the data it registers coming through but *some* part of us knows "this is what comes next." It's a visceral feeling, almost electrical. When it comes, we have to push ourselves on stage and follow it. It's time to jump in.

Even though verbal improvisation necessarily includes the cerebral part of the brain, there's a similar dynamic of learning to let impulses through. When we play "Three Things" or "Word-at-a-Time" exercises, the "success" and fun of the game comes when we let loose and go with whatever shows up. You don't have to wait for the 'right' idea. You don't have to be clever. Or funny. Or good. Just put *something* out there. Be obvious. Be average.

Trusting your impulses makes a big difference when lighting an improv show as well: you always have to have your finger on the dimmer key, ready to bring the stage to blackout. You might sense a scene has ended but if you take the time to move through a thought process to *confirm* that sense, you miss the opportunity. The moment is gone and it's no longer appropriate to end the scene. The moment the surge rises, you have to follow it.

Again, spontaneous times like these aren't where you want a longer mindfulness pause: *Oh, I've noticed that I have an impulse to pull the lights down. Let me breathe."* Or, "*Hmm, let me generate a full range of possible options."* You just want to go with it. It's like in emergency situations. If I see a child running into a busy street or a vase about to fall, I don't pause and go into a mindful reverie to consider all my options. I move and move quickly. These are instances where unfiltered reaction is good and appropriate.

## pausing in improv

Still—and this is where we step into a bit of paradox—improvisational theatre can also show us that there *are* times where the first idea may not be the best. While making internal space for uninterrupted flow, we can also recognize our responsibility to larger societal patterns and dynamics. Our work, especially when presented publicly, becomes a force that either perpetrates and perpetuates injustice or one that illuminates and liberates. While it may be true, as Keith Johnstone says, that "we are not responsible for the content of our imaginations," we do remain accountable for what we do with that content. [9]

In a workshop or a classroom? Fine. You've got a safe container to let any idea through, no matter how raw. There's no huge risk for taking the hound off leash. If something offensive, hurtful or difficult emerges, the teacher can pause the class and take time to debrief and reset. When a troupe gets on stage for a public performance, however, the rules, strategies, and standards necessarily shift. Forming new expectations isn't easy, especially because great improvisation will explore the full range of human interaction. Nasty villains will do and say nasty things. Performers who care will wrestle with these questions, though.

While on stage, I myself have had experiences on both sides of the spectrum. In one instance, I left the stage wishing I had followed my impulses more directly. That night, I was playing an employee in an old-time movie theater. I was the employee at the desk. An old man came in and we established that he was a long-time patron. I had a photo of him on the wall with his beautiful wife who was riding a horse. She was no longer living and I knew this guy always came to the theater by himself. Would I go in and sit with him in the theater while the show started? The scene took a while to develop as we got to know each other, but it was worth it. The connection made for a

---

[9] Keith Johnstone, *Impro*, p. 105.

super sweet start where the audience genuinely cared for this old man and the relationship.

Eventually, my character did go in and sit with him in the theater. Another player mentioned from off stage that the movie was starting so the old man turned to me and asked, "Oh, what's the movie?" The first thought that came to mind—immediately—was some derelict porn title, like "Va-Va-Va-Vixens." My self-censor jumped in and fumed *No, no, you can't say that.* So I came up with something saccharine like "Together Forever."

Afterward when we talked about the scene, I realized—and my colleagues agreed—that the porn title would have been hi-lar-i-ous. We had established this sweet old man and a tender relationship with the movie usher, the beautiful dead wife... and now here's this unexpected pivot. It was simply my self-editor that didn't want me to be seen as obscene.

In another scene, I remained thankful for the pause I took. On that night, we had three separate stories unfolding, each being told chapter by chapter. We would generate the first scene of each story, and then the audience would eventually vote on which two of the three stories they wanted to see move forward. In the first scene of the first two stories, it turned out that a female character had been captured and imprisoned by men. The third started to unfold that way as well. I noticed that and thought to myself, *Look at this tired sexist trope happening. Here's the helpless damsel waiting to get rescued by some worthy male hero....again.* As improvisors, we wouldn't have *chosen* to reinforce such patterns, but there we were.

As the scene continued, I was playing the bad guy who had captured the woman. In an effort to discover what came next, I reached my hand out into the imaginary wall of my evil lair, not knowing what I would find there. The first thought that came to me—what my unconscious served up--was *Oh, this is a drugged drink that I'm going to give this woman.* In that moment, I had a little mindfulness pause that suggested, *Hmm. I don't want that. I don't want to continue going down that road and make the sexism even more egregious.* So I said to my unconscious, almost like in the improv game New Choice, "Give me something else." I literally took a breath and looked again at the imaginary cup in my hand. And then a new thought came: *OK, so it's a container with sticks of gum in it. I'm going to give her a stick of gum.* Now, the female character was still captive and my character was still trying to seduce her, but at least he was going to have to use his charm rather than drugging her.

In that instance, I was glad I paused long enough to choose a line other than my first thought. I couldn't entirely undo the sexism of the scene but I could at least lessen it.

So, as improv shows us, sometimes a pause doesn't help and sometimes it does.

## going beyond "first idea" in design thinking

The world of design thinking—coming up with practical, creative solutions for human problems using the principles of effective design—offers some great insights along these lines.

Walk in the door of Stanford's graduate Institute of Design (known as the d-School) and you know right away that the place hatches all sorts of creative thinking. Rainbows of Post-it notes stream across transparent walls, brainstorm lists and idea webs reach around corners and posts, and furniture in funky shapes and arrangements invites students to meet in new configurations. The physical space works in concert with its aspirations. Here, it's clear, you can do more than think outside the box. You can redesign the box altogether.

On my conference group's day-long visit to the d-School, presenters Leticia Britos Cavagnaro and Maureen Carroll helped me understand their approach soon after we arrived. "The key to creativity," Leticia offered, "is seeing problems as opportunities. The bigger the problem, the bigger the opportunity." Our group got the chance to dive into one such opportunity by examining the harrowing experience of moving house. Most of the room groaned in recognition of this common "problem." Who wants the hassle and disruption that comes with that chaos? Our starting exercise would look to find some kind of possibility within that pain.

The d-School rubric proved helpful for the task. To build empathy, we formed pairs and shared stories of what we each had experienced when we had to move. As individuals, we then worked to define just what problem our partner was facing in this scenario. Moving into the brainstorming phase, we took time to imagine what *could* be possible, making sure to hold off on dismissing or clinging to any particular idea.

As we dug into that brainstorming phase, however, I stumbled a bit on one suggestion: "Go beyond the first idea." In d-School terms, this meant not to get locked in to the first possibility that comes to mind. My improv hackles raised immediately: *Here's another censoring of healthy impulse.* I listened and watched skeptically as Leticia demonstrated the notion by directing a group of ten volunteers to put themselves in order by birthday within the calendar year– and to do so in one minute without talking. January would fall on the left, December all the way to the right. Quickly, those who had volunteered zeroed in on a preferred method, holding up fingers to indicate which was their birth month. Those who found themselves sharing a birth month with another then counted out the day number using the same method. At the end of the minute, the group had gotten most—but not quite all—members in order.

Leticia had established an artificial urgency that forced the group to take action so there wasn't real time for a lingering mindfulness pause. At the same time, no one moved past that first idea. They could have written birthdates on paper, they could have held up driver's licenses, they could even have *sung* their birthdays. (The directive was no *talking*.) Instead, they locked into that first idea and the locking prevented the possibility of actually completing the task within the given time frame. A good brainstorm reserves judgment or evaluation of possibilities as they emerge. The first idea might prove fantastic or it might come saturated with or filtered through unconscious harmful biases. Either way, latching on too quickly to one approach could prevent other, better ideas from ever coming into view.

## from judgment to discernment

Now you see the apparent conflict between improvisation and mindfulness. On one hand, as improv usually suggests, going with the first idea that shows up might employ the unconscious mind's ability to generate creative insight from whatever lies at hand. In that way, you avoid the critical lenses that would snip off a bud of insight before it ever had the chance to blossom. On the other hand, that first idea may simply result from the ruts and patterns of your conditioning. Maybe you will only play inside the walls of the boxes you know. In that scenario, mindfully looking past the first idea keeps your eyes open for further possibility. You step out of your reactivity, break free from your patterns, and challenge your habits. So which is it, then: How can you monitor your impulses without censoring them? How can you determine what's a healthy leading from the gut and what will lead to gut-wrenching regret? Do you follow the first idea or go beyond it?

In short, one healthy answer is to move from *judgment of* your impulses to *discernment about* them. Judgment usually comes as an immediate, reflexive reaction to the impulse that has surfaced. It makes a personal assessment—usually negative in some way—with puppet-string quickness and elevates the one judging while diminishing the one judged. (This could also be one part of ourselves judging another part of ourselves.) It declares a simple "yes" or "no" and calcifies its decision in a way that resists new information or changing conditions. Because it springs so quickly from deeply grooved channels of the unconscious mind, it also often relies on prejudice or fear and thus serves dominant social paradigms. It's no wonder that tendrils of creativity would shrink in its presence.

Discernment, on the other hand, suggests a more patient, considered response. It makes a situational or behavioral assessment—rather than a personal one—and recognizes an interrelationship between the discerner and the discerned. Rather than establishing a simple yes or no, it asks, "How does this idea or impulse match my intention?" and engages in an ongoing, flexible interaction to generate more understanding. It brings the conscious mind into friendly contact with the unconscious and thus, can acknowledge prejudice and fear without giving in to them. It honors the creative. It *serves* the impulse.

In improv and in regular life, a mindful pause helps make this maneuver. An experience happens or a thought arises, one that I might register as pleasant or unpleasant, but rather than reacting in my typical way—grasping at attraction or flinching with aversion— I simply take a moment or two. In this case, the pause is neither a stammer of waffling or wimping out nor a hammer of self-restriction. It's a wider space where more possibilities and options for my next move emerge. Now I have a range to choose from. Rather than reacting, I'm responding.

We hasten this pattern of healthy discernment by trusting our stagemates—or, off-stage, our teammates and friends—to call us on our missteps and take care of us when we're hurting. We can each serve as the other's loving filter, naming without blaming "Ouch, that hurt" or "Check that out—that's uncomfortable" instead of "What the hell?" or "You always do that!" Improvisors on stage and in life can also make sense of a 'mistake' in the moment by using it and building on it. Maybe a heinous character in a scene says or does something awful, but the other characters rally in resourceful response to provide an effective foil. Or maybe together we justify the hiccup by providing a glimpse of a grittier reality. Life includes unpleasantness and obscenity. Theatre can too.

| judgment | discernment |
|---|---|
| Immediate | Patient |
| Reflexive/reactionary | Responsive |
| More personal assessment-- about others and self | More situational/behavioral assessment |
| Yes/no, be done with it | What is preferable? Establish ongoing interaction |
| More calcified in position | Acknowledges the chance of error |
| Less open to changing conditions | Flexible |
| Unconscious | Conscious |
| Relies on prejudice and/or fear | Can acknowledge prejudice and fear without being controlled by them |
| Perpetuates dominant paradigm | Opens possibility of new ways of being |

Ultimately, we're convincing—or at least asking—our muses to trust our fundamental shift in attitude. We change our internal dialogue in relation to our suggestions. We choose to hang with others who celebrate and build upon our offers and we offer the same in return. Once the muses buy in to our overall stance—*Oh, you've finally established a pattern of welcoming in whatever we send! Great, we'll send more!*—they need not shrink or flinch, even in times of discerning evaluation. Not every idea needs to be acted on. The muses get that. Once a friendly rapport has been established, the unleashed mind need not run off in crazy abandon. It can settle into contented connection, both willfully wild and open to refinement.

When we get up to perform—again, particularly in front of an audience—it's not a tightly restricted thin band of possibility and it's not a free-for-all with whatever occurs to us. Just as when we're looking to be creative in our interactions at home or at work, we're not inviting the unconscious mind to spew forth random crap. We can learn to hone our skill in honoring the contents of our imagination. As in mindfulness practice, we notice and nod to our thoughts or feelings without being beholden to them. Over time, we start to figure out which filters qualify as helpful and which get in the way.

In the end, this paradox asks you to develop a practice and work on a skill. You're not getting rid of default responses altogether, but you are *resetting* the default to something closer to what you seek. As you get more established in a steady mindfulness practice, the pause happens almost instantly. You don't need to make a big production of stepping out of flow to say, "Let me just observe this for a moment.... " It just happens. And it happens quickly.

Eventually, you start to move out of unconscious, automatic habits—your reactions, assumptions, and established patterns—and move into something more wide-ranging. By including both poles of the tension—*trust your impulses* **and** *go beyond the first* *idea*—with the same natural ease that you include an inhale and exhale with each breath, you give up on harsh evaluation while also maintaining your intention. In that mode, more resourceful responses easily emerge---*bwhooop!*—to make themselves available. You can savor the unbridled joy of creativity released. And you know that you can clean up any messes that follow as a result. What a lovely place to be.

# Chapter 3
## Impulse or Pause? *Moving from Judgment to Discernment*

### GEMS from the JOURNEY

- Mindfulness encourages us to pause so that we interrupt our reactivity and have the chance to choose a more artful response.

- Improvisation invites us to trust our impulses and unleash the creativity that comes with them. Oftentimes, those impulses come most notably through the body as a whole rather than just through the brain and its thinking.

- Going beyond the "first idea" sometimes leads to deeper insight.

- Quieting the voice of judgment and developing a wiser discernment helps us find the right balance between impulse and pause.

### PARADOX

- We can embrace our impulses and still make conscious choices about what to do or say in any given circumstance.

### GOING DEEPER

- Experiment with expressing your impulses. What happens if you say what you're actually thinking? How do others react when you act more boldly? Note whether your results confirm or challenge your expectations. Note also whether your expectations color—or even prompt—the results you receive.

- Also try noting your first impulse and generating three other options. What happens when you insert a mindful pause before reacting?

- Assemble a group of at least three friends to play "I Am a Tree" as described in the Glossary of Games.

# you, then me; me, then you:
## *building the magic of shared control*

IMAGINE GETTING SET TO STEP ON STAGE in front of 1,100 students at an elite New England boarding school. You and your colleague thought you'd have 25 minutes to present but as it turns out, there's been an unexpected delay. You'll only have 22. So that down-to-the-minute plan you'd cooked up? Now compressed, smooth logic made impossible. You've also been told that this audience has legendarily high standards. Lots of famous folks have spoken in this spot— Hollywood celebrities, intellectual titans, US presidents—so you know the students won't suffer fools, pretenders or BS-ers. As your host told you in the prep meeting the day before, "The kids will turn on you if they smell fear." So, great. This could be a train wreck. You could go down in flames. The host starts your introduction and you notice your heart rate has increased and your legs feel a bit wobbly. Aaaaaaand...go!

For many folks, such a set-up would qualify as a horrific nightmare, a certain recipe for a panic attack if not an outright cardiac arrest.[1] For Lisa Rowland and me, though, it was the opposite. Here was an opportunity to do our thing. Though we felt some nerves, we also

---

[1] They say more people fear public speaking than fear death. Situations like this make that statistic understandable.

felt confident. So much so that even with the tighter time frame, we led off with an unpredictable and risky experiment: creating a one-word-at-a-time introduction to our presentation. We didn't know what we would say but we knew we would say something. What gave us enough confidence to overcome such a daunting scenario? *Our shared practice and resolute trust in shared control.*

Here's a transcript of what Lisa and I came up with that moment in front of the boarding school crowd. This emerged at close to regular speaking speed.

**Ted:** *So*

**Lisa:** *we*

**Ted:** *would*

**Lisa:** *like*

**Ted:** *to*

**Lisa:** *share*

**Ted:** *with*

**Lisa:** *you*

**Ted:** *this*

**Lisa:** *bit*

**Ted:** *of*

**Lisa:** *wisdom.*

**Ted:** *When*

**Lisa:** *you*

**Ted:** *have*

**Lisa:** *a(n)*

**Ted:** *opportunity*

**Lisa:** *to*

**Ted:** *seize*

**Lisa:** *the*

**Ted:** *day,*

**Lisa:** *do*

**Ted:** *it*

**Lisa:** *even*

**Ted:** *when*

**Lisa:** *that*

**Ted:** *opportunity*

**Lisa:** *is*

**Ted:** *not*

**Lisa:** *what*

**Ted:** *you*

**Lisa:** *expected*

**Ted:** *it*

**Lisa:** *to*

**Ted:** *be.*

**Lisa:** *It*

**Ted:** *might*

**Lisa:** *be*

**Ted:** *a*

**Lisa:** *new*

**Ted:** *opportunity*

**Lisa:** *that*

**Ted:** *surprises*

**Lisa:** *you*

**Ted:** *with*

**Lisa:** *delight.*

That's a bit of "Word-at-a-Time," an unrehearsed, fully spontaneous intro given onstage in front of more than a thousand people. It's not the Gettysburg address, but neither is it horrible. It demonstrated what we wanted to show. And the crowd loved it.[2]

Sharing control stands out as one of the most critical practices in improv—and in a life well-lived. Neither goes so well without it. In improv-speak, "sharing control" means picking up on the offers from your partner and building on them. It also means letting go of your ideas if your partner's idea doesn't mirror yours. You adapt to what's happening rather than holding firm to what you came in with. You recognize that you'll be on a roller coaster ride of suggestions and possibilities that emerge and disappear in every moment. Each person's input informs the other's. And something new and unpredictable emerges from the partnership.

Admittedly, some folks don't prefer this cup of tea when they're first learning the form. They'd rather stick with their own ideas and work to maintain full control when they're on stage. If that preference stays stuck over time, they'll probably do better as a playwright or a solitary sketch writer. They can sit in a room and write down their ideas and... end up with their ideas. For many who do improvisation, though, the whole point is the collaboration. You create with somebody else and enjoy the surprise of where you end up together.

Of course, one can do an on-the-spot monologue and that might make a beautiful improvisation. Even in that situation (though it might be tougher to spot), shared control is still happening. The improvisor delivers her "lines" by quieting the logical brain and sharing control with her unconscious mind. Note how this differs from free association, where the unconscious takes the driver's seat and the improvisor rides in back. In this case, one offer comes, and the improvisor responds—volleying an offer in return, back to the

---

[2] For a fuller description of how to do "Word-at-a-Time" exercises, see the Glossary of Games at the back of the book.

unconscious. The unconscious sends forward another offer and the improvisor responds again. It all emerges moment to moment.[3]

This unpredictable quality is what improv audiences love most: *Ooh, we don't know where it's going. The actors don't know where it's going. How will they integrate this new input?* And they especially love when they see an improvisor start with one idea and another comes on stage and defines that person doing something else or in a different location—meaning the first improvisor has to adapt on the fly to gracefully accept what the second person has created. It's magic.

For example, if you come on stage and make a motion as if you're opening a jar, and then I come on stage to say, "Great, we only have 14 more squirrel necks to break," then the original twisting motion you were doing has become squirrel-killing. The audience sees you good-naturedly accept my offer—*Toss that squirrel aside, pick up another, and... Twist. Snap.*—and they know it's different from what you originally intended. A grisly example, perhaps, but you can see how the instant adaptation proves compelling, enough so to evoke a raw but real affection from the audience members. They fall in love with you a little bit and get excited about where we're both going next. They know for certain that neither of us has total control.

One of the most delightful aspects of improvisation—and for me, the most thrilling—is getting to the end of a scene and realizing, *That could not have happened without me AND I couldn't have done that alone.* Every player's fingerprints are on the scene. Each's influence is clear. But none of what unfolded would have emerged

---

[3] Such a one-person scene can provide a poignant, helpful balance to other scenes that have showed up that night. Still, if that's all an improvisor ever plays—if every time they come out on stage, they end up doing a monologue—their stagemates are going to get pretty sick of playing with that person because nothing ever comes back. That player has opted out of their commitment to delight in fully shared control.

without the others. And so the particular scene becomes a unique creation or combination of influences, an ephemeral celebration just for us and the audience. Together, we've formed a distinct and unrepeatable constellation of people and space and time.

I also love when this approach shows up in everyday interactions. In a conversation, can we both contribute evenly by building on the other's offers—rather than hijacking them? When choosing a spot for dinner, do we both get input—and thus surprise ourselves with the end result? In decorating a home, can we share equally in the final arrangement? Whenever the shared control works, it generates real affection and natural intimacy. Our creative songs have intertwined and their echoes now ripple out as one wave, forever.

### 'line-at-a-time'

In our weekend retreat offerings, Lisa Rowland and I have used a concentrated version of this process that happens on stage. It's called "Line-at-a-Time Muse" or "Line-at-a-Time Deity."[4]

Here's how it works: you and a partner start with a blank piece of paper and one or two pens or markers. Then you put two dots on the page about a third of the way down and evenly spaced horizontally. Maybe those dots will become eyes, maybe not. From there, one partner makes a single gesture—a line, a circle, or any other shape, linked to what's already on the page or not—and puts the pen down. The other partner picks up the pen and adds their two cents. In this way, the two of you go back and forth, taking turns, one line at a time. Maybe you continue to develop a theme you sense emerging from your partner's contributions. Maybe you go back and add to something you've already started. Maybe you

---

[4] I first learned this from friend, colleague, and UC-Berkeley Haas School of Business lecturer Cort Worthington, who may have learned it from Keith Johnstone. You can also play it as a more general Line-at-a-Time drawing where you don't know that a character will emerge. Look for a full description in the Glossary of Games at the back of the book.

start something new. Eventually, between you and your partner, an image emerges of some new being. When one of you feels the time is right, that person starts writing the new character's name, one letter at a time. In the end, you have an image and a name for this being represented in the image. It's an amazing process that inevitably generates fascinating results.

This exercise reminds me of my own tendency to grasp for control: *Aww, I just really want to make sure this goes well. I want to keep that eye specific and finish up the detail on the lips. Or, I want to make a line that is technically only one line that continues on and on, so it covers enough of the page to ensure my partner knows what this is supposed to look like. Or If I can just make it clear enough, they'll know what shape of the face or type of eyebrows I'm intending.*

Thankfully, I also usually remember to just let go and tell myself, *Just respond to what your partner is doing. You can come back to your own idea later if you need to.* When I can let go, the image comes out way better. We've each made our contribution and waited with curiosity about how it will morph, knowing that it's highly unlikely that any effort will end up how either of us anticipated or envisioned individually.

As you might predict, some of these images end up looking chaotic. That sometimes happens when we share control. That need not be a bad thing. Chaos can be really beautiful.[5] And the same is true of improvisation. It's highly messy and oftentimes bizarre and doesn't quite make sense. A lot of times it does make sense, but befriending chaos always helps the process. If we can release our ownership over how our idea ends up being used, it can grow on its own. It can breathe. It can fly.

---

[5] As you'll learn more about in Chapter 7, "Chaos Theory: Balancing Preparation and Pandemonium."

## sharing control with life

Really, that talk Lisa and I gave to the private school students was not just about give-and-take between study partners or how improvisors should include each other's influence on stage. It was just as much about sharing control with life itself. You can have a plan for your life, but life has plans as well. You can set your goals and intentions, but you should know that life will want to contribute too. If you consider your life more like a word-at-a-time conversation or a line-at-a-time drawing, where you make your mark and then get information on which to base your next move, some new co-creative magic might emerge. The trick is to stay open to whom and what life is bringing you.

Like those students we were speaking with, you may have been raised to believe you could control your own destiny. Play your cards right and you'll have the house, the spouse, the money and the fame you've always wanted. Assemble a five-year plan with clear objectives and SMART goals, and you'll be on your way.

Problem is, you're not in control of your life. You obviously have *some* influence on what happens—maybe even a lot—but you'll also encounter unpredictable bumps, bruises, interruptions and roadblocks along the way. It seems patently obvious to say, but where you are in five years depends directly and entirely on what happens between now and five years from now. And much of that you can't predict or plan for.

What you *can* do is set an intention and say, "OK, that's where I want to go." But it's better that you hold that compass point lightly—or maybe not hold onto it at all—by placing it out in the distance on the horizon. Like, that's where you *think* you're going. But the point is not that you're actually going to end up there. The point is setting out on an adventure that gets you moving. Once you're moving, you start to pay more attention to what's happening. And then you adjust. As life offers you responses in return, you'll adjust again and make another offer. You and life play together. In a year's time, you might notice that that original intention no longer fits. So you'll shift it and set another to take its place.

## boldness and adaptability

What we're talking about here forms a fascinating combination—in both life and improvisation—of boldness and adaptability. Having a bold plan or making a clear claim can provide huge help. You're putting a stake in the ground and standing by it. You've made a decision and claimed, "This is it. I'm strong." And there's power in that certainty. Again, this could be on stage: your character establishes clean boundaries of who and where they are and what they're about. *Darius, if I don't get this musket cleaned and loaded, those Redcoats are going to waltz right in and take this farm and the Revolution will have ended before it's started.* The specifics give your improv partner something to play off. Or it could be in life or at work, where this kind of boldness shows up as stating your position, offering your opinion, or naming your desire. Onstage or off-, anytime we sing our song clearly, others can more easily find the right "notes" for harmonizing. They know where to fit in.

Adaptability means following right on the heels of that boldness with radical openness. One moment, you're declaring a position with confidence. The next, you're willing to completely abandon it based on what else has actually happened. Rarely do we make a super strong move in life and then allow ourselves to drop it like that. More often, we hold tenaciously to it. We want to be consistent and confident. We don't want others to think we're "flip-flopping." That we don't have the discipline or willpower. Maybe our change of mind—our adaptability—doesn't suggest any of those negative conclusions. Maybe it's just that we've gotten more information and allowed that data to inform us.

Here's an example. One of my friends in her 60s made the bold decision to retire as a nurse practitioner, thinking "It would be great to travel with my husband, and it would be great to be available to my kids." Soon after leaving the hospital, though, she realized that she had gotten a lot of meaning out of her work. Faced with that new insight, she struggled with whether to come out of retirement and go back to work. *No, I can't do that. I retired. I should stick to it. They had a party for me.*

When she was able to reframe the situation for herself—*Look, you made a step you needed to make with the information you had: it was time to retire. Now you have new information pointing you in another direction, and you owe it to your life to follow those road signs*—her options became clearer, and she went back to work. No need to stay with a choice just because she had made it. That's boldness followed by adaptability. Act. Listen. Act again.

## wu wei: action through inaction

Choosing to share control can mean loosening one's death grip on the reins of life. Decisions and choices can start to feel a lot freer and easier. They develop a sense of flow. Committing to that approach may necessitate, then, challenging the notion that the path of least resistance is a bad thing. Thanks to whatever story we've been told—Protestant work ethic? Immigrant survival skills? Athletic competition?—many of us believe that we have to put blood, sweat and tears into every effort we make. *Grind it out. Work hard. No pain, no gain.* It's all about bootstraps getting pulled up. *Get knocked down seven times, get up seven more.* Of course, there's a bit of wisdom in such aphorisms and some of them make charming posters. But if you're getting badly buffeted by your life choices, better results might arise from a different approach. Maybe the wiser choice follows what flows, what gets the most reinforcement, and where doors open in natural time. Maybe looking for the easy way works better than a bull-headed path that insists on certainty (which is an illusion anyway).

Here, then, is another way that improv wisdom lines up beautifully with mindfulness and other Eastern philosophies. In specific, Taoism introduces the concept of *Wu Wei*, action through inaction or effortless doing. In that mindset, you move and choose your path like water, following prevailing currents that flow according to gravity's pull. In improvisation, you similarly change shape to fit your environment and maintain the flexibility of different forms. You can keep a hand on the steadying tiller of intention, but you're mostly floating with the river's direction.

Meditation tends to lead you on a similar path. Rather than preferring or resisting certain types of thoughts or emotions, you simply attend to what arises (and falls away). Again, your hand might rest on a rudder or anchor—breath, sounds, thoughts—but it does so lightly, returning to focus as needed with humor, curiosity and kindness. As you do when sharing control on stage or with others in your life, this approach to mindfulness can bring you to greater discovery and delight. You learn new things about being alive.

## taking the plunge with big decisions

Not so long ago, I was teaching religious studies and philosophy in New England at a boarding school.[6] I had an enviable life. I loved my job, I loved the kids. It was a gorgeous place. I lived in a beautiful home provided by the school. I got paid relatively well. I had summers off with generous professional development funds for exploring new ideas. All that was great. And...my heart—or life itself—kept calling out: *You need to do something more in line with your whole being. You'll never get to explore the full range of your passion for mindfulness and improvisation in this setting.* I knew that leaving would mean giving up on the community and years of

---

[6] Northfield Mount Hermon, along the Connecticut River just south of Vermont and New Hampshire. Not the same place where Lisa and I gave the presentation mentioned at the open of this chapter.

memories I had woven myself into. I'd be letting go of reliable security. Could I give up that level of predictable control and give myself over to what life was asking of me?

Patricia Ryan Madson, my improv teacher at Stanford, offered great perspective as I wrestled with the decision. Over the phone, she simply said "The great thing, Ted, is that you don't need to know the end of the story. You just need to figure out what comes next." Yes. So true. Patricia's few words freed me up entirely. I didn't know what else might unfold, but I knew for certain that I wanted to move to California, to work with Lisa, and to connect more with the renowned BATS Improv community in San Francisco. That was enough. I could ease my furious grip on the future and let life's impulses working through me take over for a while.

The few years since then have, of course, included variability and unpredictability. Some days have felt lonely and uncertain. Other days have felt exquisite and magical, like I couldn't have imagined it being this good. Wherever I have been on this spectrum on any given day, though, I have sensed a different kind of hum in the background of my life, a fulfilling sense that I'm participating in something more effortless and larger than myself. Allowing shared control feels more fully alive.

So, then, this is another paradox to wrestle with: the "path of least resistance" we're talking about might actually involve some challenges. It might not require physical exertion, but it definitely can ask a lot emotionally. *Are you willing to face your fear of uncertainty? Can you allow the vulnerability of openness? Will you trust in the generosity of the world?* In my case, I left the comfort of friends and community that I had built up over twelve years because life was giving me information that said clearly, *Go to California.* It took a while for me to screw up the courage to take on that risk, but I'm glad I did.

It can be both inspiring and breathtaking to conjure up this kind of trust in the universe. Know then, that just because you don't know what information you'll have at the next step doesn't mean you won't have it when you get there. Just because you can't see where you're going doesn't mean you'll end up stranded. You might end up having what you need. In my case, I could rely on the awareness that when I got out west, the world would look different and I would have more information with which to make my next move.

At some point, you'll also face a time where you have to give up control and take a leap into the unknown. As Mrs. Morris, a friend's wise high school piano teacher, once advised: "A trapeze artist has to let go of the bar with both hands before she will be close enough to grab the next."[7] In that moment, you're neither here nor there. You've let go of the last bar and not grabbed onto the new one... yet. In order to reach the other side, you have to trust that whatever you're going for (or perhaps some altogether different blessing) will come within reach.

Thankfully, both mindfulness and improvisation teach us how to hang out in that liminal, in-between space, enjoy the uncertainty, and delight in the shared creation of what comes next. The gap between the notes becomes a moment of possibility rather than an out-of-control nightmare. You choose to let go into that mid-air suspension and trust that life will provide the bar on the other side of the leap. You contribute. Life contributes. You contribute. Life contributes. Something great—and delightfully unpredictable— emerges from the collaboration. And that partnership feels good.

---

[7] The French poet Andre Gide made a similar point in one of my favorite quotations: "One does not discover new lands without consenting to lose sight of the shore for a very long time."

## Chapter 4

### You Then Me, Me Then You: *Finding Delight in Shared Control*

#### GEMS from the JOURNEY

- *Improvisation explicitly teaches and practices the joy of shared control: boldly picking up on a partner's "offers" and building on them—and leaving room for them to do the same in return.*

- *Just as improvisors share control on stage, you can share control with your life and the circumstances that arise.*

- *The Taoist concept of "Wu Wei"—action through inaction, or effortless doing—offers a great example of going with the flow, the way water moves down a hill or into a new shape.*

#### PARADOX

- *Skillful shared control requires everyone involved to make bold choices—make a declaration, take an action, open up an emotion—while also adapting generously to the choices of others.*

- *The path of least resistance may actually prove the most effective path to your destination. At the same time, that least resistance may require some notable effort.*

**GOING DEEPER**

- *See if you can tune in this week to the "offers" life presents you. How might you meet it with a bold offer of your own? Can you then let go of that until life returns with yet another response?*

- *Try seeking out the opinion of others and then incorporating those opinions into what you're doing, even if it's not how you would do it. How does that choice affect your relationship with that person? Do you feel more or less connected?*

- *Find a friend or get a good-sized group together to try out some word-at-a-time exercises or line-at-a-time drawings. (It could make for a great party!) You can find specific suggestions and directions in the Glossary of Games.*

# want without need:
## *balancing aspiration and acceptance*

WE'VE DISCUSSED RECOGNIZING AN IMPULSE while also pausing for a moment of discernment. We played with the notion of taking bold action through inaction. Now we get to honoring a third central tension from the intersecting worlds of mindfulness and improvisation: that between aspiration and acceptance. Take comfort: as you continue to build your capacity for holding such simultaneous truths, their seeming complexity will begin its turn to wisdom. Paradox might make a confusing partner, but Truth tends to hang out nearby. Get familiar with one, you'll soon bump into the other.

## the simplicity of mindfulness

Mindfulness practice teaches us to notice what is with curiosity and kindness. We don't have to like it, necessarily, but we seek to accept that it *is*. Reality exists. Improvisation starts with the same premise: accept your partner's offers and build on them. What your partner has added to the scene has been added to the scene. You can't change that. So, what comes next? Both traditions build the muscle of "acceptance with equanimity." And we can build that muscle with the simplest of practices.

In courses with the UK-based Mindfulness in Schools Project, teachers introduce a mini-meditation called a "dot b" (spelled ".b").[1] In the exercise, you pause—the dot is like the period at the end of a sentence, giving you a moment to take a breath—and then feel your feet and feel your breathing. You take a moment just to be. Dot (that is, pause). Be.

When I lead the exercise, I usually have folks mill about the room as if they're in a hurry. "Mind each other so you're not bumping into anyone," I caution. "But, oh my God, you're checking your list and you have to pick up the groceries and you forgot to get the kids to the store..." I ramp up the hurry and the anxiety, getting people whirring about until... "Diiiinnngggg," I ring a bell and we pause. Everyone does a .b. I have them return to milling as if they're still in a hurry, and then, "ding," invite another .b. And we do it a third time.

Usually, folks notice that, after the first time of doing the .b, their hurry changes. They're still in a rush, but it's not quite so frantic or pressured. They can move quickly without *stressing* about it. In the moment, the simple act of pausing for 10 or 15 seconds completely transforms the experience. At the end of one such workshop, one participant shared, "I was amazed at how easy mindfulness can be. Like, all we have to do is a .b, and I felt so much more relaxed and so much more present. With everybody in the room." And I thought, *You're right. It is that easy.* Pause, catch your breath, and bring yourself present. *You're here. Great!*

### not so easy

Even the micropractice of a .b can help cultivate a calm acceptance and peaceful greeting for each moment. Super efficient. Super effective. It's that easy. And, of course, it isn't. We human beings also have the natural desire to better ourselves. We want to improve

---

[1] From the Mindfulness in Schools Project curriculum for teens that goes by the same name. So ".b" is both the curriculum and the name of a practice within the curriculum.

our situations. We get itchy with how things are. And when we don't get what we want, we feel frustrated. It may seem obvious, but it's worth mentioning: these cravings and desires for something different don't disappear even when you have an established mindfulness and improvisation practice.

So, maybe it would be more accurate to say that mindfulness is *simple* rather than *easy*. Even with significant mindfulness experience under my belt, I still struggle with the world as it is. I, too, resist reality. Take the time I traveled in Turkey, for example. The jet lag had left me feeling dazed. Our hectic schedule had me bouncing around from event to event. And I couldn't get good sleep. The foreign (to me) language left my brain constantly overstimulated and overworked, trying to make sense of the world around me. Istanbul with its 16 million people, unpredictable traffic, and ongoing nightlife jumbled up my introverted sensibilities. Predictably, I felt distinctly stressed.

Even knowing that what I needed was to meditate, I had the hardest time picking up and maintaining my practice. I'd coach myself to relax, saying *OK, be here. Breathe. Just notice.* But those intentions got crowded out by a stronger-voiced annoyance. And then I got annoyed with feeling annoyed: *Why am I so frustrated all the time? Why am I so short of temper"* In the ten days of my visit, I never found an easy peace. My work went fine. I had some fun. I saw beautiful places with my friends, and I led a great workshop. But I left thinking I was a bit of an impostor with this mindfulness stuff. I hadn't escaped my desire for things to be different.

Usually, if I hear someone struggling in the same way, I calmly ask, "Well, how did you relate to not finding peace? Can you just be with that?" In talking with that other person, I bring out the mindfulness tools of curiosity, kindness,[2] and taking a step back a meta-level or two to get some perspective: *Oh, look. I'm frustrated about being*

---

[2] See Chapter 12, "Isn't That Curious? Exploring the World with Eager Eyes."

*frustrated but the part of me that is observing isn't feeling frustrated. It's just witnessing.*[3] At that point, the insights usually begin to flow. But in this case—in my own case—even that didn't work. Despite my track record, I simply couldn't get there. The frustration had thoroughly permeated my experience. Rather than spaciousness, I felt self-criticism: *I'm just not good at mindfulness. This is hard stuff, and I don't know if I'll ever be good at it.* And, as per usual, I *so* wanted to be *good* at it.

A similar dynamic often can show up in improvisation as well. On one level, doing improv can seem the easiest thing in the world. You don't have to *do* anything. You don't have to strive. You can just notice and discover. See what happens, stay present and accept offers: everything will be fine. But then that ease can turn on a dime. You can do a crappy scene or have a bad show and feel like *Oh, I don't even know what I'm doing anymore. I'm still terrible at this.* Such self-doubts run deep and can rise up at a moment's notice, even for the most experienced improvisors.[4]

Of course, improvisation will always include a big dose of mystery. Because of that, no matter how long we work at it, we'll never completely figure it out. And thank goodness! We do improv for the surprise, after all. We seek that "OMIGOD!" experience that shows up every so often. *I never could have predicted we'd go here!* On the negative side, though, we can start thinking *I did all my best improv*

---

[3] See Chapter 8, "Meta-tation: The Benefits of a Bigger Picture."
[4] Before a two-person improv show that Lisa Rowland and I performed at Phillips Exeter academy, she mentioned feeling a little nervous, as in "Am I going to be good at this? Will this work out?" I was flabbergasted. She's one of the best improvisors I've ever seen, reliably bold and delightful. "Lisa Rowland, what do you mean are you going to be good at improv?!?!?! Are you crazy? You're fantastic at this!" And yet, that feeling still arose in her, that slight but persistent question of adequacy/inadequacy. Again, these patterns run deep. They really do.

*and the scene still didn't work. Now let me figure out why.* That mystery is forever humbling and exciting—and problematic at times. Maybe it was our fault, maybe it wasn't, but we simply couldn't work our way out of it.

It's like in those old-timey cartoons where the hapless hero reaches into the quiver on his back for an arrow and pulls out a can of tuna fish. Or he reaches in again and pulls out a Bible. Everything he's known no longer works. That's how I felt in Turkey. *I've got my tools. I'll just sit for 10 minutes and catch my breath. I'll write in my journal. That will quiet things down.* But that didn't work. *I'll just eat some protein. I'll eat a protein bar.* Did that help? Nope. Normally, I might have tried talking it out, relying on my verbal processing skills, but in that instance, I couldn't speak the language! I just kept reaching back and found nothing in my toolkit. Except that damn can of tuna.

## the importance of physical well-being

Now that I have gotten some time distance from that trip to Turkey, I've also gotten a bit of perspective. I remind myself that, just as in improv, there are so many elements of daily life that can prevent achieving a relaxed, centered, resourceful, accepting-what-is feeling. The barrier could be fear, anxiety or my mind revving in overdrive. Those factors get especially ramped up in a new or unusual situation: the primitive brain kicks into gear to watch for threats and dangers. Looking back, I sense the biggest variables at play during that Turkey visit were my fatigue and disrupted food patterns.

In short, I hadn't cared well enough for my body. I couldn't find the resources I was reaching for—and thus had a hard time accepting the moment—because I didn't have a stabilizing biochemical buffer to ground me. I had crossed ten time zones in a day and a half and not had a solid meal to settle in after I arrived. At one point early on in the trip, my hands were literally shaking because I had gotten so hungry. I had a headache and felt particularly prickly. I know no meditation that could have lifted me out of that funk until I got food in my belly.[5] Even after I had something to eat, my hands were still trembling for a half hour.

Oftentimes, the benefits we seek from mindfulness practice—or from almost any self-help technique, really—are those that come from self-care. You need to sleep. You need to exercise. You need to eat well. For some (including me), eating well means not eating sugar, gluten, dairy or other system-disruptors. If I take care of getting food, sleep and exercise, I'm probably going to feel at least 50% better even before I get to any moment on a meditation cushion.

Of course, the same is true of getting on stage for a show—or getting "on stage" for any "performance" in your life. If you're tired or hungry, you won't see or hear that much of what's happening. You'll more likely get pulled into self-judgment or self-evaluation in the moment. You'll lean away from what's happening and seek self-protective refuge. Your attention is more likely to wander. You'll get cranky and resistant. And so on. Simply put, the neurons just won't fire the same way.

### the need to challenge mental defaults

So, insufficient food, sleep, and physical well-being can get in the way of a peaceful, ready acceptance of what *is*. Our mental default patterns can do that too. I mean those moments of self-judgment when we ask ourselves, *Damn, why did I do that? I know better than that.* These critical thoughts can often arise out of well-grooved habits. Over time, we've established patterns of thinking and feeling that have become like neural superhighways crossing the terrain of

---

[5] Thankfully, I did maintain enough self-awareness to know that I should stop talking. Any words coming from my mouth other than "I just need to get food" were going to come out wrong. I suppose that's worth a few "I'm good at mindfulness" points anyway.

our minds. All mental traffic gets routed that way. It is how it is with us because it's been how it's always been.

Eventually, we need to dig into our mental patterns to start constructing new routes and roundabouts.[6] That's exactly what mindfulness, improvisation, and a growth mindset help you do. Because our brains remain ever-changeable, anything can be learned, unlearned, retaught or reshaped. Old stories can get retold. Familiar images can get a reframe. In this case, you start to catch the default derision and offer up another, more helpful option. *I never do well when I have to speak up in front of other people* gets redirected to *I'm excited for the adventure of speaking up because I learn something every time I do.*

As I've mentioned before, other people can prove immensely helpful in reshaping these patterns. Friends can hear when you start going negative. Colleagues can note when you complain. Family members can point out blind spots.[7] If they can do this for you without judging you themselves—that is, with *their* curiosity and kindness front and center—then their contribution strengthens your practice and hastens your change-making.

If you take up this journey, it's wise to ask how you might find—or build—that kind of a practice community. What group do you want to align with? Are these meditators, improvisors or simply friends helping you reset your defaults? Do they help you with acceptance? If so, they're worth engaging with further. If not, you might reconsider spending time with them.

---

[6] Note that this is an important perspective for balancing impulse and pause as we discussed in the previous chapter. Without challenge or examination, the first thought that shows up may trend in one direction. Or it may perpetuate patterns of injustice or self-judgment that we're blind to because we go with the default we know—and that default is to go in an unhealthy direction.

[7] Admittedly, they'll have their own as well. ☺

## what about the desire to be good?

Here's an oddity to consider: improvisation and mindfulness both breed acceptance and release into the present moment. And, paradoxically, they can also fuel a clinging desire for excellence.

In improv, folks who have established themselves as top improvisors want to improve: they care about the craft and want to develop the art form. Beginners want to shine so they get more opportunities to perform. Or so they'll attract a romantic partner from the audience. Each desire has a certain kind of nobility or practicality. At the same time, if those wants start to outmuscle a more spacious acceptance of things as they are, they can lead to struggle. Being determined to get a particular result causes players to tense up, diminish their sensitivity and start missing cues. Scenes can go south fast.

Skilled improv teachers recognize that desire to improve and look to introduce it wisely and under controlled conditions. Ben Johnson, a former member of the BATS Company, usually conveys something like the following to his students (but only after they've been studying a while): *OK, folks, so far, we've been working to free ourselves from the part of us that would edit or trim or judge our ideas before we even share them. We've been opening a free flow of creativity. That's good and important. Now we're getting to the point where we can talk about setting a standard for ourselves. What will you shoot for?* I love the standard Ben then shares with his students, his own hoped-for quality level: 1) Do a scene where the dialogue sounds as good as if it were written beforehand, and 2) Do a scene that makes the audience cry because it's so moving or poignant. I've had other teachers introduce a question that also resonates with me: do the folks you're playing with want to play with you again? Standards like these can pull improvisors forward into greater commitment and, eventually, into higher quality performances. In improv and in regular life, we can be careful in this way, welcoming in higher aspiration after having reestablished connection to creativity.

Even though mindfulness eventually promotes equanimity and a greater acceptance of things as they are, many beginners come to their budding practice with a hopeful or aspiring agenda. They start because they want greater calm, clarity, or focus, and they know they have to get "good" enough to gain the benefit. For example, I continue with mindfulness because I want to stay present as often as I can, choose connection over isolation, and stay resourceful rather than judgmental or reactive in response to life's ups and downs. I want to become the better man I can envision. Holding on too tightly to any of those hopes or intentions actually pushes practitioners—beginners and more experienced folks like me alike—in the opposite direction. We can get caught up in measuring our mindfulness "performance," judging our results, and losing connection with the moment, with the here and now. It's as if we've forced the chrysalis open only to realize we've killed the butterfly that was preparing to emerge. Better to trust in the unfolding magic of the shapeless, mid-process goop.

Where then do you put such a seemingly wholesome desire as greater calm, clarity, and focus? Can you allow and even feed a desire to be "good" without it automatically triggering the insidious flip side of aspiration that is self-judgment? Or can you pursue a goal without creating constrictive tension in the effort?

At least four factors can ease that tendency to clamp down:

- **WHEN you feed the desire to be "good."** In improvisation, workouts, rehearsals and practice sessions offer the chance to explore your edges. With mindfulness, individual meditation or group study presents a similar opportunity. You get to expand the range of your capabilities, take notes and ask for feedback in a setting safe for apparent mess-ups. You can chisel away at the block of default behavior and start to sculpt the person you want to become. And, after a performance or a real-life situation that draws on your mindfulness and improvisation practices, you can take pleasure in the calls you made, the bright notes you hit, or the resourceful responses you found. Or, you can take stock of the ways and places you fell short. But during the performance itself—the show or the presentation or the difficult conversation with a spouse—is not the time to get caught up in the desire to be better. (And forget completely about being perfect.) Those are the moments that demand your full attention to the interaction at hand.

- *WHO fuels that desire.* It makes a big difference who stokes the fires of improvement. Does your motivation come from your highest self—*I want to be the best I can be so that I reach my fullest expression*—or does it come from the outside, some voice telling you to measure up against an external standard? The former might be a natural extension of your will to live. The latter probably just generates unhelpful comparisons. Note, too, that what you think of as your own internal motivating voice may be a smoothly recycled and cleverly disguised—but still harmful—rehash of an external voice you heard earlier in your life. Coming to greater self-awareness keeps you more easily aligned with your own self-measure.

- *Your mindset ABOUT the desire.* If your longing to improve comes from a growth mindset, it's much less likely to turn toxic. You'll recognize that getting "better" serves you more than getting "good" (again, that outside standard). You'll acknowledge that you'll have moments of excellence and moments of failure, and that you might hit stubborn plateaus where you feel stuck before you get a sudden breakthrough. That growth mindset gives you a larger context to hold your ups and downs. In this case, even strong desire can burn without the shame that often accompanies not meeting that desire.

- *HOW TIGHTLY you hold the desire.* In softball and baseball, young athletes often think that hitting the ball hard means squeezing the bat with great effort. Unfortunately, if you grip the bat tightly, your wrists get tense and you lose the fluidity to generate the whip-like action that delivers full power.[8] If you hold on more loosely, the body's wave of energy—legs to hips to ribs to arms to wrists to bat—can gather and surge into contact with the ball. The same is true for your aspiration for improvement. When you bear down and grit your way towards a goal, you set up all sorts of unnecessary tension. A more relaxed stance lets you ground and direct your power so it moves *through* you rather than coming *from* you.

### picking and choosing

This back and forth between aspiration for something better and acceptance of how things are can seem wishy-washy. *Accept what is. But then go ahead and feed your desire.* Well, which is it? Aren't these opposite pieces of advice?

Rather than thinking we're flip-flopping—and thus finding reason to judge ourselves—we can again acknowledge that we're traveling in the realm of paradox. I can desire to practice mindfulness well, to see every moment clearly and not get easily triggered by everyday events. That's a great aspiration to have. *And,* I can simultaneously see that it's important not to get too attached to that desire, too clingy or too tight around it. If I were to go that route, I'd slip out of being present with what's true now.

---

[8] And probably in cricket, hockey, lacrosse and other "stick sports" as well.

Buddhist teachings often help in this arena. In each chapter of his lovely little book *Bring Me the Rhinoceros*, John Tarrant considers a different Zen *koan*, a riddle meant to short-circuit the intellectual mind and lead practitioners to truth and wisdom. In chapter 10, "The Great Way Is Not Difficult," Tarrant offers this koan: "The great way is not difficult if you just don't pick and choose." In other words, your preferences or desires for things to be a certain way get you in trouble.

More specifically, he says:

> You might be armored against an unpleasantness that turns out not to be. Instead of wrestling towards what you think ought to be going on, it might be refreshing to approach events without armor, meeting their nakedness with your own nakedness. That might also be a kind approach, since it sets up no conflict in your own heart.[9]

If you can meet the world as it is without wanting it to be different, then something different can step forward within you. By doing so, you remove the blocks to your direct experience, and you remove the blocks to your natural powers. The great way becomes not difficult.

Going further, Tarrant introduces an audacious twist. He adds:

> Everyone knows that Buddhism is about non-attachment and people might think that not picking and choosing is about having no preferences. Yet non-attachment might lead to warfare with a part of you that enjoys the world. In this case, non-attachment would be just another tyrannical belief and itself a source of unhappiness.[10]

---

[9] John Tarrant, *Bring Me the Rhinoceros* (Shambhala: Boston, 2008), p. 114.
[10] Tarrant, *Bring Me the Rhinoceros*, p. 115.

Whoa. Say what?

> Not picking and choosing could be the opposite of non-attachment. Something more unsettling and more demanding. If someone asks you 'Vanilla or chocolate?', and you notice that today you would like vanilla and say so, that might be not picking and choosing. If you say 'I don't mind. What are you having?', then that could well be picking and choosing. You might be trying to guess what your host wants. You might want vanilla but be unwilling to reveal yourself by saying so.[11]

In other words, if your natural desire in this moment actually wants something, the "not picking and choosing" means acknowledging that desire as real. The wanting exists. Trying to project a stoic dispassion actually further strengthens a desire: that of not having desires.

Often in the mindfulness world, practitioners want so badly to remain neutral, all-accepting and fine with whatever shows up... but they are human. They (and we, of course) still want stuff! Ultimately, that *pursuit* of neutrality ends up creating a conflict with what is. If the whole point is that we're not fighting against reality, preference comes with the territory. It's part of reality. You can want something and be present with that wanting. You can acknowledge it. You can recognize that you may or may not get what you want. You could face unfortunate circumstances. You could have trouble in relationships. In that mindset, you can have your desires without clutching them, without needing them, and without armoring to protect them. You can meet the nakedness of reality with your own nakedness. And enjoy the nimbleness and vitality that comes out of it, however vulnerable it feels.

Coming back around to our earlier discussion, maybe in this moment I want to be a good improvisor or a good meditator. What if that

---

[11] Tarrant, *Bring Me the Rhinoceros*, p. 115.

desire is just what it is? What if I don't need myself to be other than what I am right now?—and that includes my desire to be other than what I am right now.

## moving aspiration from 'what' to 'how'

If swimming in the paradox of Zen koans leaves you feeling you've gone too far into the deep end, I can offer you a ladder for climbing back out of the pool. It's one that lines up nicely with a growth mindset. To make sense of the seemingly contradictory goals of aspiration and acceptance, try moving from imagining a fixed point where you want to end up to a more dynamic intention of *how you want to be in the process of getting there.* Instead of declaring to yourself, "I want to be a good improvisor!" or "I want to do meditation well!" prioritize the journey itself. *What does a good improvisor or mindfulness practitioner do? Can I do that, too? What attitude do I want for this next scene? Can I notice my breath one more time today than I did yesterday?* In this mode, the more you practice **how** you want to be, the closer you get to **who** or **what** you want to become.

Another way of describing this shift from "what" to "how" would be to shoot for becoming a good *practitioner* of improvisation or meditation (or life!) rather than for becoming a good improvisor or meditator in an absolute sense. You can live out a dedication to the craft of either practice without needing to arrive at some measurable level. You can have a life without earning an official certification as an Excellent Human. You show up for the game. You breathe with your experience. You enjoy whatever happens.[12]

---

[12] More paradox: when we can let go and just invest in the work itself, we make it more likely we'll move in the right direction. We'll get closer to the goal we would have chosen anyway. In other words, if you want to really be excellent and brilliant, you have to let yourself be average. But you can't be average *for the sake of* being excellent. You can't hope that someone notices how awesomely average you are (99th *percentile average!*). That's

## 'clover'

The word-association game "Clover" illustrates this approach beautifully. A group, standing or sitting in a circle, starts by choosing a word, any word (for example, "slingshot"). One person says the word aloud and the next person in the circle word-associates from it (perhaps saying "rock"). The next person in the circle word-associates with that most recent word, doing their best to let go of any echoes from earlier words. And so on, with the associations continuing around the circle. The goal, loosely held, is to circle back around to the original word—in this case, "slingshot." It can take a while but it will happen. Once the group returns to the original word, you start a second round using that original word ("slingshot") again. Maybe the next person now says "Daniel." And so on until "slingshot" shows up again. Eventually, you do a third round. The game becomes a playful *experience* of the dynamic we're discussing: returning to the origin word without *trying* to return to the origin word. You just word-associate. Play in the moment and say what comes next. The endpoint emerges of its own accord.[13]

In the game, the process of getting there becomes just as much a delight as the success of arriving at the destination. Words and patterns show up in unexpected sequences. People surprise each other with their oddball connection-making. Themes emerge. You *do* have to remember the original word, but even if the group forgets for a while, you simply wander off on a bit of fun diversion. Someone will eventually remember. It's all good. Or, more

---

just putting a seemingly mellow sheepskin over the wolf of grasping and grinding. You've got to actually buy into the letting go. You've got to give in.

[13] See the end of the chapter for a sample round of "Clover" and the Glossary of Games at the back of the book for a more detailed game description.

accurately, it all *is*. You don't have to be good at Clover. You just have to play.

## goals as magnets

As in Clover, it may prove most helpful to consider even your process aspiration—wanting to get better at the *how* of what you're doing—as a quiet magnet. You toss it out ahead of you and let it activate a field of attraction. You move where you choose to move without obsessing or grinding. Slowly and eventually you get pulled in the direction of that intention. The "word" that was your goal comes back around.

In that way, maybe our desires and declarations—when most healthily held—serve as compass settings. We take stock of where we intend to go, set a course, and start moving. Our initial heading prods us to get up and get out so now we're gathering new information and greater energy. At some point, we may need to pause and recalibrate—maybe it's time for another new direction— but we have remained in motion. We have stayed engaged. We're still learning.

So there you have it, people. Vanilla or chocolate. Coming back to "Clover." Have your aspirations and acknowledge them. But hold lightly to them and lean them in the direction of process rather than specific outcomes. Let the journey become the goal.

### 'clover' example

Here's an example of one complete round of Clover, as played by Lisa Rowland and me on one of our Monster Baby Podcast episodes.[14]

**Both:** *Turnstile.*

---

[14] If you want to *listen* to this exchange, visit Monster Baby Podcast episode #5, "Aspiration vs. Acceptance," at the 3:19 mark.
https://animalearning.com/2016/05/11/monster-baby-5-aspiration-acceptance/

**Lisa:** *BART.*

**Ted:** *Subway.*

**Lisa:** *Metro.*

**Ted:** *France.*

**Lisa:** *Paris.*

**Ted:** *Eiffel Tower.*

**Lisa:** *Steel.*

**Ted:** *Magnolia.*

**Lisa:** *Flower.*

**Ted:** *Petal.*

**Lisa:** *Velvety.*

**Ted:** *Bobby Vinson.*

**Lisa:** *Vincent Van Gogh.*

**Ted:** *Starry Night.*

**Lisa:** *Movement.*

**Ted:** *Dance.*

**Lisa:** *Prom.*

**Ted:** *Flowers.*

**Lisa:** *Field.*

**Ted:** *Pasture.*

**Lisa:** *Fence.*

**Ted:** *Cow.*

**Lisa:** *Moo.*

**Ted:** *Oink.*

**Lisa:** *Pig.*

**Ted:** *Swine.*

**Lisa:** *Pearls.*

**Ted:** *Jewelry.*

**Lisa:** *Jewels.*

**Ted:** *Findlay.*[15]

**Lisa:** *Finland.*

**Ted:** *Denmark.*

**Lisa:** *Scandinavia.*

**Ted:** *Vikings.*

**Lisa:** *Longboats.*

**Ted:** *Paddles.*

**Lisa:** *Doggie.*

**Ted:** *Kitty.*

**Lisa:** *Jude.*[16]

**Ted:** *Hey.*

**Lisa:** *Horses.*

**Ted:** *Kentucky Derby.*

**Lisa:** *Race.*

**Ted:** *Crowd.*

**Lisa:** *Pleaser.*

**Ted:** *Enabler.*

**Lisa:** *Alcoholic.*

**Ted:** *Beer.*

**Lisa:** *Brew.*

**Ted:** *Pub.*

**Lisa:** *Public.*

**Ted:** *Enemy.*

---

[15] I once had a student named Jules Findlay!
[16] Lisa's former cat, may he rest in peace.

**Lisa:** *Defender.*

**Ted:** (laughing) *Air Force.*

**Lisa:** *One.*

**Ted:** *Two.*

**Lisa:** *Couple.*

**Ted:** *Pair.*

**Lisa:** *Fruit.*

**Ted:** *Vine.*

**Lisa:** *Grape.*

**Ted:** *Wine.*

**Lisa:** *Women.*

**Ted:** *Song.*

**Lisa:** *Sing.*

**Ted:** *Sang.*

**Lisa:** *Has been.*

**Ted:** *Forgotten.*

**Lisa:** *Memory.*

**Ted:** *Trace.*

**L isa:** *Paper.*

**Ted:** *Factory.*

**Lisa:** *Conveyor belt.*

**Ted:** *Airport.*

**Lisa:** *Luggage.*

**Ted:** *Check in.*

**Both:** *Turnstile!* (laughing)

## Chapter 5
### Want Without Need:
*Balancing Aspiration and Acceptance*

### GEMS from the JOURNEY

- *Reality exists whether we fight it or not. Finding little mindfulness rituals—like the ".b"—can help build your equanimity muscles as you go through your day.*

- *If you haven't taken care of your physical needs, it may be even harder to find the internal spaciousness you need to accept your circumstances as they are.*

- *If you want to allow your more wholesome desires without triggering the self-judgment that comes when you haven't yet achieved them, it can help to examine four factors:*
    - *when you feed your desire*
    - *whether that desire comes from within you or from someone on the outside (the latter will likely cause more suffering)*
    - *your mindset around the desire (do you have a process-focused growth mindset?)*
    - *how tightly you hold the desire*

- *Not picking and choosing includes acknowledging the times when you actually want something. Trying to put forward an inauthentic neutrality actually further cements a desire: that of not having desires.*

- *Changing your aspirations from a goal orientation to a process orientation will likely boost your mood and, paradoxically, improve your results.*

## PARADOX

- Accepting reality as it comes can bring great peace and reduce immense suffering. At the same time, setting, stating and following through on intentions can make dreams come true. Both mindfulness and improvisation help you find a healthy, dynamic balance between the two.

- Mindfulness and improvisation both breed equanimity and help you relax into the present moment. They also can pull you into the seductive—and potentially destructive—gravity of wanting to get "good" at them.

## GOING DEEPER

- Take a few minutes to write journal responses to these questions: When and where do you find yourself feeling and feeding your desire for improvement most strongly? Is it before, during or after your "performance"? Where is the desire coming from? Does it emerge from within the highest part of yourself or from someone else's plan or directive?

- See if you can recall any goals you've set for yourself. Have you chosen an outcome-related goal or a process-related one? If the former, how would switching to a process orientation affect your motivation and/or mood as you go after those goals?

- Play a full round of Clover as described in the Glossary of Games. Pay particular attention to any desire to "goose" your word choice to accelerate coming back around to your starting word. Can you instead hold more loosely to the game's intention?

# part three
## *a new mindset emerging*

Congratulations! You made it through the dense territory of all that paradox. There's a bit more to come, but now that you've done the heavy lifting, the rest should feel like a refreshing breeze.

Our task now? To keep rewiring your neural patterns using more inquiries from the worlds of mindfulness and improvisation.

- How does choosing a positive frame affect our experience of life?
- Some uncertainty makes life interesting, but what do we do in the face of chaos?
- What wisdom comes from choosing a wider lens on the events of our lives?
- How do we deal with change?
- What does it mean to stay present—truly present—with the people and places we encounter?

In this section, we'll explore those questions by living them. You'll try on some rose-colored glasses, get some tools for finding the calm eye at the center of any storm, and then pull back for a bird's eye view on life's troubles and stresses.

You'll also make friends with change and find a sweet spot of presence that lets you connect with others more easily and gracefully.

You've been building a mindset. Time to strengthen it further.

# the power of positivity
## *creating a delightful default*

WHEREVER YOU GO AROUND THE GLOBE, you'll find a strong instinct—or at least a default—among many theater improvisors: to make negative choices at the beginnings of scenes.[1] So often, players start by responding through an unpleasant lens. They complain. They notice what's wrong. Their character harbors a suspicion or a resentment for another character on stage. That tone then sets the stage for the rest of the scene. Players remain mired in conflict. Little moves forward. And the audience grows tired of it.

Many of us carry a similar attitude about life. Maybe you do, too. You grumble about little pains and aches. Your attention gravitates to what upsets you rather than what delights you. You gain sympathy (or aim to) by squeezing mileage out of every bit of suffering. Or you bad-mouth those around you—as your inner critic does to yourself. This negativity need not show up as wailing or railing, either. It's often a low-level background noise, a subtle-but-still-toxic cloud that hangs in the air and poisons our breathing. You keep it going because it's familiar. There's reassurance in having some sense of how the story—or your day or your life—will go.

---

[1] This is especially true for beginners and intermediates. It also holds for a saddening number of seasoned veterans.

## why the negative default?

Of course, we may have evolutionary reasons for such a tendency. We notice what's wrong so we're prepared for any life-threatening situations. Back in the stone age, that tendency might have prevented our getting eaten by a saber-toothed tiger. Today, it might protect us from a less dramatic—but still real—threat. Your leg hurts so you go get it checked out and make sure there's no gangrene. Sharing a story of getting scammed on Craigslist alerts others to that same danger. And even complaining with the neighbors about the local team might form a social bond that comes in handy when a hurricane strikes and you have to clear your street of debris. On one level, we tune into what's "off" so we can ensure we get back "on."

Improvisors have additional reasons for this tendency to lean negative, especially at the beginning of scenes—but they may not prove so helpful.

### *"This won't be interesting without a problem."*

Many improvisors fear that their work on stage will stall without a dilemma to resolve or discomfort to ease. They believe a story needs to involve *conflict* (rather than rely on the more fundamental concept of *change*). Heads must butt. The stage poetry we speak must create waves of tension: Human vs. self. Human vs. human. Human vs. nature. Such performers think if everything is fine, nothing is happening. And they think that's a problem, that the audience will lose interest. This, we have found, is simply not true.

In "real" life, we might also wonder if our struggles make us more interesting. Maybe we end up in a my-misery's-worse-than-yours competition. Or maybe it sets us up to make our journey seem more heroic. In any case, it's an interesting experiment to see what kinds of connection show up when we drop the default and stop complaining.

***"If I try to go positive, I'll leave my comfort zone, skill-wise or story-wise. I know how to do conflict."***

Improvisors often make these negative choices because they fear moving out of their comfort zones. Saying yes leads to action and adventure. Action and adventure then lead to the unfamiliar. And the unfamiliar might require expanded abilities that expose the improvisor as not-yet-fully-formed. Or it might cause them to freeze-up or blank-out. Saying no maintains control. They don't have to change. If they start with a problem, at least they stay on familiar ground—they've got a leading hook, *something* to deal with.

When we've taken on a negative default in our daily lives, the same can hold true. We stick to the conflict because at least it's familiar. We know how to get into the mess and we know how to get out of the mess, even if we have to repeat the process and stay mired in the mess. That much we can do. It keeps us occupied.

***"I will look bad."***

Ultimately, it's not just the fear of where the story might take us that leads to a negative default. Even more prevalent is the fear of not being good. Each time I step on stage, I've got some fear that I won't perform well, that the audience won't like me, they won't think I'm a good improvisor. And I really want them to think I *am* good. As we've discussed before, that comparative mindset locks down one's creativity. Blinders up, I'll unconsciously look to protect my vulnerability—and then conflict will naturally emerge.

For many—if not most—people, even the most basic interaction can bring up a bit of anxiety. We're social creatures. We want to fit in. That anxiousness, like most fears, can cause us to tighten up. Tension constricts our breathing. And less oxygen puts us in a me-first survival mode so we get less friendly, less generous. In other words, more negative.

Since these gloomy patterns have had thousands of evolutionary years to settle into our neural pathways, it's no wonder they show up at the beginning of improv scenes and even ordinary conversations. That we understand why these default patterns exist doesn't mean we shouldn't challenge their sticking around, however.

## reasons to reset the default

Some say the best improv comes when we have no rules. Start in a moment and allow the magic to unfold, even if that means a scene or story initiates with whining, complaining, or conflict. The best improv teachers counter that notion. Good things come from a default of starting scenes with characters who come on happy, healthy and whole. In the beginning, it helps to have a positive intention.

Here's why.

### creating 'platform'

If you want to tell an effective, engaging story with a meaningful arc—whether a long-form narrative over 45 to 90 minutes or a short-form snippet told in three minutes—you need to start with a bit of "platform," or set-up. In other words, begin with what's "normal" in the world you're creating. *Who are the people? What do they do? How are they related? How are things when everything's fine?* In the beginning, you're just laying out information, no big developments. Think of it as the "Once Upon a Time" that sets up the rest of what will follow. Staying neutral-to-positive gives your audience a chance to revel in that introduction, to take a breath and settle in.

### opening up possibility

If you can get that basic introduction out without conflict or attached problems, then your scene has more places to go. Negativity constricts possibility, immediately narrowing and magnetizing the scene into dealing with *that* issue. That negativity can come as a complaint—"*When will the bus get here? It's always late.*"—or as a small conflict—"*Didn't I tell you you're not supposed to come out here?*" Or "*You forgot again.*" From the start we see hostility. And now that has to get addressed. Start more positively and you preserve an infinite range of other storytelling options.

## making available more of our senses

Starting negative also constricts our senses. We tunnel into the conflict and put up (nearly literal) blinders to everything else. When we open scenes with humor, kindness, and contentment, our sense detection opens up. We see more. We hear more. The world comes alive. We're more likely to name and endow things in our setting because we're relaxed. In that mode or mood, things appear. We don't have to *find* them. And the world starts to make more sense for the audience and all the players on stage.

Imagine you were dropped in the ocean and couldn't swim. You're drowning and your only goal is survival. You're just trying to keep your head above water, so you've got no bandwidth to notice anything else. It's all about the urgency. If instead you're placed gently on the beach, you can wade or paddle around in the shallows to get a sense of—and enjoy—the location. You have time to notice the sunlight sparkling on the waves, the feeling of sand between your toes, the sound of seagulls or the weight of water bobbing you around. If you're caught in having to defend yourself from negativity, you miss all that richness.

## creating investment in the characters

In the same way that we don't like hanging around with Debbie and Donnie Downers who complain all the time, audience members would rather watch characters who get along, at least to start. We like it when characters seem happy, when they're not heavily burdened. Eventually, of course, some difficulty will challenge these characters. They may find a conflict. Something could go wrong—

and hopefully (almost certainly), it will. But when it happens further down the storyline, we've developed a reason to care about these characters. We've spent some time together and so have generated an affection for them. Maybe we've even come to *identify* with the characters, to see ourselves on stage. Now their trials and tribulations carry more weight. They have more import. Now it all matters because we care about—or, in some sense, have *become*— what we're seeing on stage. Had the characters just been complaining all the time, we wouldn't care if something bad happened to them. We might even prefer it![2]

Colleague Lisa Rowland relays a great example of this dynamic she experienced during an improvised musical at BATS:

*We were doing a long-form film noir musical and one of our actors was playing a character named Malcolm. He was a henchman, the big boss's employee tasked with looking after the boss's wife. He was supposed to follow her around, make sure she got where she needed to go, but also protect her and make sure she wasn't getting into anything the boss wouldn't want her doing. Malcolm was a very sweet character. He wasn't very smart, but it was clear that he kind of pined for the wife. He was kind of in love with her. And that was very endearing. Well, there came a moment when the whole plot unraveled. The wife was trying to leave her husband and hired someone to kill him. It ended up that Malcolm got killed. He got shot. And the*

---

[2] Note that this dynamic holds true even when the complaining is sharp and witty. As audience members, we're likely to think, *Well, these characters are funny but I don't really want to hang out with them for very long.* When the characters get along and care about each other, we get to the end of the night and think, *Ahh, I want to see those people again. I want to live in their world again.*

*audience gasped. An audible shriek of sadness went up at their losing him.*

*The only reason that happened is because we spent time getting to know him. He wasn't a total downer of a character. There was this sweetness about him. So, he had worked his way into the audience's hearts, and then they cared when he died... because in that moment, they were genuinely mourning the loss of Malcolm. They weren't just watching improvisors try to come up with something good.*

Each of these reasons for starting positive in an improv scene also holds true in most human interactions. In the arc of a conversation, for example, it can help to establish a bit of honest, open-hearted connection before digging into the twists and turns of more difficult topics. It's why we exchange pleasantries or why it makes sense to start an e-mail with an acknowledgment of the reader: this link between us forms our norm. Establishing that solid foundation then leaves us a wider range of possibility in interaction. We're not gossiping about what we don't like or solidifying judgments of others. When we're more relaxed and more pleasant, we take in more of our conversation partners. We're not worried about survival. As a result, we can let down our guard and show more of who we really are. That lets the people we're with care more about us. We take the risk of showing affection and vulnerability. And that forms connection that others invest in.

### the psych ward

Choosing to start positive—in life interactions and on stage—can also counteract the normal nervous tension that comes with beginnings. In improv, that choice impacts both audience and cast. One time, Lisa's group, The Improv Playhouse of San Francisco (IPSF), began a long-form three-act stage play. As part of that "Naked Stage" format, each night the audience suggests a single location that could fit on stage and will house the whole storyline—

something like "gas station," "surgery theater," or "university library." On this particular evening, one audience member came up with "psych ward" and the IPSF players accepted that suggestion.

An audible in-breath from the audience demonstrated a shared trepidation about that call. *Eeeee, they're going to do a psych ward? Is this going to get offensive? Are the actors sensitive and knowledgeable enough to take that on? Are we going to be making fun of dementia patients or the mentally ill? This could get real ugly, real fast.* Thankfully, the players didn't get pulled into that fear and managed to start positive.

Ben Johnson came on stage first and began playing a character sitting in a lounge reading magazines. That was all we knew. As we found out after the show during the Q & A session, Tim Orr was waiting backstage at that point, making a positive choice. Tim decided that the only thing he would know before going on stage was that his character liked Ben's character and that something good had just happened. So, Tim entered and said, "The meeting went well. The group went well. I got to lead the meeting for the first time." Right off the bat, the audience relaxed: *Oh, we like these guys! We want to know more about them!* Everyday was OK. They weren't stereotyping "crazy" people or demonizing attendants. It was all good. And the rest of the show unfolded from there, one of the most poignant, beautiful, thrilling, and meaningful improv shows I have ever seen.[3]

## mindfulness: open to what is without complaining
Now you can see how and why skilled improvisors often make the choice to see the positive in any given moment—or at least to start with it. What kind of corollary exists in the world of mindfulness or

---

[3] To watch the full "Psych Ward" show, check out
https://www.youtube.com/watch?v=mbQmDLA2Zko.

in regular life? How does using a positive lens affect the unfolding "scenes" of your life?

In mindfulness, practitioners look to what's present in the here and now. You might allow yourself to notice a challenge or a pain or suffering. But you're not locked into that observation because you know it will change (since everything does, guaranteed).[4] Rather than getting wrapped up in complaining about the challenge or ruminating so it snowballs, you bring a sort of curiosity and kindness to the whole experience of being alive. *Huh, look at that. What's happening? What's true? What can I discover?*

As we saw earlier, practicing mindfulness means "paying attention on purpose to the present moment and things as they are with curiosity and kindness." And it's that last phrase that sets the tone for the whole practice. You *could* pay attention to the present moment with a judgmental mind: *Oh, this is wrong. I'm noticing that I'm itchy. I'm noticing that it's raining. And I don't like it. The weather sucks this time of year.* But you could also make the choice to just get curious and say, *Oh, it's raining. How about that!* Or even *It's raining and I don't like it. How about that! What don't I like about it? Does my preference change as I sit here and observe that I don't like it? What's the nature of this dislike?* You're kind to yourself and to the very circumstance.

Suddenly, the discomfort and the suffering loosen up a bit and shift more towards... normal. Or neutral. It's not so bad anymore. You're just dealing with everyday experience.

## not necessarily great, just not-wrong

Returning to the world of improvisation, let's note that when we talk about starting positive, it doesn't have to mean starting with orgasmic elation: *"God, life is the best!!! I love you!!! We won the*

---

[4] More to come on this dynamic in Chapter 9, "Ch-ch-ch-changes: Learning to Go with the Flow."

*lottery!!! I'm so happy we're best friends!!!"* You don't need so many exclamation points.

Rather, it's that you're *not* starting with a problem. The beginning of a scene could be perfectly mundane. A guy could be checking his mail, placing his keys on the counter and putting groceries away. But he's not checking the mail and finding an eviction notice. Or finding bills that will send him over the edge into bankruptcy. When he puts the keys on the table, they don't scratch the surface. That's just where they belong. He doesn't step on the cat or the dog when he opens the fridge. It's non-negative. Everything is fine. And the next actor then receives a full range of possibilities for what to bring to the scene.

### 'positivity/negativity spectrum'

Lisa Rowland and I came up with a fun game to introduce making room for such options in our responses—whether to a partner's scene opener or to life's experiences. It's called the "Positivity/Negativity Spectrum." We set up a line of five people facing the audience and allot them numbers 1 to 5. A sixth player goes up to person number 1 and offers a neutral line of dialogue. Nothing noteworthy, just something factual. Like, "The guests will be here at six o'clock." Or "I decided to sign up for ballroom dance class."

Each of the five players then gets the chance to respond to that neutral prompt, making sure to proceed as if the line were real and true. (In improv jargon, not "blocking" the offer. The person responding won't deny the reality of what's been presented.) But there's a slight twist: Person Number 1 responds super negatively. Person Number 2 responds with mild negativity. Number 3 responds neutrally. Number 4 comes back with mild positivity, and Number 5 rejoices with wild positivity.

It might go something like this:

**neutral offer: "Francine, it looks like we're going to have to go to the market today."**

*Person #1:* "Uggh! I hate the market! It's always so crowded and all the produce is always rotten already."

*Person #2:* "Oh did you forget to go on your way home from work? Again?"

*Person #3:* "OK."

*Person #4:* "Oh good. We just ran out of potatoes, so we can get some more."

*Person #5:* "Perfect! We can bring our reusable bags and walk home along the coast afterwards. How does that sound?"

Or like this:

**neutral offer: "I brought another log in to help make a fire."**

*Person #1:* "Dammit, I just cleaned up the fireplace and finally got rid of all the old ashes. Arrrrgggghhh!!

*Person #2:* "So the oil company never came to refill the furnace? They're so unreliable."

*Person #3:* "That sounds reasonable."

*Person #4:* "Thank you. That was very sweet of you. We'll use that."

*Person #5:* "Yeeeeeeaaaaahhhhh, baby!!! Bonfire buuuuurrrrrnnnnn!!!!"

When we talk about starting scenes with a positive opening, we don't mean a level 5 sense of glee. The first offer could come in at a 3 or 4 level. And the first response to that offer could do the same.

*Oh, another log. Great. That'll give us more time to snuggle.* We open on the positive side of neutral. That keeps our senses open and our possibilities limitless.

### reframing 'negative' storytelling—the power of suspending judgment

The "Positivity/Negativity Spectrum" exercise helps demonstrate what powerful and instant storytellers we are. Our minds take the facts of everyday experience—the stuff that happens—and spin webs of meaning, justification and prediction, all in the space of seconds. One of the gifts of mindfulness practice is learning to pause for a moment before (or maybe just after) that whole mechanism whirs into action.

This happens across the spectrum of preference, with your pleasant experiences and, of course, with what we traditionally call negative experiences. Let's say you get into a car accident. All sorts of things could be true about that, about why it happened and what it will mean going forward. Your mind might tell you, *You're such a bad driver.* Or *That guy's an ass.* Or *If I just hadn't stayed that extra five minutes at the yoga studio...* Or your mind might start to fret: *My parents are going to kill me.* Or *This will send my insurance rate sky high.* Or *I won't be able to go on vacation now.* A million stories can happen in that instant and quickly snowball into an avalanche of ruminations and worries.

In such moments, though, you've also got a choice about how you deal with the unpleasantness, how you meet the apparent negativity. If you can catch yourself, pause and take a breath, other options for self-storytelling show up. Maybe your reaction becomes slightly positive: *Well, here's a growth opportunity.* Or *Here's a chance for me to react in a way that I'll be proud of down the road.* Or maybe that's too far along the positivity spectrum for you and you have a more neutral (but sill curious) *OK, that happened. What comes next?* You suspend the interpretation and instead remain alert to the kernel of possibility contained in what is actually occurring. If you can do that, some path becomes available that wasn't there before.

For an even simpler example, imagine you send a text message to a friend. It's a little vulnerable, maybe you've asked that person on a date. And then... they don't get back to you for 15 minutes, an hour, an afternoon, and on into the evening. What stories does your mind generate? *I shouldn't have done that. That was too intense. I'm too intense. They're probably pissed. Or offended. They don't like me. I'll never go on a date. I'll never be in a relationship.* And on it goes. These negative stories regenerate, mutate and spawn even more negative stories. They stick to us like Velcro hooks stick to loops.

But the reality could just as easily be that the person just doesn't have their phone with them. Or it ran out of charge. Or they're really excited and want to respond in a way that requires some quality reflection. Or whatever. Unfortunately, such positive interpretations tend not to stick—they slip away like fried eggs on Teflon—leaving us to fend off the negative thoughts once again.

Rather than getting caught up in either interpretation—negative or positive—it might help most to suspend all the storytelling and take that mindful pause. In the texting scenario, all we know is that that person hasn't returned the text. What if that fact stays right there? What if it doesn't have to *mean* anything, at least not yet. No need to get worked up. No need to spin the wheels. You have a data point and you can't know what the next one will be—until you do know.

In a sense, this practice actually promotes the power of neutrality— or at least a mild positivity. It's the power of openness and curiosity. Of soft focus. Of faith in the unfolding. It's like a 3.5 on the Positivity-Negativity Spectrum, a steady sense of "it's good" without a whole, steaming pile of evaluation and judgment towed behind it. It's a simple experience of feeling gratitude for the specifics of now.

## what to do when someone else goes negative

Once you start to reset your own negative default to something more positive—at least Level 3 neutral—you may begin to encounter a tricky dilemma: what happens when those around you start or go negative? On an improv stage, maybe that person's fear has kicked in or they're working in a different style or with a different set of ethics. In regular life, maybe someone is generally grumpy or is going through a particularly rough patch. What then?

For one, you can avoid ramping up the tension. Just because the other person has stepped into a gray mood doesn't mean you need to join them. You can allow for their discomfort without getting swallowed by it. You can offer sympathy (*I can understand what you're going through*) without needing to feel empathy (*I feel the same way*).

You also can avoid getting into a fight about it. When you stay out of the fray, you're trying to restore your neutral-to-positive energy by draining the venom from the situation. If your partner starts with, "Arrgh, it's raining again," you might feel tempted to respond with, "But the rain is pretty and we've been in a drought." This puts you in opposition, wrestling for the "right" interpretation of the established reality that it's raining. While you are offering an alternative response to the fact that it's raining, you are replacing their negativity with outright (though mild) conflict.

Better to find a way to normalize the negativity. You can soften the edge of the discomfort by saying something like, "Yeah, it just started up. Hey, we should get the tarp up." You acknowledge the complaint and make it not a big deal. Or maybe that person regularly grouses about the weather: Old Man Gunderson sitting on the porch, as he always does. In that case, the negativity registers without it being a problem. We know this guy and his curmudgeonly self. And we have an affection for him. He's lived in our world for a while and we like that.[5]

Note that you could normalize the bad thing but do so at the other person's expense. If you respond, "Dude, it's Seattle, of course it's raining," you've declared that, while the rain might not be a problem, the character (and the other improvisor) is. *They're stupid or illogical or overreactive. They shouldn't have done that or said that.* As an improvisor, that kind of thinking tosses a wrench into the system of story-making—even if it's said with a laugh. On-stage and off-, it sets up opposition, conflict and holier-than-thou judgment. In reality, we're all in this together and we need to treat each other well.

Another option along those lines: you can just choose to love these cranky characters who show up from time to time. Love the crap out of them. Lisa Rowland told me about a time when taking this avenue made the most sense on stage:

> *I played a show with an improvisor from out of town, and his style was far wittier and a little more cutting, a little more sarcastic. Quicker, zippier. Whereas my style was slower and more attentive, really focusing on the platform. Because this other improvisor came from out of town, we didn't get a chance to really dig in, warm up together and understand each other. We couldn't bridge that gap before the show. So, the first show we did, I was really hit in the face with our difference in style. And I had a really hard time. I tried to convince this improvisor to play in the way that I wanted to play, trying to communicate, Everything's fine, isn't it? And don't you care about this? We will be positive! I kept grabbing our interaction and trying to force it to be OK. And that did not work. I did not have a good time. The show did not benefit.*

---

[5] We all have a family member who fits this category, don't we?

*Then, the second night, I made a really conscious choice that "I'm going to love this character." Whatever else happened, my character was going to love that negativity. I was going to love it. All of his offers were going to crack me up. So, I aligned myself with that attitude. Sarcasm, negativity, witty quippiness, all that stuff: I just chose to love it. And I had a way better time. I didn't join him in the negativity. I didn't give up my wanting to be OK. I just met his upset with, Oh yeah, you're great.*

One last way to bring a negative offer back to neutral or positive without rejecting it, setting up an opposition or making your partner look bad is to notice that the negative represents just one part of the current reality. The negativity or unpleasantness becomes one of the things happening. It's not the only thing happening. You're neither erasing nor elevating the anxiety. You're simply painting a fuller picture.

## normalizing the negative: clouds moving along
Mindfulness helps you reset these neural-pathway defaults in regular life as well. When you notice something "wrong"—an itchy patch of skin, a wave of grief, a delay in travel—you pause and simply name it. Something's off-kilter? *OK, there it is.* You neither get caught up in nor carried away by the difficulty. You normalize the negativity by naming it, and in doing so, you encourage it to transform.

It's like clouds moving through the sky. The general background for the world stage? Blue sky. Not radiant sunrises or spectacular fireworks. Just basic blue sky. Things are fine. Goodness. Contentment. A thought or emotion comes by, a cloud blocks a bit of the blue. It changes shape. It can come in different sizes or intensities. But it's there and eventually it moves along. That's part of how weather works. Clouds happen. Thoughts and feelings rise and fall away.

I find that my emotions sometimes stick around until I consciously acknowledge them. So, I might feel that basic blue sky one day. Then I go several days without checking in with myself and lots of emotions have rumbled across my sky since then. Maybe I'm excited for some upcoming travel. Nervous about finances. Frustrated about not sticking to a dietary plan. Sad on the anniversary of a long-ago loss. If I don't acknowledge those moods, the clouds stick around and the blue sky turns a dreary gray, darker and heavier. I get grumpy. Or lazy. As soon as I do register their presence—*Oh, excitement. Oh, anxiety. Or, frustration. Oh, sadness.*—they move on their own and the blue sky returns. Again, neither avoiding nor elevating or enthroning those emotions. The moods remain transient events, not permanent facts.

## is this closing off the shadow or simply resetting a default?

Note that this approach avoids veering into the realm of repression or denial. When we say we're wanting to choose positive starts to scenes or look toward what's good in life, we're not rigidly trying to seal off the negative, the difficult or the unsavory. We're not seeking to lock up that vital, if risky, Monster Baby part of ourselves. If we were to bury what psychologist Carl Jung called the shadow—that unwanted, unacceptable part of ourselves that we try to keep hidden—it's only going to leak out in ways that prove even more dangerous or destructive. This is true in both life and in improv.

If I get dogmatic as an improv teacher or an improv player, and I'm trying to compress my teammates into a mode of *always* starting positive, then maybe there's some negative impulse that's going to show up elsewhere. And maybe it doesn't show up in that scene or that particular story, but it creates a tension between us as improvisors in our troupe. Where are we putting that negative energy?

That said, the negativity that we're talking about here, the kind that shows up as a default, probably doesn't represent some ominous expression of the dark shadow that desperately needs a witness. It's more likely a response to fear. Rather than develop the habit of things starting OK, we've gotten into the habit of things starting wrong, tangling in conflict from the get-go. We can reset the default from one of negativity to one of positivity.

Again, it's not that we shouldn't recognize that life includes negativity, challenge and conflict. It's that the positivity gets us to saying yes—and that leads us on adventures. It moves us forward. Something happens that creates delight. This simple element can show up in a basic park bench scene. One person sits on a park bench and another person comes in. As the scene unfolds, they meet each other and get to know each other. One person might ask, "Would you like a soda?" By default, the other might respond "No, thanks." That could be the character speaking—maybe they've got good reason to be cautious—or it could be the improvisor—*I'd never accept food or drink from a stranger.* But why not just say "Yeah, thanks."? We can choose to be pleased by what our partner just did—it propels us forward, after all. Now there's more of a connection between those two characters. Now something else can unfold. Either direction could be authentic. And we have a choice.

When I coach beginning improvisors in scenes like this, I often find myself saying, "*Sure, you can do it.*" Or "*Go ahead.*" Or "*Yes, you know how.*" Especially at the beginnings of scenes—and of relationships in real life—we seem to need to have a little problem. Maybe it's because we're a bit afraid of what might happen. We're nervous. We've gone out on a limb, and we protect ourselves by finding a problem. As my improvisor friend Pam Victor likes to ask, "What if everything's fine? What if nothing's wrong? What if you don't need to get anxious about this?" We can ask those questions of ourselves and our characters.

### every moment a positive start

By starting positive in scenes and in life in general, we're choosing to reset our negativity default. Rather than letting events trigger an avalanche of assumption and interpretation, we pause and take stock of what is—including the negative and the positive—and then ask ourselves, *Do I live from the good, pleasant and wondrous or do I gravitate toward the rough, the unpleasant, the aggravating?* Each day marks a new start. Each moment initiates a new possibility. And whatever practice we choose eventually turns into habit. That habit then becomes character—whether a character on stage or the character that guides our choices and actions.

---

**Chapter 6**
**The Power of Positivity:** *Creating a Different Default*

**GEMS from the JOURNEY**

- *Most of us carry a bit of a default negative approach or attitude through life. We pay more attention to what's wrong than what's going well. There are good evolutionary reasons for that. However, choosing a more positive frame sharpens our senses and relaxes us into a wider sense of possibility.*

- *You need not take on a manic or Pollyanna enthusiasm for every situation. Sometimes remaining intentionally neutral—that is, not negative—makes enough of a shift to rewire those default negative circuits and give you more choices in life.*

- *Suspending judgment on life's events—rather than getting caught up in your mind's knee-jerk storytelling—helps you see more accurately and respond more gracefully to what's actually going on.*

- Your good cheer or even keel can neutralize another's negativity without conflict. You can imagine their negativity arising and moving on, like clouds traveling across the sky.

### PARADOX

- You can hold the intention to start positive or look for the good while allowing room to recognize what's difficult. In fact, positivity helps create the space to allow what's difficult. It just does so much more effectively when you can start with it.

### GOING DEEPER

- Before you enter a room, take a moment to bring a pleasant thought or memory to mind, especially if it's one having to do with the people in the room. How does that change your experience of what comes next?

- Get a group of six people to try the Positivity/Negativity Spectrum exercise as described above and in the Glossary of Games. What insights does it generate for you? How could you apply those insights in the different venues of your life?

# chaos theory
## *balancing preparation and pandemonium*

MAYBE YOUR LIFE FEELS LIKE a massive, swirling black hole of randomness. Or maybe you've got it neatly tucked and buttoned in crisp rows, at least temporarily. Whichever end of the spectrum you occupy—and even if you move back and forth depending on your circumstances—both mindfulness and improvisation offer valuable perspective for exploring the tension between chaos and order. Well-informed and well-practiced, you can draw on the value of both poles to serve you when you need them.

### overpreparation saps the life out
When we record an episode of the Monster Baby Podcast, co-host Lisa Rowland and I sometimes start with a skeleton outline for the conversation. More often we only have our chosen topic. The flesh fills in naturally through our improvisational riffing in response to that theme.

Relatively early on in the podcast's evolution, we tried an experiment: we (or more accurately, I) generated a more detailed plan of where the conversation might head: talking points, examples, intended transitions and flow, and the like. I'd also listed sub-topics to cover and had crafted a sample timeline to follow.

As we chatted, Lisa and I successfully hit all those intended bullet points on our list, but the episode came out flat: disjointed, not as free-flowing or satisfying as our previous episodes. We hadn't gone anywhere in the conversation that we didn't expect to go. Rather, it was more like we knew what we were going to talk about, we said it, and then we marched on to our next point. Tell one story and move on the next. It all felt inorganic, like we were trying to write an academic essay rather than going on an adventure. Less our intended "curious romp" and more of a by-the-numbers goose-step. In the end, we did not publish that particular podcast.[1]

We discovered that day just how much we prefer our conversations to cover uncharted territory, replete with surprises and unpredictable twists and turns. We'd rather listen for and follow the random leads that emerge than tick all the boxes in a playbook. For us, the episode doesn't really happen until the chaotic element of surprise shows up. You can't plan for it—by definition, we're doing improvisation!—but you *can* leave space for it.

## minimum scaffolding?

Our process that day led to an interesting question: to what degree can we engineer or encourage that more magical discovery? Too much organization can stifle the freedom we aim for, as we discovered with the thoroughly planned episode-that-wasn't-an-episode. At the same time, too much freedom might leave us wandering aimlessly. *What provocative questions might we consider? Do we want a poem or quotation to get us going? What's going to make sense for the listener?* However minimal the bare-bones frame, maybe it would help to have *something* to work from and bounce off.

In the improv world, such scaffolding comes from a troupe's agreements when they're first deciding to play together: accept each other's ideas, make bold offers, listen well, and so on. Without such baseline tenets, improvisors would most likely generate a bland, frustrating soup of too many storylines, unclear characters,

---

[1] We both agreed that it sounded OK but we hold ourselves to a higher standard than "sounds OK."

and unending conflict. The players would become like newborns in a world streaming with color, sound and texture—there's a ton going on and none of it makes sense so they just flop about from shiny object to shiny object.[2]

Mindfulness teacher and colleague Charisse Minerva Spencer explores similar edges when she leads improvisational music-making circles. She'll arrive at a group with a huge bag of percussion instruments so that each participant can choose one of their own: a small drum, a triangle, a tambourine, wooden blocks, a zither, or whatever. Then, one at a time, everyone joins in and begins to play. Often at first, it's complete chaos. Some people bang as loudly as they can while others hold back in timid, arrhythmic restraint. There's little cohesion or support. It just sounds like noise. For my quiet-loving, more musical mind, those first few moments prove constitutionally disturbing. As in, make-me-want-to-leave-the-room disturbing.

Once Charisse sets us up with just a few basic principles, though—*listen to each other, find an empty space to play in, you don't need to make sound all the time*—then everyone starts to synch up and a deeper groove emerges. The group finds a shared rhythm within the sea of sounds and people fill pockets with syncopation and subtlety. Charisse doesn't know what's going to happen, but she trusts the music will rise and fall in its own time—and she's always right.

Not surprisingly, there are gradations all along the way. Charisse could just invite folks to come in, popcorn style, whenever they're inspired and ready to join. Or she could hold more order by asking folks to enter one at a time going around the circle. She could exert even more influence by asking new entries to wait at least four measures of music before adding their sound. Or she could set a timer to indicate when the next should join. Figuring out how much

---

[2] And probably leave some metaphoric mess on the stage as a result.

chaos makes for too much chaos has a lot to do with what the group can handle—and with the personal preferences of the facilitator.[3] In the end, what matters most is noticing which "controls" on the chaos enable or foster greater beauty and imagination and which constrict them.

## 'three-words-at-a-time poems': facilitating with different levels of control

Here's another example of such differences in approach using a variation on the word-at-a-time and line-at-a-time exercises we discussed earlier. In "Three-Words-at-a-Time Poems," all participants start by sitting in a circle, each with a blank sheet of paper and a pen or pencil in front of them. After a bit of instruction, each person writes the first three words of a poem—maybe it's a two-word title and the first word of the rest of the poem or maybe it's the first three words of what will end up as a seven-word title. It's up to that first writer. Once finished with those three words, each person passes their incomplete poem clockwise and the next person adds the next three words of the poem, looking to justify, support and build on what's already there. Then each poem gets passed again, until it makes its way around the circle once or twice. Each author who started a poem gets to finish it—with only three additional words.

One could choose to play the game with the direction, "Pass the poem on when you're done with your three words." Or one could choose to play with the instruction, "Hold your poem and we'll all pass together." The first lets folks move at their own individual speed and trusts in the process to right itself so the group stays

---

[3] It's safe to say, as Monster Baby listeners know well, my co-host Lisa Rowland would welcome more chaos than I would. As she once said to me when we discussed this notion: "Maybe two [people]...come in at the same time and maybe they'll clash a little bit, maybe we'll see what happens then. There's that extra bit of 'I don't know, it might be a total train wreck' that I like."

reasonably coordinated. If a bottleneck forms, the person will realize he should go faster and that's okay. There's natural consequence to give us feedback about how long we're taking. The second makes sure the poems remain in order, preserving the pattern of start-and-finish. It prevents any stress-inducing logjam from accruing behind a single person. And it keeps folks involved throughout the process. Either approach can work to create delightful, hilarious, and even poignant poems. Which approach you prefer probably depends on your own personality as a facilitator. How comfortable with chaos are you?

## myers-briggs perceivers and judgers

The famous Myers-Briggs typology test offers one way to answer that question.[4] The psychological assessment measures test-takers on four spectra:

1) Extroversion (E) vs. Introversion (I)

   Do you recharge by hanging out with others or by going inside yourself?

2) Sensation (S) vs. Intuition (N)

   Do you primarily get your information through tangible perception or through a more ephemeral "sixth sense"?

3) Thinking (T) vs. Feeling (F)

   Do you make logical decisions based on objective criteria or subjective preference?

4) Perceiving (P) vs. Judging (J)

   Do you prioritize taking information in or getting something done with that information once you've got it?

---

[4] Some question the scientific validity of the test, describing it as a good-enough parlor game but nothing to make big decisions by. Others swear by its usefulness for understanding individual preferences and group dynamics. Whether it's a scientifically reliable measure or not need not prevent us from considering its insights.

Anyone who takes the test comes out with one of sixteen possible four-letter personality types, as in "ENFJ" or "ISTP." For the sake of our conversation here, that last letter—the P for Perceiving or J for Judging—says a lot about one's preferred (and likely, default) relationship to chaos.

Because they prioritize taking information in, Perceivers tend to leave their options open until the last minute—and sometimes beyond. *Oh, I'll just explore the chaos and see what happens.* They tend to be a little bit messier in their homes and cars. They're the creatives with the cluttered desks.

Judgers are the crisper folks who prefer things on time. They show up on time and leave on time. They know exactly how many ingredients are supposed to be in the recipe. They stick with directions rather than "winging it." A P-person would probably prefer the first Three-Word-at-a-Time approach (pass on the poem as soon as you're done) . A J-person would prefer the second (everyone passes on their poems at the same time).

Oddly enough, such designations—or at least the tendencies they point to—can alter, depending on circumstance. When I attended business school, I often played the part of the Perceiver, slowing our study groups down to ask about greater contexts: *What about social and environmental impacts? How are we relating as a group? What can we say about our interpersonal dynamics and how they're affecting our outcomes? Why are we doing this? Can we just slow down?* Years later, when I attended Divinity School, I played the opposite role, beseeching my classmates to get something done. *C'mon, here. Can we just make some progress? Let's go!* In the first setting, I showed up as a P in comparison; in the second as a J.

## the need for space for contemplation

The improv stage shows us that it actually is possible to welcome the unknown, to dance in uncertainty and to allow ambiguity without chaos taking over. In trying to bring that learning to life in general—where chaos can create real and persistent anxiety—it might help to ask this important question: can you cultivate a stillness or equanimity in receiving or meeting chaos? Can you find a grounded, more spacious rhythm in your life so you remain resourceful in the face of changing challenges—and do so whether you're a Perceiver or a Judger?

If you're not used to finding stillness, that may prove a growing edge. In some families and cultures, silence gets employed as a restriction. *Children should be seen and not heard. You'll speak when spoken to.* That kind of tone. Or, loved ones stop talking as a punishment: silence becomes a shut-out or abandonment. In other settings, silence can seem dangerous or emotionally risky. *If I quiet the constant whirling of my life, I'll notice the quieter voices of vulnerability, sadness, longing or anger that I carry within—and that will feel even more disturbing.* In any of those cases, silence or stillness can carry a negative association.

If such associations sound familiar, it may take time to overcome your built-in prejudices against stillness or quiet. Of course, that's where mindfulness practice can come in. You can train your mind to hold its focus so you can navigate through the flotsam and jetsam floating on the currents of circumstance—including whatever feelings of aversion to that quiet might show up. You can learn to watch the chaos from a distance as it swirls in front of you, noting any reaction in your body and mind without getting carried away by it.[5] That self-possessed focus allows you to stay strong in the face of

---

[5] We'll talk about this more in the next chapter on "Meta-Tation."

whatever chaos arises in your regular life, without getting rigid or militaristic about it.

## simple, yet difficult

It's helpful to register that this intention of honing your focus has a simple directive. You can choose an "anchor" for the spotlight of your attention—physical sensations, the breath, sounds in the room—and simply see what unfolds, returning to that anchor whenever the mind wanders. But that's *really* hard to do.[6] Even the "best" meditators' minds wander. What matters is that they keep coming back to their anchor once they realize they've wandered.

## beginner's mind

As we so often find in the worlds of improvisation and mindfulness, we recognize the value of maintaining a beginner's mind. The more we know, the more we come to know what we don't know. The more refined our focus gets, the more skillfully we see the subtle ways in which our mind wanders again and again. I can speak with some clarity about what mindfulness is, how it helps, some of its benefits for individuals and groups, and so on. And I can remain fully aware of how little I know about the practice of mindfulness. I can notice that, as a performer, my hit rate for "good" improv shows has increased—and stay fully connected to the truth that, ultimately, I have little idea what makes this improv stuff work. People finding and creating fully fleshed stories in the moment? Even for so-called experts, it can feel like sorcery, created by the magical mixture of opposites. Chaos and order both. At the same time.

---

[6] Cultivating physical stillness can serve as a valuable first step. As the body and breath come to a deeper calm, the mind often follows. But not always. And that's where learning to work with thoughts comes into play.

# Chapter 7
## Chaos Theory:
### *Balancing Preparation and Pandemonium*

## GEMS from the JOURNEY

- *While preparation often proves immensely helpful, overpreparation can sap the life out of presentations, conversations, or any creative endeavor. There's vitality in spontaneity.*

- *Ironically, having some "scaffolding"—agreements for process, shared values, and the like—can encourage more magical discoveries and serendipities than might otherwise emerge from pure chaos.*

- *Developing a reliable inner stillness through mindfulness practice helps you handle—and even thrive in—more turbulent times in your outer world. Doing so may first require sorting through and clearing out any negative associations you have with silence or stillness.*

## PARADOX

- *On group projects, it may make sense to prioritize clear direction and getting stuff done. Other times it will make sense to prioritize the feeling of connection between group members.*

## GOING DEEPER

- Sit in stillness for some time every day. Maybe it's for 10 minutes or 20 minutes. Maybe it's just for 20 seconds. Notice how your mind and body respond to that choice, both during and after.

- Check in with someone else about that practice each day, someone who can ask you how it went, or what got in the way if you weren't able to get to it. Ask them to send you a celebratory GIF or sing you a little song when you remember to practice. Any fun reinforcement will help!

- Notice any times during the day when you feel like things swirling around you have gotten too chaotic. Are there places where that sensation shows up more often? What about times of day? Or the length of time since you've eaten a real meal? Notice any patterns that emerge, and play with them. Can you reduce the feeling of chaos? Can you take a deep breath and let it swirl around you without getting pulled into it?

- Try leading Three-Words-at-a-Time Poems as described in the Glossary of Games and experiment with different levels of control over the timing. How do your choices in facilitation affect your experience of the exercise? How do they affect the group's experience?

# meta-tation
## *the benefits of a bigger picture*

WHEREVER YOU ARE, WHATEVER YOU'RE DOING, there's always some part of your awareness functioning as an observer. Or at least there's part of you that's capable of that. In this chapter, we'll look at that looker, see that see-er, and grow in awareness about that awareness. You'll get to explore where this "meta" perspective proves most applicable, where it doesn't, and how it can help you grow insight, humor and spaciousness for a more fruitful life.

### going 'meta'[1]

The prefix "meta" comes from Latin and suggests "next to" or "off to the side of." A meta-position gives us the opportunity for perspective, to look in on the thing we have sidled up against. It lifts us up and lets us peer down. It creates a wider boundary and a broader field of vision.

For example, let's say you and I are talking. Eventually, we start examining the dynamics of our interaction—which of us is speaking more, how funny or entertaining the content is, how quickly our pace moves along, and the like. At that point, we've moved into a meta-conversation: a conversation about the conversation.

---

[1] To be distinguished from "Metta," a term that those with Buddhist or Hindu connections will likely recognize. *Metta* with two t's comes from Pali, the language the Buddha spoke, and means "loving kindness." It's a lovely quality to promote and an even lovelier one to inhabit. Alas, it's not the focus of this chapter.

Similarly, if you filmed a documentary about the history of documentaries, it could qualify as a meta-documentary.[2]

## a fundamental tension

Playing with meta-perspectives leads us again onto a paradoxical spectrum that's both fun and helpful to stay aware of. On one hand, in life and especially on stage, we want to remain fully open to the moment, *experiencing* everything it's got to offer: all the thoughts, all the feelings, all the perceptions and reactions. That means fully doing whatever task lies at hand, getting engaged and embodied rather than stepping back for a larger view. We want to *be* the experience rather than working to *see* the experience. On the other hand, cultivating a larger meta-perspective helps us rise above the limitations we set for ourselves or the limitations given us by bosses, families, spouses or our culture. The meta-view has the power to stabilize, calm and even heal the psyche. As such, it gives personal development a chance to take root more firmly.

The helpful side of a meta-perspective gets most effective when we're wrestling with challenging thoughts or difficult emotions. So often, small sparks of doubt, self-criticism, fear or frustration can ignite and grow into wild blazes, surging across the canyons of the mind, spreading destructive power in much wider swaths. Choosing a meta-perspective gives us the chance to airlift above the flames and away from their heat. Rather than having to panic in the wildfire's path, we find ways to wall off its advance. We see the anger or self-judgment for what it is, and simply observe with curiosity and kindness. Without our adding fuel, the fire burns out, the soil settles, and new growth can begin to emerge.

---

[2] If you made another informative film about how you chose which documentaries to put in that first one, you'd have a meta-meta-documentary. We could go on forever. ☺

Maybe the fire image doesn't work for you but other metaphors can offer a similar wider lens. In Chapter 6, "The Power of Positivity: Creating a Delightful Default," you learned about seeing emotions as clouds passing by and how naming those emotions allows them to move through and open up a blue sky of natural contentment. That's using a meta-perspective to find peace. Alternatively, if you imagine yourself sitting alongside a street, watching the traffic of your mind pass by, neither road-blocking unpleasant thoughts nor trying to ride along with pleasant ones, you might find similar benefits. Most likely, the traffic will begin to thin and slow on its own, leaving behind a more stable calm. Or, you can think of thoughts and emotions like leaves floating on a stream. You park yourself on a streamside rock and simply let the leaves pass by. Maybe they get caught in an eddy for a while. Eventually, they move along.

In more specific or clinical emotional terms, as when you're grieving a loss, reeling from a betrayal, or roiling in anger from a violation, you can simply witness those thoughts and emotions—*Huh, look at that. There's grief. There's betrayal. There's anger.*—and let go of *doing* anything in particular. Your internal witness need not grieve, reel, or roil. It can simply rest in its own awareness.

Occasionally, difficult thoughts and feelings prove sticky enough or painful enough that we need multiple levels of distance before we find that place of stillness in their presence. After the major Loma Prieta earthquake in San Francisco in 1989, for example, I was literally and figuratively shaken up. When the quake hit,[3] I had come home from my senior year of college classes and was just putting my head down to take a nap. I quickly jumped up and braced myself in the doorway as I watched the room lurch around me: bookshelves and speakers crashing to the floor, windows breaking, fire alarm sounding in the hallway behind me. Once the trembling stopped,

---

[3] 5:04 pm PDT, October 17, 1989. Certain details get locked in.

part of me thought to search around for emergency supplies to take with me out of the house. All I ended up grabbing was the teddy bear my high school girlfriend had given me before I left home.[4] Our co-operatively run house got condemned and our tight community got scattered into emergency housing all across campus and throughout Palo Alto. It was a rough time.

Not surprisingly, the trauma stuck with me. For months moving into years, I'd hesitate whenever I went to lay my head down before falling asleep. If someone bumped my chair or if I felt the floor rumble from a passing truck, my heart would start pounding and I'd get short of breath, a surge of fight-or-flight hormones coursing through my system. Every innocuous jolt told my system an earthquake was starting up.

Eventually, I found my way to a healer who used Neuro-Linguistic Programming (NLP). NLP studies the way we store and access our thoughts and emotions in our brains and bodies. It then tries to find new patterns for doing so that support our fullest resourcefulness and greatest excellence. In this case, my NLP therapist used a helpful meta- technique.

He started by observing my response to a neutral stimulus. How did my facial muscles and my breathing react if I imagined myself walking on a safe path along the ocean back home in New England? OK, that was a baseline we'd try to recreate. Then he invited me to imagine the scene of the 1989 earthquake on a movie screen. This was a meta-move for sure. He told me, "You're in the audience watching this scene play out up there on the screen." He quickly noticed from my facial and body language cues—pursed lips, tension around the eyes, flush in my skin tone—that even this perspective remained too intense. So, he paused and suggested, "OK, why don't you put yourself in a projector booth watching

---

[4] Randolph and I had been and have been through a lot together.

yourself in the theatre, watching this on screen. Then replay it."
Again, he noted my reaction and saw that I was still agitated. He
then added, "OK, imagine yourself in the lobby watching yourself in
a projector booth, where you are watching the guy in the theatre,
who is watching the scene up on the screen." Each layer further
removed "me" from the original trauma.

As it turned out, that last meta-level provided enough distance.
From there, I could run the "movie" and even play some disarming
games with it, such as running it forward and backward until it
became nonsensical. Eventually, he also had me make it funny: "I
want you to imagine everybody in this movie of the quake has a butt
for a head. Just a big old bubble butt sitting atop their neck." So,
now when I played the scene on screen, people were stumbling and
bumbling, getting bounced around in their lopsided imbalance. I was
still watching an earthquake play out, but now it was making me
laugh. I finally had enough distance from it.

To close the session, my NLP practitioner had me shut down each
scene one at a time and move toward fully embodying the story:
"OK, now imagine yourself stepping from the lobby into the theatre
booth... Then go on into the theatre and watch the screen... Now
finally, can you jump back up into the scene?" By then, we had
healed my traumatic reaction enough that I could step back into my
own memory.

Since then, I haven't felt any panic about earthquakes. I actually lived
through one a couple of years ago while leading a retreat in the
mountains of northern California. At 3 a.m. in the morning, I woke
up with a start wondering if the ground had been shaking. But it was
a simple wondering, not an adrenaline rush. I pulled out my phone,
pulled up the U.S. Geological Survey app, saw that an earthquake
had happened 100 miles away... and then went back to sleep. All
good. All those layers of distance from my 25-years-earlier NLP
session had allowed me to get perspective on the panic and put it in

its place. I had found a place where I wasn't agitated, so I could be with the agitation in a different way.

## Ben Johnson's meta-perspective for improv scenes

Balancing both sides of the tension around meta-perspectives—being *in* the experience while also being above it—can also prove immensely helpful on the improv stage. Maybe a character hides a knife in a closet in an early scene, a promise for some dramatic unfolding later in a story. If everyone in the cast gets completely consumed by the moment and forgets that earlier moment with the knife, something's diminished. The audience might consciously forget as well—or they'll generously forgive—but they'll feel the disappointment of the unfulfilled teaser. If someone has the meta-perspective to remember and reintegrate that dramatic promise, however, it creates an incredible thrill. When the knife gets reincorporated into the story, it gets gasps of delight.

Ben Johnson, former company member at BATS and improvisor extraordinaire, describes how he manages his "meta":

> When I'm on stage, I want to be thinking the thoughts and feeling the feelings of my character. That's the only thing that I care about. I'm climbing into their experience and responding as honestly as I can from their perspective, their point of view. When I'm off stage, I'm an improvisor thinking about the story. I'm a writer, I'm a director, I'm thinking about promises that we've made, I'm thinking about what does the story need in order to fulfill the promises that we set out. Did we say we're going to do a film noir, promise that we're going to do a mystery or a romantic comedy? Whatever it is, have we done it? What suggestions from the audience do we have that we haven't used yet?[5]

---

[5] As relayed to Lisa Rowland.

In other words, when Ben's on stage, he's staying in the flow. He's a puppet. When he's off stage, he gets the perspective to consider who's pulling the puppet strings—and whether he wants to pull some himself.

## creating 'offstage' moments in real life

In regular life, then, we can create such "off-stage" moments for ourselves with conscious reflection. We live fully in the moment, and then maybe we go for a walk to reflect on what we just did. *How was that? Did I say the things I wanted to say? Was I generous enough?* Maybe we do some focused contemplation in the shower. Or maybe we write in a journal before we go to sleep. Whatever way we choose, we consider our actions and whether we might want to change them next time. We note what promises we have made that need to be fulfilled: things we said we'd accomplish, connections we intended to make, loops we've yet to close. Having done that, we then answer the question: *What comes next?*

## i am playing 'i am a tree'

On one of our retreats, Lisa Rowland and I reconfigured on old improv standby game to illustrate this notion of meta-perspective. In Chapter 3, "Impulse or Pause: Moving from Judgment to Discernment," we mentioned the game "I Am a Tree." In that activity, one person steps into the center of a circle, takes the pose of a tree and declares "I am a tree!" The next person steps in to take on the shape of something that would be with a tree, like "I am an acorn!" A third person does the same, connecting the first two—"I am an oak leaf!"—and now a complete three-part tableau has emerged. The first person in, in this case the tree, chooses one of the others to take with her back to the outside of the circle—"I'll take the oak leaf"—and the game starts over with the one left behind redeclaring his identity and shape: "I am an acorn!"

In this version, which we called "I Am Playing 'I Am a Tree'" (see what we did there?), we started with the same rules but encouraged the participants to play with meta-perspectives. Once the first element in a particular tableau had been established, could folks find a viewpoint that was either further out or further into that first prompt? For example, in the original version of the game, if someone said, "I am a soldier," another might say "I am the soldier's gun" or "I am a tear running down the soldier's face." Both those responses show up in the soldier's immediate environment.

A meta-perspective might pull back further: "I am a general who is assessing troop movements at command headquarters." Or, "I am the director setting up his Oscar-winning shot."

In a reverse meta-move, the perspective could dive further in: "I am the soldier's nervously beating heart." Or, "I am the soldier's memory of his son back home."

A more horizontal meta-step could also take us away from the immediate environment: "I am the horrors of war." Or, "I am the metalworker who made the soldier's gun."

In each of these cases, we look for opportunities to jump, whether playfully or poignantly, to a new angle or a new perspective.

For some reason, whenever we've introduced this 'meta' element, the game snaps into new life. The varied perspectives amplify the likelihood of surprise. We get context shifts and... whoop! We're in a new world that's both funnier and more meaningful.[6]

## Joanna Macy and deep time

In her despair and empowerment workshops, Joanna Macy—long-time philosopher, eco-activist and Buddhist teacher—introduces a related notion called Deep Time. Within that frame, she notes how our culture's emphasis on speed and short-term thinking causes great harm. We rush around in adrenaline-fueled frenzies that

---

[6] You can find full descriptions of both versions in the Glossary of Games.

exhaust our bodies and put great stress on our relationships with each other and with the Earth. With that narrow focus, we stay blind to long-term disasters coming our way, digging our heads in the sand when our senses and conscience suggest we should act otherwise.[7]

In contrast, Deep Time sees our existence within the vast expanse of Earth's history. We stretch our awareness back to our emergence from original elements and galactic gases, moving through human history out into the future of our descendants and other beings yet to come. Macy writes:

> Could future generations... discover a way to communicate with us? If so, what would they say? Perhaps they could only do this if we played our part too by extending ourselves forward in time to meet them. We can do this through our imagination. We don't know whether the communications we would receive this way are real or imagined—and we don't really need to know. They still offer useful guidance.[8]

When so much of life on earth is hanging in the balance, taking that creative meta-leap could prove a source of great comfort and creativity. What could those future beings show us? Or, in the other direction, what wisdom could we glean from our stardust ancestors? Or from the multicellular organisms that emerged from water to evolve eventually into us? Widen the lens and we gain both perspective and motivation.

## part of a larger story

As I mentioned in my story of the earthquake, meta-moves can provide supportive context for challenging times. If you step back to see your life as a story, each downturn becomes a chapter—an

---

[7] As is true with human-made climate change.

[8] Joanna Macy, *Active Hope: How to Face the Mess We're In Without Going Crazy* (New World Library: Novato, CA, 2012), p. 158.

obstacle to overcome rather than a permanent curse to suffer through. Each challenging moment gets a larger container: *Oh, this is the part of the story where things get really dark. This is where I feel like crap.* You're no longer a victim, you're the hero getting tested on your journey. You know there's more to come.

It's like watching a horror film. If you notice the fear riling you up past the point of fun, you can pull out to recognize the filmmaker's craft. *Oh, listen to this music. Check out this camera angle. That's how they're ramping up the audience's fear.* Again, you need not get consumed by any painful or frightening moment. It's OK if you're feeling bad or scared or lost or stuck. This is not the end of your story. You're somewhere in the middle.

## going meta makes you laugh (maybe)
Meta-perspectives can also generate humor and insight by showing us the absurdity and predictability of patterns we fall into. If we'll be able to laugh at some calamity 15 years in the future, why not take on some of that perspective right away and lighten the load now?

I first recognized the comedic value of such leaps at the Falcon Ridge Folk Festival back in the summer of 2002. I was lounging in the sun in front of the hillside main stage and a new-to-me a cappella group called Da Vinci's Notebook bounded up to the mikes. With super-tight harmonies, mischievous smiles, and infectious energy, they launched into a set of irreverent songs that poked welcome holes in the audience's stodgy folk sensibilities. The best of their set was a meta-level boy-band send-up that left me literally rolling with laughter. Earnest-eyed, it started like this:

> Declaration of my feelings for you,
> Elaboration on those feelings,
> Description of how long these feelings have existed,
> Belief that no one else could feel the same as I.

*Reminiscence of the pleasant times we shared together*
*and our relationship's perfection*
*Recounting of the steps that led to our love's dissolution*
*Mostly involving my unfaithfulness and lies*

With all the typical boy-band musical trappings, they continued on into a suspense-building bridge:

*Penitent admission of wrongdoing*
*Discovery of the depth of my affection*
*Regret over the lateness of my epiphany*

Before landing on the punch-line chorus:

*Title of the song*
*Naïve expression of love*
*Reluctance to accept that you are gone*
*Request to turn back time*
*and rectify my wrongs*
*Repetition of... the title of the song* [9]

That last line especially cracked me up because it took a second-level meta-leap, calling out the repetition as it happens. Meta-level funny. Good stuff.

Some presenters have taken a similar approach with the typical TED-talk mini-lecture format. For example, cheekily self-declared "thought leader" Pat Kelly describes the process of his talk as he's giving it—without ever really saying much of anything. After firing up his laptop (because "a presentation seems more legitimate than it actually is if... there... are... slides"), he goes on to report, "I'm

---

[9]Lyrics from Da Vinci's Notebook, "Title of the Song" from *The Life and Times of Mike Fanning*, Uncle Buford Records, 2000; used by permission. Take a listen to this link and you'll laugh with the other meta-level cleverness they included in the song. Make sure to enjoy the comments as well. https://www.youtube.com/watch?v=734wnHnnNR4

now going to come back to the center of the stage and give you some unremarkable context about how I became a thought leader." There's no "there" there, but he maintains authority because he leans on the familiar physical and vocal tropes that any regular TED Talk viewer will recognize: "Coming back to the center and... slowing... my... speech... lowering the volume of my voice... by looking at you directly... and by making a list on my fingers... I've made you believe there is a point." It's a seamless, artfully delivered satire that, like "Title of the Song," uses the genre to create a talk about nothing but the patterns of the genre.[10] The meta-level approach makes us laugh—and exposes how such talks usually rope us in.

### putting in your 'meta-' reps

Humorists pull us to these meta-perspectives for the laughs they generate. Improvisors choose them backstage for storytelling prowess. Therapists or meditation instructors employ them for their healing potential. Given their widely beneficial applicability, the question becomes: can everybody learn to generate such meta-level leaps? Could you train yourself to see from such perspectives? The easy answer to those questions? Absolutely!

Mindfulness practice develops this mental muscle, for one. We notice the breath coming and going. We listen for sounds as they rise and fall. We watch our thoughts and feelings come and go,

---

[10] "Pat Kelly, 'Thought Leader,' gives talk that will inspire your thoughts," CBC Radio, Published June 8, 2016.
https://www.youtube.com/watch?time_continue=241&v=_ZBKX-6Gz6A.
In a similar presentation published online on January 15, 2015, New York-based comedian Will Stephen also delivered meta-level laughs in his "How to Sound Smart in Your TEDx Talk." In it, he promises his audience, "I have nothing for you" but narrates "I'm going to do this with my hands and then do this with my glasses"...as he gesticulates and adjusts his glasses. As he refers to a simple pie chart, he proclaims, "What you're going to see is that the majority *far* exceeds the minority." Ha, ha, yes indeed.
https://www.youtube.com/watch?v=8S0FDjFBj8o.

moving along like leaves floating down a stream or traffic moving down a highway. Even when that flow gets clogged or stuck, we generate the ability to observe our processes with dispassion, with perspective and insight.

Then, whenever we notice ourselves getting consumed by our thoughts and feelings, the curiosity and kindness we've developed can soften our harsh reactions even further. Rather than thinking *He's a total jerk who wants to screw me over*, we can notice *Oh, he really pushes my buttons, that's interesting*. We don't have to ascribe malicious intent; we can stay present instead. And each time we do that, we're developing and reinforcing neural pathways that make a magnanimous response more likely in the future.

In improv, playing meta-level games—like "I Am Playing 'I Am a Tree'"—offers another avenue for building up meta-muscles. When we practice seeing and making these leaps, our brain creates a more flexible, wider-level default filter for the world. And doing narrative-based improv—where we jump back and forth between being *in* the scene and making choices *about* the scene—takes everything to yet another level.

When we do build up this capacity, we almost always find we're better able to enjoy the best parts of our lives, and we can find humor or spaciousness to handle the rocky times too. We get more skillful and more graceful whenever and wherever we step on life's stage. It's a valuable faculty to develop, one of the greatest gifts of both mindfulness and improvisation.

## Chapter 8
### Meta-tation: *The Benefits of a Bigger Picture*

### GEMS from the JOURNEY

- Some part of your awareness always maintains the capacity for a "meta" mode, a wider perspective on whatever challenge you're facing or experience you're having. That wider perspective can ease anxiety and provide psychic space for dealing more productively with intense emotions.

- Watching your thoughts and emotions come and go—like leaves floating down a stream—helps you realize they're more events than facts. That insight alone loosens their restrictive grip on your life.

- Thinking about our human connections to our ancestors and our future descendants—stepping into "Deep Time"—can also provide resilience in the face of great challenge.

- You can build the capacity for such meta-awareness by (surprise!) practicing both mindfulness and improvisation. ☺

### PARADOX

- Mindfulness encourages you to remain fully present, fully embodied in your experience of the moment. That said, sometimes you need to step out of that first-person perspective in order to avoid getting swept up in emotional reactivity. Both staying fully present and using a meta-perspective help. A life well-lived calls for us to discern when each approach proves most helpful.

## GOING DEEPER

- Sit for 10 or 20 minutes and notice the thoughts moving through your mind as if they were those leaves on a river. Can you name the thoughts as they come and go without getting carried off by them? If you do get carried off, can you come back to your seat to start again?

- Watch a great stand-up comedian's routine to see if you can identify any humor generated by a "meta-move" where they look at life's curiosities from a wider angle.

- Bring the buddies who played I Am a Tree with you back together and add in the meta-twist of I Am Playing I Am a Tree. See the Glossary of Games for a complete description.

# ch-ch-ch-changes
*learning to go with the flow*

CHANGE WILL HAPPEN. Sometimes you'll like it and sometimes you won't. In either case, your relationship **to** that change will drive the direction of your experience **with** it. In this chapter, we'll investigate that relationship, name what's difficult about change, and discover how to work more skillfully with it. If you're going through a big shift in your life—at work, in a relationship, within your sense of self—you may find helpful ideas here. If you're not going through such change, wait a bit. You soon will be.

### the inherent stress of change
Change—and especially the refusal to accept that change—can generate great suffering. Something shifts from what you anticipated, and you get thrown off your rails. Your car breaks down. Your employer lets you go, and you have to face a world without a reliable income. Your sweetheart decides he or she just wants to be friends. *Ouch, right?*

Or maybe it's that things have remained a certain way for a long time, and they suddenly crack into a new reality. Your grandparent dies. A flood wipes out a part of town. A beloved childhood forest gets cleared. When such changes go down, it can be tough to heed any advice to "just roll with it." You've lost something dear.

Even with a *positive* change, there's inherent stress. When life stays steady, you don't have to evaluate so many variables. You know how things work, hit a groove and sail right along. As soon as change rears its head, however—even when it's welcome—that easy default mode no longer works. New capabilities and new possibilities still force you to make sense of new information. You have to expand your bandwidth to handle the emerging demands: *Oh, what's actually happening? What do I need to pay attention to? What's relevant?* Even at its best, change can slow you down.

Given all this, it makes sense that we might develop a default "no" to life's offers, rather than a more adventurous "yes." We think that by resisting change, we can avoid the pain of loss and the increased demands on our mental and emotional systems.

## change changes the story

Improvisation offers radical lessons for dealing with this reality. In the world of improv, nothing is bad information. It's all just new data that helps you decide what comes next. Of course, that new data could prove completely different from what you were anticipating. And change can happen in the blink of an eye. You thought you were a doctor preparing tools to enter surgery, and your partner comes on stage to say, "Well, once you get settled with your coffee, I can show you the catalytic converter readings. It looks like you actually *will* need a new carburetor." Suddenly, you're a customer at Midas. There's no time to respond with resistance—*No, no. That's not what the scene was!*—because the show must go on. In order to stay present with what's happening, you have to immediately let go of what you imagined was happening. And reset your reality. In almost every moment.

Of course, maybe part of you wants to resist the change because you were really enjoying how you were portraying a doctor. Or you were excited about that doctor's growing urge to bust out of the hospital hierarchy. After all, her growth *mattered.* But if you ignore what just happened on stage—that your scene partner has tilted the axis of your world—you risk fighting with each other through your characters, and no audience wants to watch that. The more skillful approach means shifting from a mindset of *No, no, I have to fix this* to one of *OK, I'm rediscovering the story. I thought I had an idea, but now I don't.*

Are there times in improv when this certainty about accepting unexpected offers moves from black and white to shades of gray? Does it ever make sense to resist a change in plot or character? (Or in life?) Maybe. Perhaps the whole troupe has established a certain momentum with an unfolding story and another player comes on stage to make a disjointed call from out of left field—and everyone else basically continues telling the story as it had been. In unspoken fashion, they refuse to let the loopy additional offer undo what they've already established. More often, though, such resistance will grind the scene to a halt.

On stage, we've got more direct, more easily malleable control over how we react to the unfolding twists and turns in storyline. In real life, you may not get that kind of flexibility, and you may feel far more attached to whatever outcome you're wanting. No matter how strong your attachment, however, change still shows up. What's happened has happened. Resisting a change will never undo it.[1]

## 'metamorphic circle'

One improvisation exercise provides a great vehicle for playing with change—and with your tendency to resist it. "Metamorphic Circle" starts with all players standing in a ring. One person, Player A, begins by passing a simple sound and movement combination—opening the arms wide, tilting the head back, and exhaling with a "Pwwwwwwaaaaahhh", for example--to the next person, Player B. Player B then turns to Player C and passes that same sound and

---

[1] Resisting can never undo what has happened, but it might alter future outcomes. In some scenarios, like in political or legal arenas, resistance to change becomes mobilization—which can then undo whatever change had been implemented.

movement combo as best they can. Player C does the same, sending it along to Player D. And so on.

Here's the rub: however imperfect a reproduction of what was received, whatever gets passed along represents a new "perfect." Change has happened. There's a new normal. So, each player's job is not to correct or go back to what they think the original was.[2] Their job is to lovingly and accurately recreate what they have actually received.

The game works well to illustrate what we're discussing because change *will* sneak into the mix. Even if I receive and imitate your movement perfectly, subtle shifts will still come into play. My body will move in different ways than yours did. My voice will introduce a different tone or inflection. My face will contort without my awareness. Can you step out of your expectation in order to discern and then acknowledge the change as it happens?[3]

## anicca and anatta

A steady mindfulness practice also dives into this concern head-on: the more you practice noticing the present moment, the more you come to see that things change. Thoughts change, feelings change, self-perception changes, experience changes, circumstances change. Buddhism calls this truth *anicca* (pronounced a-NEE-cha), or impermanence.[4] Like the breath, all that we take in rises and falls, comes and goes, adapts and evolves. Even a mountain that seems so permanent wears down or erodes away if we choose a long

---

[2] Trust me, though, that's almost *certain* to happen. Someone will get caught up in their expectation of what *should* have happened and then try to cling to and restore that perception of the "correct" movement.

[3] See the Glossary of Games at the back of the book for a more complete description.

[4] *Anicca* in Pali (the language the Buddha spoke), *Anitya* in Sanskrit.

enough exposure for our "camera."[5] That transience and evanescence is true. It's real. We can try to fight that reality, but we won't win. We'll only generate suffering, including our own.

This kind of suffering can come in response to events—trying to hold on to what we love or prevent what we don't want to happen—and it can come from our notions of self and identity. We tend to view ourselves as stable personalities. Pay closer attention, though, and we come to see that our constructed "self" comprises a vast range of non-self elements. (In Buddhism, this fundamental truth is called *anatta,* the idea that there is no separate identity.[6]) We are all made up of water, air, sunshine and food. It follows that we're thus made up of rivers and oceans, hurricanes and breezes, seasons and light patterns, as well as seed and soil. We're also formed by our friendships, families, social connections, places we've been, teachers we've experienced, books we've read. You, reading this now, are being changed by what I have written—and I, the author, may ultimately be changed by your engagement. Anyone we influence will never be the same after our having "met." It's not that the self doesn't exist. It's that it doesn't exist in isolation from everything else, and it doesn't stay the same. Again, you can try to hold fast to who you are, but that holding can't last forever. Eventually, you'll tire yourself out by swimming against the tide of reality.

Ideally, when you learn to relax into these two truths—that all things change, including this interconnected pattern of being that we call "you"—it can take much of the sting out of any transition. What seems disconcerting can move through your mind and body like a wave, entering and leaving on the other side. You become like an embodied, happy ghost, a constellation of pattern and light that

---

[5] Watch a months-long time-lapse sequence of boulders moving down a rockslide and it moves just like a river.

[6] *Anatta* in Pali, *anatma* in Sanskrit.

allows objects and experiences to pass into and through them without resistance. You change with the changes as a murmuration of starlings shifts in flight[7]—expanding, shrinking, swooping and surging—and yet you remain recognizably you.

## handling big change

Making peace with the truth of impermanence may not prevent the pain of unwanted change, but it can at least provide a guidepost when we're weary of facing it, a salve for our suffering. If we get kicked off a team or suddenly lose a beloved pet or family member, no amount of accepting that this has happened can fill the hole in our hearts. It will still feel devastating. But understanding *anicca* (everything changes) and *anatta* (there is no separate self) means that the sadness of that empty space need not lead to *extra* suffering.

When I taught religious studies and philosophy, Buddhist monk Issho Fujita used to visit my class during our unit on Buddhism. Each time, he offered a helpful equation to illustrate this idea. With the students watching intently, he would silently write on the board, "Suffering = Pain x Attachment."

He'd wait a few beats, and then explain to the kids that, in other words, if you want to end suffering, you have two options. First, you could avoid all pain. Zero pain would mean zero suffering. Of course that's not actually possible, but even if it were, it would probably mean shutting yourself off from most of the delights of the world as well. Good things come to an end, and that end hurts. Does that mean you would want no joy?

Your second option in that equation is to reduce attachment. In this case, attachment means wanting things to come out a certain way—

---

[7] Check out this video for a gorgeous example that includes some awesome audio of the starling phenomenon as well. Amazing. https://www.youtube.com/watch?v=8VkpDCD6fms

or wanting to slow or accelerate the tides of change. In other words, to whatever extent you cling to a particular result, you magnify whatever pain shows up when you pursue it. If you're not attached to things being some other way, then you just have the pain but not the suffering.[8] Hurt—or sadness—becomes an experience in itself, one worth knowing and exploring. That pain might be inevitable, but the suffering remains optional.

In times of bigger losses, maybe you have permission to feel extra emotional for a while. Even a long while. Maybe the grief rises up at inopportune times. But if you allow it room to be and surrender to its power, then that rising up washes over you and simply drains back away. You recognize (and maybe even welcome) the grief as a visitor—*Oh, look, my heart has opened*—and let it leave when it chooses. Now pain, now not pain. No gnashing of teeth or self-pity (*Oh, why am I in such pain? When will it ever be over?, etc.*) needed.

Once you start allowing the change and applying your curiosity to it, you might also start to see how the pain itself shifts. What started as a sharp stab of sudden loss may morph into an ongoing ache of absence or lost opportunity. The first pulls you up short. It's jarring and shocking, a stunning violence of sorts. Then, as you get further from that initial moment, you come to recognize the repercussions of that loss. You won't travel down that cherished road on the way to work anymore. You'll no longer hear that friend's voice in a message. You and your family will have an unfilled chair at the holiday table. Your former partner's side of the bed will stay empty. So the initial ache takes new shape. It becomes a twinge that flares and recedes with regularity but no longer overwhelms in the same way. Noticing the specific qualities and sensations of the hurt as it shifts can give us that meta-perspective, that larger picture we need.

---

[8] Many folks who exercise recognize that the pain of a good workout can 'hurt so good,' for example.

Eventually, the hurt might fade imperceptibly into the distance or even disappear altogether.

Of course, this growing awareness and perspective may arrive at a bewilderingly slow pace. You can grasp this notion intellectually— *Oh sure, stuff happens, just go with the flow*—without your whole mind-body-emotion system getting on board. Some of us move like steamships: it takes a lot to get us going and then, once we're in motion, it takes a lot to change course. (And by "some of us," I also mean "I.")

## nature's wisdom

Nature also makes a great change coach, offering up valuable perspective for working through loss. The slow dying of autumn eases into winter and eventually makes way for the bloom of spring which in turn leads to the abundance of summer. Likewise, the moon comes and goes, waxing and waning, disappearing from view and then returning to fullness. We can find comfort in these reminders woven into the fabric of our physical universe. *This too shall pass. To every season, turn, turn, turn.* Paradoxically, change itself becomes a constant you can count on.

The rhythm of the tides can offer a similar perspective. Look out a seaside window and, depending on the time of day, your water horizon will shift. One time, boats and docks will be lifted high. At another, the tide will have retreated, exposing rocks and seaweeds. It's an hours-long rhythm, but it marches on. In and out, in and out. On a shorter cycle, each wave that makes up the tide does the same. In, out. In, out. In both cases, it's like the ocean just keeps breathing. Always changing, yet also constant.

The tide's instruction gets particularly clear whenever you need to travel by human-powered boat. In Casco Bay, Maine, if you need to get from Birch Island to Little Goose Island, and you try to do that when the tide is coming in against your direction of travel, it will take you four hours to get there—and you'll be completely spent in your effort. If you time your trip as the tide heads back out, it will take you twenty minutes—and it will feel like a gentle carnival ride. Adapt your behavior to the changes rather than fighting them and life gets easy (or easier, at any rate).

## shifting to curiosity

The biggest shift that both improv and mindfulness make in terms of confronting change is to move from an attitude of control to one of curiosity.[9] Instead of asking *How can I fix this story?* or declaring *This shouldn't be happening*, you drop into a more relaxed, more open investigation: *Oh, is that what's unfolding? Interesting. What might come next?* Rather than digging your heels in and resisting a stage partner's choices or life's unfolding, you prepare yourself to remain nimble and engaged with the new reality. Now you're learning and growing in ways you wouldn't or couldn't have predicted.

Friends and colleagues who have attended Burning Man—the annual countercultural festival that since 1986 has drawn thousands for ten days of heat, dust, music, and psychedelic consciousness in the California desert—have recounted similar dynamics and lessons about change there. Over the last ten years, some longtime festivalgoers have come to moan about the event's growth and commercialization: "It used to mean something but now the newbies (or tech bros or outsiders) have ruined the Burn. This is not what it was."

Literally, that last sentence is true. It is not what it was. But it is what it is. And the people who arrive fresh for the experience of Burning Man will have their own Burning Man experience. It may not match what they would have experienced 10 years ago or 15 years ago, but

---

[9] We'll explore curiosity more fully in a later chapter. For now, we'll just consider its connection to change.

it's what they'll know of the festival. They will create and play and love and discover—and find sand in places they wouldn't have thought possible when they get home—in their own way.

One could say sarcastically to the old-timers—those resistant to change—"OK, you hang onto that and stay riled up for however long you like. Or, if you're too angry, go seek the experience you want elsewhere." Either way, holding onto the outrage will sell short what the festival has become or can be. That clinging stands in the way of discovery and potential for this moment. In contrast, getting curious opens up new waves of possibility. *What is Burning Man now? What's available that wasn't before?*

## when should you resist change?

It's one thing to surrender to what's unfolding on an improv stage or in meditation, but what about the really unpleasant stuff that shows up in life? What about changes sponsored by greed or injustice? Whether on a personal, societal or even global level, what do we fight for?

Take our human loss of contact with nature, for example. It was only a few years ago that our human species crossed the line from a mostly rural population to an urban one. Meaning, more of us now live in cities than in more natural settings. I lament that so few young people will ever witness old-growth forests or fully mature ecosystems. They'll never have their breath taken away by those particular experiences. And that loss of intimacy means they'll not care the same way, further compounding the concern as ecosystems come under even more threat.

Using the tools we've extolled in this chapter, one could retort "Sure, they don't get to see those old-growth trees, but they do get to see the trees that are here now. Or the city skyline." But those kids aren't just losing an experience (and gaining another one), they're losing a breath-taking capability and capacity that they won't even imagine was possible. The same is true with the loss of species. Due to our consumptive choices, vast swaths of biodiversity are disappearing, certain arrangements of limbs and wings and colors and songs will never be seen or heard again. The boundaries of our imagination continue to compress—and we'll never even recognize that the dimensions have shrunk. Do we just give in and let this change happen? When do we fight and when do we acknowledge that fighting is like trying to force a square peg through a round hole?

### grieving losses and recognizing when to let go

Here's the thing. Recognizing and accepting that change is happening doesn't mean that you can't choose differently going forward. Have we lost old-growth forests and entire animal species? Yes, we have. We can accept that reality without needing to like it. Do we need to continue our self-destructive acceleration on both fronts? Absolutely not.

In this case, you can acknowledge the change, see it clearly, and feel your feelings honestly—all these allow you to act with greater clarity, courage and conviction going forward. You can wake up and face the facts with an engaged curiosity. *Hmm. Given that this is happening, how do I want to participate?* Again, we circle back to that notion of being fully invested without getting attached to the outcome.[10] You put your heart and soul into your intention, ideally making use of the currents of change passing through your mind and body. You do the work in concert with the tide and then let go. Or come back to do more work. You're never guaranteed how it will end. But that work and your attitude about it are what you do actually have control over.

---

[10] See Chapter 5, "Want Without Need: Balancing Aspiration and Acceptance."

If, for example, a relationship seems to be dissolving, maybe you stay and fight for its survival a bit longer—and do so lovingly and gratefully rather than fearfully. That it's changing need not mean it's done. Go to counseling. Take temporary space from each other. Recommit to kindness. Then, if it's still not working after that time of honest effort, maybe you realize you're holding on at the cost of your own happiness. You come to see that staying together stifled in misery actually reduces you and your partner more than the temporary pain or shame of breaking up ever could. Maybe this was meant to be a two-year or five-year or seven-year relationship.

Having made an honest effort, you might say as you would with any change in your life: *It's OK, it's time to move on.*

---

### Chapter 9
### Ch-ch-ch-changes: *Learning to Go with the Flow*

#### GEMS from the JOURNEY

- *Change happens. Your relationship to that change will directly determine the quality of your experience of it.*

- *Even positive change can prove stressful or disturbing. Given that, it's no surprise that we sometimes want to resist transitions.*

- *Living the Buddhist truths of anicca and anatta— impermanence and the absence of a separate self— takes much of the sting out of change. If we aren't attached to things staying the same, we may well feel pain, but we won't suffer.*

- *Adapting to big changes can take a long time. It's helpful to remain patient and kind with ourselves and with others during such transitions.*

- *Nature makes a wonderful change coach. Getting outdoors gets you in contact with wisdom beyond words and human constructs.*

## PARADOX

- Accepting change doesn't mean that you can't or shouldn't work passionately for a different outcome going forward. You probably can't go back to the way it was, but you might be able to shift what happens in the future on a personal, societal or even global level.

## GOING DEEPER

- If you live where you have a view of the sky, try keeping a moon journal for a month. Look up as often as you can, day and night, and notice the moon's size and location. What has shifted in its appearance since the last time you saw it? What has shifted in you?

- Alternatively, if you live near the ocean, pay attention to the tides for a month. Where's the high water mark? Where's the low water mark? What moods arise in you at different tide levels? How do you feel when the tide is coming in versus when it's going out?

- Next time you find yourself resisting a change in your life, ask yourself if you're resisting reality in any way. Is there any truth in the situation that you can acknowledge and release? Is there any component to the change that remains uncertain and would be worth fighting for?

- Try out the "Metamorphic Circle" game described more fully in the Glossary of Games. Take particular note of when you and others resist when people make seeming mistakes of interpretation. What helps you or the group stay ready and accepting of whatever shows up?

# got presence?
*moving into second circle*

PRESENCE CHANGES EVERYTHING. Get present and the world opens the full range of its gifts to you. You see more. You feel more. You grow more. Even better, when you're fully here—in *this* moment, in *this* place, with *these* people—you offer your best in return. You listen more closely. Your words land and connect. And your very being automatically activates others to become their best selves.

Presence lies at the heart of both mindfulness and improvisation. This chapter will show you how to develop this elusive quality in yourself—and how to share it with others.

## 'presence' versus 'present'

Because its meaning can get a bit fuzzy, let's start with the word itself. If someone walks into a room and we say *"Oh, she's got **presence**,"* what exactly do we mean?

Maybe it's that she's comfortable with herself. She's positive and open. She wants to be where she is and doesn't wish anything were different. She could have a grace in movement, a radiance or a kind of energetic shine. You don't have to talk with her to sense she's there—though you'd like to stand near her, if only to bask in that great energy. She's dynamic, engaged, and fun to watch. There's a power and a generosity. There's a buzz and hubbub. There's a magnetism or an attraction.[1] In short, she is **here with** you and everyone else. Fully embodied and deeply connected.

It's curious—and perhaps important—to note that one can be physically present and even fully attentive without necessarily conveying this wider quality of "presence." Maybe someone quietly observes from the corner of the room. He's focused. His mind stays steady and he catches what passes before him. He contributes astutely when called upon. But he's not someone who would necessarily draw our attention when he steps into the space. He might struggle a bit to play a leading man on stage—improvised or rehearsed—but he'd likely offer great support. To get to this other, deeper level, he'll need at least some element of openness or engagement with others added to the equation. He'll need to reach out. Said another way, you can be **present** without having **presence**; you just can't get to presence without being present.

## Patsy Rodenburg and changeable presence

Many people assume that either you have this "presence" or you don't. The 6-year-old girl who wows us all in the national singing competition. The 3-year-old golf prodigy who can demonstrate a sweeter swing than most adults. If you're not given the gifts at birth, you won't ever get 'em.[2]

Renowned UK-based voice and acting coach Patsy Rodenburg asserts and teaches otherwise.[3] As an acting student of her own, she

---

[1] Note that the attraction could be sexual but doesn't have to be.

[2] Remember Carol Dweck's work from the Relationship to Failure chapter? This is classic Fixed Mindset thinking.

[3] Rodenburg has coached most of the modern luminaries of British acting: Sir Ian McKellen, Dame Judi Dench, Hellen Mirren, Nicole Kidman, Daniel Craig, Ewan MacGregor, Lawrence Olivier, and the like. She has worked with the Royal Shakespeare Company and taught at the Guild Hall. She has also trained the world champion national rugby and women's field hockey teams and coached the Royal Air Force and people in Parliament—all folks who need to know a thing or two about presence.

often found herself frustrated by instructors and directors who decided quickly that a student either had "it" or did not. Those with the "gift" would get showered with attention and opportunity. Those without would get second-class treatment and often find themselves quickly bounced off the advancement track. That unfairness led Rodenburg on a journey to crack the code for effective presence. What tweaks and levers could lead ordinary folks to uncover *their* natural charisma and unique vocal power? What postures and breathing patterns could bring *anyone* most alertly into the present moment?

## three circles of awareness

Eventually, Rodenburg landed on the notion of three circles of awareness or energy, three ways of being, three attitudes. Each has its strengths and limitations, but one ultimately represents our most effective home base.[4] We'll cover 1st and 3rd Circles to start because they pull us away from our natural presence. After that, we'll return home to the greater resourcefulness of 2nd Circle.

*1st Circle: The energy of self-absorption and withdrawal*

In 1st Circle, your concentration turns inward, pulling outward events into your sphere. When activated healthily, 1st Circle represents an energy of introspection or self-reflection, the kind of mood you'd choose for writing in a journal or doing some forms of meditation. Or maybe it's a skillful moment of "disappearing" so as to escape being bothered or harassed. Rodenburg recounts a story of Marilyn Monroe being in a department store with a friend. When no one came up to them for an autograph, the friend was astonished and asked what was happening. Monroe said something to the effect of "I'm not 'on,'" shifted her stance and presence and stepped into her

---

[4] For a fuller explanation, check out Rodenburg's *The Second Circle: How to Use Positive Energy for Success in Every Situation* (WW Norton: New York, NY), 2008.

"Marilyn" persona—and a crowd quickly gathered. She had been skillfully standing in 1$^{st}$ Circle, hidden in plain view.

More often, 1$^{st}$ Circle energy represents a hesitation or unwillingness to engage, a retreat so that the heart or body doesn't get exposed. 1$^{st}$ Circle shrinks from contact and fears taking up too much space. It apologizes for even being. In the body, then, 1$^{st}$ Circle brings the feet close together, maybe one or both sets of toes pointed in, one or both arms across the body, hips back and shoulders curved in so the head faces down. Muscles remain weak or toneless. Joints might stay locked.

When in that mode, you often come across as dispassionate, self-absorbed or aloof—even callous—and can deplete the energy of those around you rather than raising it. Hang out in 1$^{st}$ Circle a lot, and it may feel comfortable—as in, familiar—but you'll also likely feel more sadness, loneliness, or anxiety. Ultimately, living primarily in 1$^{st}$ Circle lessens your influence. And, though it feels like a protective maneuver, it can actually put you in greater danger because you're not fully tuned into the risks around you.

If 1$^{st}$ Circle seems like home for you, you may have been harassed out of your natural presence by criticism, cruelty or unwanted attention when you were younger. (Note that there's no shame now in noticing what you've needed to do to feel safer or to avoid ridicule!) Or, maybe others felt threatened by the fullness of your powers. Whatever the root, you have likely learned to hide your presence to escape notice.

### 3$^{rd}$ Circle: The energy of bluff, force, and intimidation

In contrast, 3$^{rd}$ Circle blasts its energy outward, like an aerosol can spraying into a room. Your attention leaps outside yourself and into the world but without focus or specificity. To the good, 3$^{rd}$ Circle can crank up a party, rally the team or clear a wider path—think an ambulance siren—and it can prove compelling or entertaining, at least for a little while. It can also help to defend your privacy or deflect unwanted attention. Eventually, though—and maybe quickly so—3<sup>rd</sup> Circle begins to wear listeners (and even presenters) down. Because it looks past or down on its audience, it misses nuance and subtlety and cannot bring its energy back in. It lacks intimacy and takes up too much space, the proverbial bull in the china shop.

In the body, 3<sup>rd</sup> Circle over-widens the stance, with toes pointed further away from each other. The hips sling forward and chest opens wide with the chin faced up. Maybe workouts have sculpted the muscles to ripped status. 3<sup>rd</sup> Circle can appear confident, but like 1<sup>st</sup> Circle, still contains a prominent element of fear. Rather than hiding you away, however, 3<sup>rd</sup> Circle tries to protect the heart by keeping *others* away, acting as a determined shield.

If 3<sup>rd</sup> Circle sounds familiar, you might feel alone, even when with others. You might need to control your world without allowing anyone to help. Maybe someone came after you early on and rather than shrink away, you chose to come out swinging. You regularly fight to be seen and heard, resisting anyone who would cut you down—or who would dismiss you altogether.

*2<sup>nd</sup> Circle: The energy of grounded connection and full presence*

2<sup>nd</sup> Circle finds the sweet spot between the other two. Here, focused energy extends out toward your object of attention and then kindly returns, having touched and then been amplified. It moves skillfully and wisely, like an animal in its natural habitat, reaching out with curiosity and purpose. When in 2<sup>nd</sup> Circle, you take up your fair share of space, ready to connect with and influence the world—and to be influenced by it in return.

In 2<sup>nd</sup> Circle, your body remains both strong and flexible, relaxed and alert. The feet rest comfortably under the hips, knees softened, weight very slightly forward to the balls of the feet. The arms hang freely from the shoulders and your gaze remains open to the world.[5] Because it values balance and equality, 2nd Circle generates real intimacy and signals authentic trustworthiness.[6] It calls forth our wisdom, patience, humor, insight and compassion. It puts us in our power.

If 2nd Circle seems like home to you, congratulations. You've either had loving support in your life or have worked hard to create it for yourself. You're probably someone that others turn to in need—and you maintain boundaries well enough to take good care of yourself. As with the other two, however, 2nd Circle comes with a caveat. Having this kind of presence and charisma doesn't necessarily lead to ethical choices. You could use your charm to seduce someone inappropriately. Twisted leaders have leveraged such powers to lead acolytes to heartbreaking ends. 2nd Circle is *likely* to call forth compassion, but it can also do real damage.

As you just learned, each of the circles has its own physical qualities. Each also has its own breath and vocal quality. The model extends even further into wider ways of being: we can reside in and move from 1st, 2nd and 3rd Circles in our word choice, our emotional stance or our spiritual beliefs. What would it mean to take a 2nd Circle approach to a physical object we're handling? Or a tough conversation we're having? Or a choice that lies in front of us? As with so much wisdom from the worlds of mindfulness, the more we learn to practice 2nd Circle awareness and presence, the more we see the potential for its impact throughout our lives.

## the power of posture

The quickest way to generate the benefits of 2nd Circle is to take that physical stance and breathe into it. Relaxed alertness creates and

---

[5] Those who do yoga might recognize as a 2nd Circle posture.

[6] If you are in some foreign place and you need directions or feel under threat, you will most likely turn to the person who looks like they are in 2nd circle. They seem safe—confident, without being arrogant or dangerous.

reinforces an attitude of openness, curiosity, kindness and support: *Here I am. What can I do to help? What's needed?*[7] We don't have to expend energy protecting ourselves because we remain open. We don't hide away. We don't push against. We cultivate the kind of readiness that waits in the wings and knows the right time to enter the stage—whether literally or figuratively. Because we're connected, we notice more. We sense when someone is upset, or see when our words cause a ripple that appears to have hurt or stung the person we're speaking with. Put your body in the position of openness, and you help the process along.

We know the body responds to the brain. Win a race and you're likely to take the open-armed victory stance—think Usain Bolt crossing the finish line at the Olympics. Suffer a humiliating defeat and you'll shift into a slumped-shouldered, head-down "failure flinch" as we discussed earlier.[8] The experience leads to the posture. The body responds to the experience.

But the signal can travel the other direction as well: the brain will respond to the body. Take the victory stance and you'll feel more triumphant. Open into a Circus Bow "Woo hoo!" and enjoy your resilience. Smile and you'll feel happier.[9] Alternatively, slump in defeat and you'll start to feel like a loser, even if you don't want to. Or take a position that says "I don't want to call attention to myself" and you'll start to look—and feel—like prey.

Because the body can affect our mood in this way, a 2nd Circle stance offers one way to communicate with our brains when we're under special or stressful circumstances. In order to convey what Speech Skills founder Kara Alter calls "visible credibility," we have to tame

---

[7] Note: a great attitude for improvisation!
[8] See Chapter 2, "Take a Circus Bow: Changing Your Relationship to Failure."
[9] Go ahead. Try it. Try smiling with a huge grin and then say out loud "Life sucks. I'm just so miserable." You just can't generate the same depth of suffering, can you?

the adrenaline coursing through our system from the fear of public speaking. *Yikes! I'm about to get on stage in front of 1200 people!* That adrenal system won't respond to reason—it's based in the lizard stage of our evolution, for Pete's sake—but it *will* respond to physiology. So, you take up your space, balance your stance, position your shoulders above your hips, elongate the spine—and take a breath. This sends a message to your system that you can handle what's about to happen. *We're fine. I'm under no threat here.* Eyes on the horizon, head level, symmetrical in stance—all of that feeds back into the body-mind system. And the system responds. *Oh, she doesn't need any more adrenaline. It's cool. Call it off.* The posture helps you get your body chemistry pulling in the same direction as your intention.

Over the last few years, Harvard Business School social psychologist Amy Cuddy has earned a great deal of attention for her research demonstrating such effects. In a TEDGlobal talk in 2012, Cuddy outlined her findings, offering a "free, low-tech life hack that takes two minutes" as part of her presentation "Your Body Language May Shape Who You Are." Though the full applicability of her research has since come into some question, the video remains well worth watching.

Cuddy's main argument ran something like this: if you stand in a space-taking manner (3rd Circle) for two minutes, you raise testosterone levels—the hormone that helps us act with courage under stress—and lower cortisol levels—the hormone that makes us feel stressed out. If you collapse your posture so that you minimize your space (a la 1st Circle), the reverse happens: testosterone levels drop and cortisol levels increase. In other words, if you prepare for a test or a big moment hunched over your notes, you'll create a biochemical hindrance to your ability to handle the stress. If you extend your limbs outward beforehand—think Da Vinci's man in a circle—you'll have more stress-handling resources available.

Note that because Cuddy conducted her research through a lens of social dominance rather than one of grounded connection, her work overlaps with but doesn't perfectly match Rodenburg's. A 2<sup>nd</sup> Circle Mountain Pose might generate similar biochemical resourcefulness, creating a sense of calm and a relaxed approachability free from overtones of dominance, for example. That said, the more basic point still holds: how you carry yourself physically fosters your attitude. When you're conscious about this, you can start to reset your default behavior and thinking.[10]

## posture, breath and voice

Not surprisingly, changing your posture also changes how you breathe. When you open up and relax into a natural abdominal breathing pattern, neither clipped nor puffed up, you get more oxygen into your system. You think more clearly. You get better ideas. You find more courage. Again, use your posture to tell your system "everything's fine," and more resources will show up to make it so.

And, of course, any time you change your breath, the voice shifts along with it. Move into 2<sup>nd</sup> Circle and you can start to *feel* your voice in your chest, belly and back. You're no longer trying to hide. You're willing to be vulnerable so the authentic voice shows up, freer, richer and more resonant. You've got a wider range, so more of you comes through. At that point, speech becomes the most natural expression in the world. You breathe in and then, what are you going to do with that breath? Well, you could speak. And if your voice remains free, what you say will more truthfully convey your experience. Your words will impact the listener. They may even change the world.

## moving to unconscious competence

Part of you may feel exhausted starting to consider all this. *Do I have to pay attention all the time to which dang Circle I'm in? Do I ever get*

---

[10] See Chapter 6, "The Power of Positivity: Creating a Delightful Default."

to just give up, lie down on the couch and relax? That's understandable. If we haven't worked our presence muscles in a while, they're likely to tire quickly. And even realizing we're "out of shape" can stir some frustration.

Still, the point isn't to create a tense hypervigilance that generates more stress than it relieves. You're resetting your default: from an absent-minded, disconnected autopilot to an engaged connection with yourself, others and the world. You're building up a foundation of open readiness and participation that eventually becomes your home state. And you're moving through a sequence of learning so that this all happens on its own.

To this end, it can be helpful to recognize four states of learning. We start with **unconscious incompetence**. We don't know how to do something (in this case, find $2^{nd}$ Circle), and we don't know that we don't know. $2^{nd}$ Circle has never crossed our radar as something to consider so we remain blind to the possibility.

Once informed, we move into **conscious incompetence**. Now we recognize that we've got something to learn. We're aware of our inability. This stage may feel particularly frustrating because we experience failure and fatigue over and over. It may seem like we'll never quite get it. *Will I always live in $1^{st}$ and $3^{rd}$ Circles?*

Eventually, we move into the realm of **conscious competence**. Here, we can maintain a skill when we pay careful attention to it. *Ok. Feet pointed straightforward, knees soft, hips above the balance point, shoulders and arms relaxed, gaze straight ahead.* We work through the checklist and get our ducks in a row so we can perform the task at hand: finding that more connected stance and breath.

In the end, we make our way into the realm of **unconscious competence**. Here, we have developed a stable skill, attitude or way of being, and we need not occupy conscious bandwidth to maintain it. We can run the learning in the background. What we've strived for has become our new default.

Ideally, this is where we come to over time with our $2^{nd}$ Circle practice. We don't have to think about presence. It just happens because we've made it the new normal. Our be-here-now muscles have become both strong and flexible, ready and nimble for whatever comes before us.

## ensemble presence

Once we've begun to develop and refine our personal presence, another tantalizing question starts to bubble up. What could become possible if a whole group of folks committed to such presence *together*? If we expand our intention past our own boundaries with others who are doing the same, what kind of magic emerges? What transcendence takes shape?

To my eye, it's what leads to the most powerful of sports teams. Watch Coach Steve Kerr of the multiple-time NBA Champion Golden State Warriors talk with the press and his players and observe how the team stays connected to each other. Go see a top-notch improv troupe like the Improv Playhouse of San Francisco or Impro Theatre in Los Angeles and notice how the performers pick up on the subtlest of cues. Catch Bruce Springsteen and his band or Brandi Carlile and hers and witness the way they offer vulnerability to their audience even as their light shines brightly. Open. Ready. Connected.

When the "Angelica" touring cast of the musical *Hamilton!* came through California, they demonstrated this kind of ensemble presence to a T. From top to bottom and start to finish, the actors, orchestra and stage crew made an exquisite team. Joshua Henry, playing the lead narrator and pivotal character, Aaron Burr, strode on stage grounded in breath and body with an acute attention to detail that never subsided. All the other performers locked in as well, remaining fully in character, even as they waited in the wings to reenter. The dance crew stayed equally invested whether in focus at the front of the stage or offering support in the background. I saw the show several times and this unity remained even when understudies took over. These *Hamilton!* cast members weren't playing their roles, they were living them. As a team, they together created an elusive, shared 2$^{nd}$ Circle experience, one that brought the audience along with them. Ultimately, this is what theatergoers hope for, to come into the present moment so we can feel fully alive. *Look around, look around at how lucky we are to be alive right now.*[11]

## it takes commitment

Patsy Rodenburg knows that creating a true 2$^{nd}$ Circle ensemble takes a commitment and dedication that most of us aren't used to making. That's why, in her workshops, she sets such strict expectations. *Put your phones away. Don't get up or rustle around when someone's presenting. Drop your concern about taking notes and capturing what's happening for the future. Keep your eyes up. Stay connected to what's here now.* It's exhausting, but it works.

The more I participated in Rodenburg's setting, the more finely tuned my own sense of presence became. Normally, I'm a big note-taker—I want to remember particular phrases or ideas for future consideration—but I could start to feel how even that impulse pulled me away from full attention to what was happening in front of me. Or, if someone—against the agreements—checked their phone, even if they sat 15 feet away and managed to stay silent, I could *feel* a disturbance in the force. My senses had heightened.

Rodenburg had us try an exercise that illustrated these new abilities in astounding fashion. We all stood in a ring so we could see everyone else. Then we all got ourselves in a 2$^{nd}$ Circle posture, breath, and awareness. (We all tuned in.) She asked us to close our

---

[11] A recurring lyric from the *Hamilton!* soundtrack.

eyes and said, "I am going to tap somebody on the shoulder, and that person is going to put their body into a 1$^{st}$ circle posture or 3$^{rd}$ circle posture or maybe step out of the circle a little bit. But I want them to do it quietly." As she continued to speak, she walked around so we wouldn't know whom she had tapped. After a minute or so, she said "Now, with your eyes still closed, I want you to point to where in the circle you sense the disruption." Everybody pointed somewhere. Holding that gesture, we eventually opened our eyes and, 75 to 80 percent of us were pointing to the one person who had shifted out of 2$^{nd}$ Circle presence. Wild!

Our small choices to stay connected with or detach from a group have an impact. You may think, *Oh, I'll just check my email really quick*, and that it won't affect what's happening. But it will draw down the group's vitality. It will sap some power from the moment. The ship may not sink, but it will spring a temporary leak. When you commit to staying present, the ship continues to sail cleanly and powerfully in whatever direction it's heading. No unintentional drag. When we're part of a dedicated 2$^{nd}$ Circle group, it actually becomes easier to support each other because we quickly and intuitively sense when something's off or when someone has particularly good news to share. And maybe most importantly, we can stay open to the shared-control creativity that's moving through us all.

## impact on others

That kind of group commitment also creates a healing power of its own. Group members feel safer and more comfortable. Fewer ego battles arise when everyone feels seen and heard. We get less tired and have more fun. We maintain mutual curiosity. We get better.[12]

---

[12] Research has shown that with doctors, psychologists and other caretakers, the single best variable for predicting patient success is the quality of that provider's personal presence during the treatment, checkup, acupuncture, therapy, or whatever. See Kelly, Kraft-Todd, Schapira, Kossowsky, and Reiss, "The Influence of Patient-Clinician Relationship on

The key variable is simply having another person—or ideally, a group of people—say, "I see you. I hear you. I am here with you and for you."

If what makes a difference in people's healing, growth and development is feeling seen, witnessed and cared for, it would make sense for all of us to get better at that particular ability. Of course, that's what this chapter's been all about. Step by step, conscious choice by conscious choice, you build your presence muscles and endurance so you can enter this moment—this moment, now—for yourself and others. You may doubt yourself along the way or feel that you've not made much progress. It may even seem that you've backslid. But surely, you will improve at staying present. You'll get better and you'll get more relaxed about it all. 2nd Circle will start to feel like home. From there, you can let the rest unfold. And what will unfold will be different than you could ever discover hiding in hesitation or coming on too strong.

---

### why i'm not looking forward to the future

It may seem sacrilege, but that header at the top of this text box is true. I've stopped looking forward to the future.

It's not that I've become a pessimist or a Donnie Downer. My internal curmudgeon knows how to flex his muscles, but he hasn't yet commandeered my internal rudder. Generosity and gratitude still captain the ship.

It's just that, as mindfulness practice encourages, I'm trying to live in the present.

---

Healthcare Outcomes: A Systematic Review and Meta-Analysis of Randomized Controlled Trials," PLOS One. 2014; 9(6): e101191 for details.
https://www.ncbi.nlm.nih.gov/pmc/articles/PMC3981763/

Because of that, I'm now catching myself. In times and places when I would have said I'm really looking forward to something, I adjust my language. What's actually happening is that I'm excited *now* for something I anticipate will arrive. I'm noticing my current experience.

I love the shift for two reasons. One, it simply seems more accurate. As someone who delights in language precision, there's immediate gold in them that hill. More importantly, it takes the future off the hook. With this adjustment, I'm no longer setting myself up for deflation if what I'm anticipating doesn't come true. I don't need the future to happen the way I want in order to gain the benefit of enjoying my excitement now. I can relax my inclination to control. The positive vibes get banked. If disappointment arrives down the road, I've got a buffer to soften the blow.

A similar dynamic can apply with looking back on fond memories. Rather than get caught in clinging to what was, I can notice and enjoy the pleasure I still gain—here, now—from the echoes of that experience. I'm not gripping for that goodness. I'm letting it wash over me, still in this moment.

Some might say I'm blinding myself with a semantic smokescreen. The linguistic shift doesn't keep me from lingering. That may be true. And... I notice a significant difference whenever I remember and choose different words. My anticipation gets lighter and sweeter. My planning gets more creative and less fearful. And my memories slough off their baggage while leaving their lessons.

Try it for yourself. See what you think. And, if you like, let me know how it goes. In this case, I don't need to look forward to enjoy the possibility. I'm excited **now** to learn what insights you gain.

# Chapter 10
## Got Presence? *Moving into Second Circle*

### GEMS from the JOURNEY

- People with true presence have a power, grace and magnetism that leads to deep connection with others and with the larger world. Thankfully—and contrary to popular opinion—we all have the capacity to rediscover that kind of presence within us.

- We humans tend to live in one of three "circles" of presence or personal energy. 1$^{st}$ Circle represents a hesitant hiding away. 3$^{rd}$ Circle pushes away through puffery and dismissal. 2$^{nd}$ Circle—a balanced attitude of open, ready connection—calls forward our most grounded, most resourceful and wisest way of being.

- The posture of your body greatly affects your mood and the quality of presence you communicate. It also directly affects the quality of your breath and, in turn, the openness and range of your voice.

- Most learning involves moving through four stages:
  1. unconscious incompetence
  2. conscious incompetence
  3. conscious competence
  4. unconscious competence

- Ideally, it helps to get to the fourth stage, where you don't have to think about how to enact the new skill You just do it. In the case of 2$^{nd}$ Circle, your connected presence simply comes as a natural expression of who you are.

- Groups who make a disciplined commitment to stay fully present with each other have the power to reach inspiring heights of performance and cohesion.

**PARADOX**

- Full presence includes a balance of internal awareness and connection with the world around you. Though there's scientific evidence to suggest you can't place your attention in both places simultaneously, perhaps you can toggle back and forth so smoothly and so regularly that it looks and feels like both are happening at the same time. Or maybe it's like breathing, simply moving from one to the other in a relaxed rhythm: present with yourself, present with others, and repeat

.

**GOING DEEPER**

- Go on a people-watching expedition to see if you can pick out who's moving in $1^{st}$, $2^{nd}$ or $3^{rd}$ Circles. Which people are you most drawn to? Who seems to have the most confidence and the most magnetism? Whom do you feel safest around? And how do other people treat the person you're focused on?

- Watch Amy Cuddy's *"Your Body Language May Shape Who You Are."*

- Consider all the things that you have learned, are learning now or want to learn. Where do you fall on the four stages of learning? What do you know how to do with ease now that you used to struggle with—or even better, that you didn't even know you didn't know how to do?

- Next time you go out to dinner with friends or family, convince the whole group to turn off and put away their smartphones while you're sharing each other's company. How does the group's choice to remain present affect your experience?

# part four
## *four more qualities (and one last paradox)*

You got yourself ready to romp by coming to understand the terms—and the practices—of mindfulness and improvisation. You stepped into the messy wisdom of some tricky paradoxes. And you continued acquiring a new mindset of skillful readiness.

Now, before you head back out into the open territory of your life, we've got four final inquiries and one last paradox for you to explore. Taken together, these inquiries will cultivate valuable overlapping qualities—adventurousness, curiosity, gratitude, courage, and humility—that will grace your life with even deeper connection.

# adventure time!
## seeking the joy of new experience

HEAR THE WORD "ADVENTURE" and vivid images from a Patagonia catalogue or *National Geographic* magazine might leap to mind. Ropes and carabiners supporting a floating hammock off the side of a cliff. Sturdy, sun-weathered, leather-clad dudes plunging horseback across a swollen river. Or an astronaut sending photos back home from her spacewalk outside the capsule.

Or maybe your sense of adventure hums at a less fevered pitch. Not quite so costly or involved, but still exciting or slightly dangerous. Maybe it's a simple journey into the unknown needing just a bit of bravery: traveling abroad or entering a new relationship, pushing past a previous physical limit or finding a new route on your way home from work. Whatever the form, you go out into the world and try something different. You choose an unusual path so you can generate wisdom and insight—and then bring more love, creativity or boldness back into your life.

In all these cases, this sense of adventure stems from a state of mind: *What's out there? Let me explore!* You choose to engage with the world in a state of open readiness—Second Circle!—and you roll with what shows up. You don't know how the adventure will turn out, so there's some element of risk and no level of guarantee. You might get in a tight spot. You might feel awkward or rejected or bad at the new thing you're trying out. With an openness to what comes, however—and with the insights of mindfulness and improvisation—

you can comfortably rely on learning. And growth. And transformation.

## those who say yes

Keith Johnstone, the improv founding father I've mentioned before, speaks directly of this kind of mindset:

> There are people who prefer to say 'Yes', and there are people who prefer to say 'No'. Those who say 'Yes' are rewarded by the adventures they have, and those who say 'No' are rewarded by the safety they attain.[1]

In other words, when you go on an adventure, you sacrifice some element of safety. When you say yes, you're temporarily abstaining from a protective no.[2]

Because improv trains us to engage and strengthen our yes-muscles, it propels us into an adventurous life. Characters say yes to each other's ideas, and a scene moves forward. Your character arrives at the mouth of the cave, and rather than stand there debating the merits of different weaponry you might take in with you, you just *go into the cave.* That's where the fun will lie, for both the performers and the audience. Enter the cave. Meet the monster, baby.

In a scene set in pre-historic times, this could be a literal directive to enter a cave. In most scenes, it's metaphorical, as when improvisors hesitate because they don't know what they'll find. They haven't decided or declared yet. Or they have a sense of what might show up but some part thinks they're not smart enough or capable enough to handle it. They keep the excitement at bay. Here, going into the cave means diving headlong into the complex *relationships*

---

[1] Keith Johnstone, *Impro: Improvisation and the Theatre* (Methuen: London), 1981.
[2] Note that there are definitely times when saying no is the wiser choice. We'll cover that in more detail soon.

unfolding in real time rather than skating on the surface. Get to the juicy part. Don't hedge, bridge or stall. Just go. Do it. Figure it out on the fly.

More often than not, the same wisdom applies in regular life. As you step up and into your personal unknowns—*What do I want to go after? What waits for me? What have I stalled around?* –you can take on the improv mindset of saying yes to adventure. In that mode, you recognize that you don't *need* to know what will happen. You get better at a) not knowing what comes next and b) staying present if things don't turn out great. You remove your barriers to the new, growth-inducing experience. You trust that you'll have what you need when you arrive. You can go into the cave and see what happens. In real-life terms, you quit the job. Have the tough conversation with your parents. Ask the dude out. It's all an adventure.

## joining the Quest

Improv legend Del Close created a fantastic experiential structure for welcoming in this spirit of adventure: The Quest.[3] Whether choosing a three-hour experience or one that stretches over a weekend, participants begin The Quest by gathering with a group of people to learn the (improvisational) skills and mindset needed to carry it out. As an individual, you reach into a bag to select two stimulus words or "prompts" to inspire your journey. Once you've got those words—usually a color and a shape or common object— you literally set off into the world—the city or landscape around where the group is gathered—and explore whatever emerges from that inspiration. In a sense, those two words become your compass for choosing which direction to head next. You might get "gold" and "circle." Or "blue" and "diamond." *What will that combination lead*

---

[3] I first learned about The Quest from my wonderful Applied Improvisation colleague, Jeanne Lambin. For more about her work with this form, check out https://www.thequest.rocks/what-is-the-quest/.

you to see? With whom will you speak? What do you notice when you take the words literally? What about figuratively or metaphorically? Where does that lead you next? In the end, after a certain amount of time, the group re-gathers to share stories of what each person discovered. One need not have any experience with improvisation to enjoy The Quest, but an openness to discovery makes a huge difference.[4]

On my first Quest, our group met in the age-old town center of Oxford, England. When I chose my key words, I pulled out "red" and "mirror." With that charge in mind, I set out solo into the streets and alleys to see what I could find. I looked to the horizon for anything that might fit "red mirror": *Oh, there's a red reflective sign, I'll go there.* Once at that spot, I looked around again. *Oh, there's a mirror in that clothing shop across the street. I'll check that out.* Eventually, I got to places or displays that made me want to talk with the people I found there. *What's the story of this tavern? How long have you worked here, and what do you like about it? What's challenging about the customers who come in?* I'd just ask whatever came to mind. Sometimes, folks would seem frightened or concerned. More often, they lit up for having a real, live, active engagement with someone. The Quest has that kind of vibe: adventure wakes us up.

Along the way, I wrote and sketched in my journal and took photos as seemed appropriate, both for the artistry of it and for preserving stories so I could share them with my Questmates when we got back together. Because my attention got so turned up and dialed in, I

---

[4] It also helps to have an experienced guide or facilitator. As with so many learning modalities—like mindfulness and improvisation—it's easy for anyone to set up a shingle and say they're a teacher. On one hand, it's great to encourage potential teachers to try stuff out—adventure!—and to share the joy of what they've learned as soon as they want to. On the other hand, to really engage these practices to their fullest takes some intention, training and thoughtful set-up. Dabbling may not prepare you for the risks you'll encounter. Accessibility does not mean mastery.

noticed tiny moments of beauty and intrigue I otherwise would have missed. *The curve of the gunnel on the taxi boat in the side canal. The twisting reflections of the mobile in the window.* My visual field had popped into more vibrant relief. The landscape came alive. When we reassembled as a group, that vitality came through people's voices as they relayed the stories and insights they'd come across. And we all felt closer.

Later that year, I tried another Quest with my buddy Dave, a super-sharp tech executive living in Seattle. The two words we drew, "silver" and "sphere," made us think of a pinball machine so we decided to start our Quest at a downtown arcade. From there, we traipsed the waterfront for hours. Another time with my friend Karen in Baltimore, the prompt words led us to climb a city park fountain, play with cool patterns in the sidewalk, take in the beauty of urban trees, and play a game of chess on a massive chessboard in front of a café. The delight kept unfolding. In both cases, the adventure relied upon my previously established connections with these friends. It also gave them fresh strength.[5]

### adventure in everyday life

Having experienced The Quest several times, I now try to choose this improvisation-informed approach whenever I'm walking around, whether I'm in a new place or a familiar haunt. Going to the grocery store, heading to the chiropractor, walking through the airport: they're all fair game. For example, one recent evening, I emerged from the cinema just after midnight. Surprisingly, there was a huge crane parked in front of the box office with one man high in the sky attending to the theater's neon marquee lights and one

---

[5] I think The Quest would make a great exercise for prospective romantic couples or business partners. Can each person contribute to the adventure? Can they make space for the other's preferences? How well do they hang with uncertainty and moment-to-moment unfolding? How strong is their playfulness and sense of humor?

man on the ground. My sense of adventure kicked in and eagerly whispered: *Ooh, this is interesting. Let's find out more!*

So I stopped and struck up a conversation with the guy on the ground. I discovered this project represented a routine maintenance for movie houses these days, removing neon to install brighter and more energy-efficient LED lights. With a few simple questions and more attentive listening, I also learned about changes in the lighting industry, how his work crew has to get permits to get around municipal parking requirements, and how it's hard for him to get skillful help.[6] Each of these bits of information emerged easily from my simple curiosity and openness to every response. Now, each time I go by that theater, I think of that conversation and have that extra bit of familiar affection. I know my place better.

You can probably see how this way of encountering the world matches the improvisor's mindset, yes? Because you don't assume what you're looking for—you don't know what "scene" will unfold—you know not to narrow your scope. Instead, you hone the skill of staying open to whatever's coming at you, assuming that every "offer" asks to be engaged with. *Sure, I'll play with that. Let's try it.* Any moment gives you the chance to learn. There's something to gain from every interaction.

## we love what we're curious about

Mindfulness offers the same perspective: choose to pay attention to what's here and stay curious and kind about it. It also tends to produce the same result: what we pay attention to, we grow fond of. If I send my attention to any object for half a minute--say, a lamp across the room—I will have a different connection with that lamp

---

[6] It turns out the man's son was up on the ladder doing the work—and smoking. When I said I was surprised he was allowed to smoke on the job, the man said, "Oh you're not supposed to. But that's my kid up there. If I didn't let him, he wouldn't work for me. And I need him to work for me." As always, complex ethical decisions on the job.

than I did before.[7] I will likely notice something distinctive or interesting about it. Or I'll grow an appreciation for its function. Engagement leads to affection.[8]

In his environmental activism, Andy Middleton—applied improvisor, handsome charmer, and founder of an outdoor education training outfit on the rugged coast of Wales—relies on this notion of attention developing affection. He recognizes with clear-eyed vision the ecological dangers we're up against with climate change and a fossil-fuel-based economy. And he wants to turn around the madness of our consumptive mindset that fuels such dangers. His solution? Get leaders and young people to develop a love for the land and sea so they'll work on the planet's behalf. His method? Engage them with adventure:

> If we stop and really pay attention to the natural world when we're on the trail or when we're on the coast, we grow a love for it. We're registering it. We take it into our hearts. Especially if we add in that element of adventure, if there's a sense of risk, you get your senses heightened and the motivation gets deeper.

The heart softens, the senses awaken, and the mind snaps into alert mode. You've got more channels open for a wider bandwidth of life. The sense of adventure helps you see, hear and taste more in every moment and, as a result, you develop a greater intimacy. You care, so you'll protect.

### some preparation required

An adventurous mindset leads us to embrace the unknown, to welcome what can't be predicted. That said, welcoming adventure need not mean—and maybe even *should* not mean—flying by the

---

[7] This is especially true if I offer the lamp 2nd Circle attention.

[8] This makes me curious about the term "engagement" as it applies to couples. What a lovely time to be paying close attention to and developing more affection for a future spouse!

seat of your pants. Even in the heroic stories of yore, we can usually find some element of preparation. It may not be a complete strategic, fully-insured lockdown—a white-knuckle controlled defense against the chaotic—but a basic training before setting out. Wonder Woman completes her regimen as an Amazon warrior before she becomes the superhero we know and love. Luke Skywalker practices with the light saber before confronting Darth Vader. The jazz musician knows her scales inside and out.[9] In other words, adventure might show up on your doorstep before you're fully ready, but that doesn't mean you can't start preparing for the day it does.

In this instance, such preparation might mean developing and strengthening a mindful improvisor's mindset through formal means. Take an improv class. Join a mindfulness group and sit with them regularly. Go on a Quest. (Heck, finish reading this book!) Many options will get you moving in the right direction.

You can also cultivate this mindset in informal ways, creating a new default through small choices you make every day. Rather than a robotic *I head to the bathroom. I brush my teeth and don't pay attention. Da da da da,* you take a different tack. *I'm willing to notice my experience today—what's it really like to brush my teeth?* Maybe you get off the highway and take a side street on your way home— and, gasp, choose not to use the GPS in doing so. Or you strike up a conversation in the grocery store. Or pause to enjoy some detail of a light display that you'd not noticed before. Whatever the specifics, you keep looking for opportunities to step out of your plan, to put down the script or the *mind-less* routine that hypnotizes you into autopilot mode. You reset your default patterns in the little moments to train yourself for bigger moments.

---

[9] If you remember, we conducted our basic training for this curious romp by defining terms and exploring our relationship to "failure" before setting out, as well.

## the Stillgoe approach

Much of what I know about taking on adventures comes from a book I first encountered in graduate school, *Outside Lies Magic*. The author, John Stillgoe, a professor in the history of landscape at Harvard, gets his students to learn by sending them out into the world with open eyes. He asks them to discover the history of a place by noticing the remnant stories hidden within its built landscape. He starts the book with a great passage:

> *Get out now. Not just outside but beyond that track of the programmed electronic age, so gently closing around so many people at the end of our century [the book was written in the late 1990's]. Go outside, move deliberately, then relax, slow down, look around, do not jog, do not run, forget about blood pressure and arthritis, cardiovascular rejuvenation and weight reduction. Instead, pay attention to everything that abuts, the rural road, the city street, the suburban boulevard. Walk, stroll, saunter, ride a bike and coast along a lot, explore. Abandon, even momentarily, the sleek modern technology that consumes so much time and money now and seek out the resting place of a technology almost forgotten.*[10]

Whether connecting with a physical landscape or the interpersonal topography of a relationship, this notion of resting in a simpler "technology" of body-wisdom holds great value. Instead of speeding through temporal reality and staying in a climate-controlled metal box, you can slow to a pause. Get out of the car. Let the rain fall on your face and the wind whip your hair.[11] Inevitably, as you begin to really see what surrounds you, you notice more. And experience more.

---

[10] John Stillgoe, *Outside Lies Magic* (Walker Publishing: USA, 1998), p. 1.
[11] Or, if you're bald like me, you can let it swirl around your dome.

Sometimes, that willingness to step out of rutted tracks means stepping into a bit of danger—going into the cave, as we mentioned earlier. It means sneaking beyond the No Trespassing sign. That said, I'll be the first to admit that such an approach to life—no matter how rewarding—does not come naturally for me. Physically and in relation to most civic laws,[12] I've always been super risk-averse. As a kid, I felt pain deeply and thus thought of myself as fragile. I wasn't the sort to race my bike down a mountain, scale a tree or jump from bollard to bollard. Doing something illegal seemed a bad, bad idea. In my mind, no promise of short-window fun would ever outweigh the looming potential (even if small) for a consequence I'd never recover from. Just one head injury or prison sentence could make for a lifetime of miserable existence.

In order to start taking some healthy risks in my life—including even lightly charged ones—I had to go back and work through some of my childhood memories that had crystallized around such fears. At one point, for example, when I was around 11 or 12, I had gone to play football—tackle football without pads—with my older brother and his friends, who were all 14 or older.[13] I so wanted to make a good impression and to be seen as one of the guys. I remember the first time the ball was thrown to me, I rose up in front of the defender to snag the pass. For a split-second, I had the joy of *Yeah, I made this play!* Then he slammed into my chest and pummeled me into the ground. Immediately, I felt great pain, but, even worse, I couldn't breathe. I'd never had the wind knocked out of me, so as I gasped for some air, any air, I thought I was going to die. I headed to the sidelines to recover tearfully and never played tackle football again. That was it.

---

[12] I say "most" because speeding has never particularly evoked the same concern.

[13] Note that for most kids, those two years are crucial for boys in terms of size and strength.

Not until therapy years later did I go back and work with that memory. My therapist at the time, a great and insightful guy named Jim, helped me see that, in fact, I had survived that collision. I hadn't died. I got up and walked again. Now, when necessary, I can bring to mind the inspiring image of football players, wide receivers especially, who get hit really hard and enthusiastically pop back up with a hoot and holler, as if to say, "WOO HOO! Yeah, bring it! Let's go!" Both literally and metaphorically, I can now get the wind knocked out of me and still get back up. I can still breathe. I can keep playing.

Weebles, the old children's toys—are you old enough to remember them?—offered a similar lesson. They were shaped like weighted eggs so you could bop them over and they'd pop right back up: "Weebles wobble but they don't fall down," went the jingle. They embodied early on what social psychologist Carol Dweck came to teach about mindset.[14] Yup, you might fall down, but that's part of the game. You can go ahead and mess up, and then pull yourself off the floor. You're learning something new, and, by gum, you'll learn it best by continuing to try.

With each bounce-back over time, my little risks have started to become more exciting than scary. I'm still pretty cautious about physical dangers and don't want any legal trouble, but when facing the challenges or risks of potential adventure, I've got insights and attitudes to counter any fear. I've got more gumption, and, as a result, I get to have more fun.

### the importance of the 'nope!'
Throughout this book, we've played with the notion of paradox: both sides of a coin can have value, even if they seem to point in opposite directions. Along those lines, even though we've been

---

[14] Again, check out Chapter 2, "Take a Circus Bow: Changing Your Relationship to Failure."

extolling the virtues of an adventurer's mindset, caution still matters. You can't always take risks. Sometimes you might feel like you can't even take small ones. You simply don't have the resources to recover if things go awry. In such instances, you need to say no.

Playing the improv game "What Comes Next?" offers a great way to practice both choices. In the game, Partner A starts a story by asking, "What comes first?" Partner B responds with a short sentence. Partner A then asks again, "What comes next?" Partner B continues to respond until Partner A hears something she's not delighted by, in which case she responds with a wide-eyed smile and a high-pitched voice, cheerily declaring "Nope!" Partner B then asks, "What comes next?" and Partner A now gets to continue the story. They continue until A makes an offer that doesn't delight B, and B says "Nope!"

Here's an example that Lisa Rowland and I generated spontaneously during one of our podcasts:

**A:** *What comes first?*

**B:** *We are race car drivers.*

**A:** *What comes next?*

**B:** *We are in the middle of a very high-stakes race.*

**A:** *What comes next?*

**B:** *We come around the bend and notice our arch-enemy is just ahead of us.*

**A:** *What comes next?*

**B:** *We decide we're gonna take her down.*

**A:** *Nope!*

*(Partner A wasn't delighted by that possibility, so now Partner B picks up the questions. She might have been piqued or mildly curious, but the game's asking for something stronger.)*

**B:** *What comes next?*

**A:** *We pull up beside her.*

**B:** *What comes next?*

**A:** *We signal to her that we want her to pull over.*

**B:** *What comes next?*

**A:** *She shakes her head angrily to refuse.*

**B:** *What comes next?*

**A:** *We turn to each other with a look of consternation.*

**B:** *Um... Nope!*

**A:** *What comes next?*

**B:** *She speeds off with renewed fervor and determination to beat us.*[15]

In this game—as in life—it always helps to remember that you have "Nope!" at your disposal. You get to start an adventure and then realize *Oh, I'm no longer delighted by this.* When Lisa and I teach this game, we make sure to emphasize that you don't need to know why you're not delighted by what came before. You don't need to explain it. You don't need to justify it. You don't have to know what you would rather have happen. Your hesitation doesn't even need to make sense to you. You just have to track your inspiration, and if it doesn't light up at the suggestion, you get to say, "Nope!"[16]

Though the "Nope!" can be given freely, it's also important to note that it shouldn't get hostile, angry or dismissive. You're not insulting or berating the person who offered the suggestion. You're expressing a preference, and you're still in the game together. A

---

[15] To hear the full version of this "What Comes Next?" story, listen to Monster Baby Podcast episode #20.
https://animalearning.com/2017/01/05/monster-baby-20-adventure-time/
[16] In that way, the game becomes a great mindfulness practice, too.

light-hearted "Nope!" rebuffs the offer but keeps you connected. Imagine a friendly, still warm-eyed *No, thank you. Not that.*

You can extend a similar lightheartedness to life outside of improv any time you're choosing what comes next. Do you want to stay at the party? Order the pasta? Go see the action movie? When you make such an inquiry, listen for your internal response. If it's a "Yup!" go for it. If it's a "Nope!" choose something else.

Though there's admittedly greater complexity, you can even apply the pocket-sized practice to life's bigger questions. *Should I stay in this job? Does this relationship delight me? Should I keep living in this apartment?* Having developed your sensors for what really lights you up, you may hear a clearly contrasting internal "Nope!"—and then loop back to the adventure-continuing question: *What comes next?*

## just do it!

Ultimately, the trick for developing an adventurous, improvisational mindset is simply to start. Choose an adventure or set one for the near future. Start looking for the smaller adventures in your everyday life. And then get out. Enter the cave. See what's there. Wrestle with it. Play with it. Learn from it. You can opt into a different adventure anytime you want—and you've always got the "Nope!" arrow in your quiver. And then, when you're done, come back to your town and your people and share your stories. Bring us your lessons. Grant us your wisdom.

*What comes next?*

## Chapter 11
### Adventure Time! *Seeking the Joy of New Experience*

### GEMS from the JOURNEY

- *Adventure comes in all shapes and sizes. It might mean rugged outdoorsy expeditions. It might mean a simple choice to try something new. In all cases, though, adventure includes an attitude of openness and engagement: let me explore!*

- *As improv teacher Keith Johnstone says, "Those who say 'yes' are rewarded by the adventures they have. Those who say 'no' are rewarded by the safety they attain." There will certainly be appropriate times to say no. But if you want adventure in your life, you'll need to start saying yes more often.*

- *The kind of mindful curiosity that leads you on adventures also tends to generate a real affection for whatever you've decided to explore.*

- *You can prepare for deep, big-picture adventure by cultivating an adventurous mindset in the little everyday choices you make.*

### PARADOX

- *Stepping into adventure can bring great vitality, eye-opening perspective and valuable teachings. It makes for a great life. At the same time, honoring your own boundaries around risk-taking—learning to say a healthy "Nope!" when appropriate—also represents a crucial part of a life well-lived. You can invite more adventure into your life without needing to push yourself out of any planes, actual or metaphorical.*

## GOING DEEPER

- *Take on an adventure or get one on your calendar. At minimum, set an intention that magnetizes a sense of possibility for you and spices your day with a bit of pizzazz.*

- *If you line up a future adventure, remember to hold its prospect lightly so as not to close yourself off from any spurs-of-the-moment that might present themselves. And keep in mind that your excitement for the future can feed your life in the now. No need to look forward—the prospect is already giving you juice you can enjoy!*

- *Also, remember that your designated adventure can come in big sizes, like a capital-A Adventure—a safari, a road trip, new relationship—or it can fit into your everyday life like a small-a adventure—striking up a conversation with the guy selling hot dogs on the corner.*

- *Resolve to "enter the cave" more often. Inertia will always have a pull. It's attractive and safe to stay where you are. But starting something different creates an energy of its own, resetting inertia to a momentum of movement. Once you're on your way, you're more likely to stay on your way.*

- *Play "What Comes Next?" with an improv partner. Pay special attention to the possibility of "Nope!" so you start to tune into what types of adventures truly delight you and which truly delight your partner.*

# isn't that curious?
## *exploring the world with eager eyes*

IF YOU'RE LIKE ME, you have friendly feelings about curiosity. And if you've thought about it at all in relationship to mindfulness and improvisation, you probably realize how it's clearly, readily, and joyfully relevant to both. *Curiosity helps create a life well-lived.* In this chapter, we're going to get curious about curiosity.[1] Hopefully, doing so will generate even more of the adventures we talked about in the last chapter—and bring all sorts of other delights into your life.

### fundamentally helpful

If I had to choose the two most important qualities of a person I want to connect and associate with, I would choose honesty and kindness. If we're not telling the truth and we're not looking out for each other, then what's the point of engaging at all? Coming in close behind those two? Curiosity.

If you're curious, you've always got entertainment. You can simply look around or listen in and wonder *What's **that** about?* You can make engaging conversation. You can dig for the meaningful details contained within everyday experience—even the dull or unpleasant. If you notice feeling bored but remain curious, you ask *Why am I bored? What does this boredom suggest? Where in my body do I **feel**

---

[1] Kudos to those who recognize that we could call this meta-curiosity. ☺

*the boredom? How is the sensation changing?* Getting interested in your boredom defuses its annoyance immediately.

When improvisors perform, snapping into curiosity mode helps in a number of ways. For one, it prevents any one individual from pushing a particular agenda. As Chicago improv luminaries T.J. Jagodowski and David Pasquesi suggest, you don't need to *create* the scene. It's already happening. You're stepping into the river of a story to help it on its way. You **discover** what comes next rather than creating or imposing it.

With this approach, any hesitation, panic, or urgency melts away. Rather than spinning your wheels, you stop, look around, take in your partner and say what you notice. You say what you see and then get curious about that. It could be a question or an observation. *You seem troubled. What's on your mind?* And just that little bit pushes the scene forward in a virtuous cycle. The noticing leads to curiosity; the curiosity leads to noticing.[2]

Exercising that mindset *before* you get on stage rather than in the middle of a show helps even more. Every life encounter offers an opportunity for character research. Start to interact with the internal mantra *What's it like to be this person?* and questions begin to flow freely. Everyone you meet gets more comfortable because you're actively and intentionally connecting. And they sense your larger, deeper acceptance. The kindness generates a mutual comfort, compassion and understanding that leaves them wanting more. Each of those interactions then provides you with more

---

[2] Some improv teachers suggest that players shouldn't ask questions in a scene. Some even make it a **rule**. That's a bit off-target for the mode we're talking about here. Sure, questions that don't offer any new information or that off-load all responsibility onto another player (like, "Oh, what's that in your hand?") won't help. But a specific, information-rich question (like, "How much longer will you fend off my marriage proposal, Sylvia?") can and will move the scene forward.

inspiration, more material to work with the next time you get on stage.

## we see more when we're curious

Curiosity mode also helps in real life. Our spotlight of attention is always pointing in some direction. Usually, we don't choose where it goes. That old puppy mind gets highjacked by whatever shiny or flashy object crosses our path. If you consciously decide to point your attention at something specific in your environment, that choice will likely generate more curiosity. Take a look around you now. Suddenly all sorts of objects jump into your awareness in greater detail than you had noticed before. Most likely, you could generate dozens of questions about any of those specific items you perceive. *Where did this come from? Who designed it? What would that texture feel like? Why did it come in that pattern?* Again, the observation jumpstarts your curiosity, which leads to more observation... and so on. You see more. You take in more. With more information and insight at your disposal, your inner sleuth gets stronger. Suddenly, you can show up at any scene in your life and find additional information for answering life's trickier questions.

Curiosity also tends to have a natural quality of acceptance to it. When you investigate the object of your attention with an open mind, you don't need it to be any different from what it is. You're just checking it out. You're withholding judgment. Or if you form judgments, you're letting them fall away like any other passing thought. With that approach, your observation goes deeper with whatever's there.

Some mindfulness instructors have mastered this approach in the way they teach. Saki Santorelli, former executive director at the Center for Mindfulness at the University of Massachusetts, helps his students examine their own experience by asking questions. He might ask, "What did you notice in your seated practice during the week?" and a student might respond, "Well, I noticed I felt anxious."

An incurious teacher would stop there, happy to have gotten, at least, to an emotion. Saki goes further, "And what does 'anxious' mean to you?" Then the person might offer more detail. "I noticed my breathing was faster than normal." "Where else, if anywhere, in your body, did the anxiousness show up?" Saki will continue. And they'll respond, "Well, my hands got a little sweaty." He's genuinely interested, and that interest helps the learner to notice more because he's accepted her reality. The kindness in his curiosity opens previously closed doors. *Oh, there's a whole new world here! I didn't know **this** was available!*

---

### can curiosity be hostile?

Usually, when we teach mindfulness, curiosity and kindness go together. Remember our original definition: *paying attention on purpose to things as they are with curiosity and kindness.* It *is* possible for curiosity to carry a hostile or damaging intent— think voyeurism, *schadenfreude,* cross-examination, gossiping or bullying—where the inquiry makes the subject of the questions uncomfortable. Maybe that's more accurately called "investigation" or "interrogation." Or more simply, judgment. The asker wants to get information to use it against the subject. For our purposes, curiosity carries a kinder intent, honoring rather than weaponizing whatever information it discovers.

---

### building curiosity when it doesn't come easily

Some people have a seemingly natural ability to engage with curiosity about others. It's a friendly quality and one that draws conversation mates near. Others—like me—might feel curious about the world or people but struggle to actually generate and ask exploratory questions. If others bring concerns forward, we're happy to interact, but we wouldn't usually *initiate* the inquiry unprompted. For those in the second camp, challenging our default and developing this new mindset can lead to better friendships and improved relationships. When we balance the scales of curiosity, holding up our fair share, we can enjoy the rising reciprocal energy (shared control!) of getting to know someone better. We can become our better selves.

Cab rides (or Lyft or Uber rides) make a great place to practice this new curiosity. You've got a limited amount of time with a predetermined end to the conversation—the risks of getting trapped go way down—but you have enough time to make some inroads. You might hear some great wisdom, you might hear some foolishness. Either way, you get to learn and you get to connect. "Tell me about the ring on your finger" might lead to an extended monologue about your driver having had anger management issues as a child and his getting sent to a local village shaman who gave him a sacred stone as a reminder of the spirit journey that then guarded him from the ten levels of demons on the astral plane.... or you might hear about a touching reminder of his daughter back home in another country. Whatever the content, you've learned about that other person's world view. You've connected, if only for a few moments —and you've given the connection priority.

### next-level curiosity as an expression of love

Comedian, improvisor and storyteller Chris Gethard makes an art of this kind of curiosity on his podcast, "Beautiful Anonymous." On the show, he simply spends an hour on the phone with someone he doesn't know. He doesn't learn their name. He doesn't know where they're from. He might have learned beforehand some idea of what topic they'll cover. At other times, he has no idea. The podcast might start with, "Hi, how is your day going?" and move on from there. "Did you wake up early? Are you usually an early riser? Oh, so you have trouble sleeping?" And so on. He pulls one little thread and discovers others as he goes. The podcast stays fascinating because he clearly has a love for the people he speaks with. His curiosity expresses that love.

In that sense, curiosity expresses the core improv and mindfulness belief of "there's something in the bag" —there's something there and it's of value. In this case, the message is *You're worth knowing. You're worth this hour of conversation. You're worth my questions.* Especially when that curiosity comes without an agenda—*I'm not trying to sell you something or leverage our interaction for self-satisfaction*—it represents a wild and grand generosity. It's a beautiful thing.

It may be that, as with a cab driver or an anonymous acquaintance like Chris Gethard's, it's easier to express such pure curiosity with folks we do not know. Perhaps our past experiences with friends, family or colleagues has created a layer of assumptions and knowledge that prevents our seeing them afresh. We think we know them, so we forget to be curious.

In her book *Mating in Captivity,* sex therapist Esther Perel talks about the importance of challenging that assumed familiarity.[3] Yes, we want comfort, intimacy, safety, security, shared experience and shared knowledge in our relationships. But (and!) we also want newness, novelty, and mystery. And it's that second piece that maintains the spark in a connection. If we can remember that we can never know everything about our partner, the relationship stays lively, exciting and even sexy. It maintains a vitality. *What else is there? What **else** is there?*

Turning such next-level curiosity into a fun challenge may make it easier to practice. *I wonder what I can learn about somebody that I think I know super well.* In that case, maybe we dive in less for *information* about our friend, partner or colleague—the vital chronological stats—than we do for *meaning* and *impact.* Rather

[3] Esther Perel, *Mating in Captivity* (Harper: New York), 2006.

than asking about the who, what and where in their stories, we ask more about the how and the why. We get more directly into the juicy stuff that electrifies the conversation—for both the asker and the one who is asked.

## 'advance-color-emotion'

The world of improvisation (again) offers a helpful exercise for practicing this kind of curiosity. It's called "Advance-Color-Emotion."[4] One could do the exercise in a structured, formal fashion or use its principles more informally to guide which questions to ask in a conversation. In either case, the idea remains the same.

Let's start with the background for the exercise. When creating a story on stage, improvisors will often try to balance three different elements:

*Advance*—The plot needs to move forward. Things need to happen.

*Color*—The picture needs filling in. Who are the characters? What's their setting, the timeframe and the like? What do they see? What sounds surround them? What do they smell? What's physically in their way?

*Emotion*—The scene needs to matter. What feelings are coming up? How are the characters being moved or changed by their experience? Why do they care? This part of the story allows the audience to connect with the characters.

When all three components stay strong, the story on stage stays exciting. The audience remains invested. If any of the elements lag, the scene will too.

---

[4] I first learned the game from the wise and talented Dan O'Connor of Impro Theatre in Los Angeles. See the Glossary of Games for a complete description.

In the Advance-Color-Emotion formal exercise, Partner X listens to a meaningful story from Partner Y's life. She can pause Partner Y at any time she wants to hear more about another one of the three components. If X asks for "Color," Y might share what the people in his story were wearing, what the landscape looked like, what aroma was in the air, and so on. If X calls for "Emotion," Y may recall how he was feeling at the time or how he imagined others were feeling. When X swings back to "Advance," Y moves the story along in time or logical sequence.

That structure creates a neat dynamic for both the storyteller and the questioner. The speaker sees, hears and feels direct assurance that the listener cares and wants to know more. Also, he might stumble on some new perspective or insight on an otherwise well-worn story. He gets to learn something new about his own journey. And the questioner gains a bit of control to maintain her own interest. Whenever she senses her interest flagging, she can ask for more details, more emotional interest or more vulnerability. If she feels the story dragging, she can ask for more developments. She gets to influence the story's pace and design while still delighting in the moment-to-moment unfolding of its final destination.

Notice that whether in the formal exercise or in regular conversation, we don't use curiosity as a weapon for usurping control. In other words, we don't make the story about *us*. The spotlight of attention remains firmly on the other person's experience—at least, until that section of story comes to an end and we maybe trade places.

For those of us who don't have a naturally-curious-about-others gene,[5] using the Advance-Color-Emotion structure can give us conversational training wheels. We can ask for more details or

---

[5] I know. Those of you who have it are saying "Whaaaaattt? How is that even possible?" Trust me, it is.

inquire about the emotion. We can ask excitedly about how things turned out. We get practice for asking questions the other person can talk about. And in doing so, we demonstrate that we actually *are* curious. We do care.

## open and honest questions

Another helpful frame for those new to expressing curiosity—and for ensuring the inquiry feels generous rather than injurious—is to ask what Quaker educator and philosopher Parker Palmer calls "open and honest" questions.

An open question expands rather than restricts the topic being explored. It's not pushing or nudging the responder toward a particular feeling or frame for their experience. It's likely to encourage a longer response rather than a yes/no or other single word reply.

An honest question means the asker couldn't possibly think "I know the right answer to this question and I'll see if I can get you to give it to me." There's no hidden agenda. Maybe it's a bit nutty or nonsensical, but that non-linearity might lead to interesting insight.

Want an example of effective open and honest questions? Here are a few:

- *"What body sensations, if any, show up as you tell that story?"*
  The asker doesn't make assumptions about the responder's experience and gives them room to name it for themselves.
- *"What did you mean when you said you felt 'frustrated'?"*
  This offers the responder a chance to elaborate on their own meaning-making, to go deeper.
- *"If this situation had a soundtrack to it, what kind of music would it be?"*

Maybe no answer comes immediately to mind, but some surprising response might bubble up, eventually opening a whole new window of meaning.

And here are some questions that don't match the ideal:

- *"Why do you seem sad?"*
  The asker tells the responder what they're feeling rather than drawing from more observable data. As in, "I notice you have a tear in your eye. What's going on?"

- *"Have you ever thought about getting a divorce?"*
  Here, the asker promotes his own agenda, disguising advice in the form of a question. It could also elicit a simple "yes" or "no" answer and get the conversation nowhere.

- *"Isn't this just like what you described with your brother?"*
  Again, this forces an angle—the asker's angle—on to the responder. It's an assertion and the asker thinks she knows the answer. A more open-ended version would be "How does this compare with what happened with your brother?"

Open and honest questions serve both the asker and the responder with *kindness*. They're a gift to connect someone with wisdom they might not know they carry within.[6]

## what about the cat?

This whole chapter, I've been extolling the virtues of curiosity. You can entertain yourself. You see more. You learn more. You enjoy more. There's just that one nagging question that might have been lurking in the background for you all this time though: what about

---

[6] For more on Open, Honest Questions, see Parker Palmer, *A Hidden Wholeness: The Journey Toward an Undivided Life* (Jossey-Bass: San Francisco, CA), 2004. In particular, see pages 132-134.

that old aphorism that warns "curiosity killed the cat"? Don't we need to stay cautious?

Fair questions. Sometimes poking around does lead to trouble. You open the medicine chest and uncover a detail about a friend's history that should have stayed secret. You sneak a glance at a partner's email inbox and find something you wish you could un-see. You start believing a conspiracy theory sounds reasonable, and your status quo gets knocked upside-down.

That's why almost every society has its own cautionary tale about curiosity. The Greeks warned about Prometheus and fire, Pandora and the box, and Icarus and the sun. Fairy tales caution about children who wander too far into the woods. Heck, even Curious George's handlers thought he needed reining in—and he's got "curious" in his name! There are boundaries to maintain that serve to keep a society stitched together.

At the same time—and I submit we all know this in some deep part of ourselves—our souls long to break free of such chains. We want to learn. We need to connect. And curiosity helps us do that. Great questions can break the ice when we're meeting someone for the first time.[7] They can uncover truth that needs exposing. And—if they're properly titrated for slowly-building intimacy—they can even help us fall in love.[8] In the end, curiosity calls us—cats included—to a more connected, more exciting life. If you don't want

---

[7] See Claire Lew, "The 25 most popular icebreaker questions based on four years of data," , accessed October 15, 2018.
https://m.signalvnoise.com/the-25-most-popular-icebreaker-questions-based-on-four-years-of-data-893df9b27531

[8] Mandy Len Catron, "To Fall in Love With Anyone, Do This" from "Modern Love" in *The New York Times*, January 9, 2015, accessed November 10, 2018.
https://www.nytimes.com/2015/01/11/fashion/modern-love-to-fall-in-love-with-anyone-do-this.html

closeness, close it off. If you don't seek adventure, shut it down. Otherwise, stoke the curiosity up and fire away. [9]

---

### 20 questions

Just for the heck of it, here are twenty great questions you could use the next time you're wanting to kick start a conversation but wonder what to ask:

- What's been your closest encounter with someone famous?
- What's the first thing you bought with your own money?
- Seen anything lately that made you smile?
- If you were to pick a city whose character best represents your own personality, which would you choose?
- What has been your greatest conquest in life so far?
- What possession means the most to you and why?
- Which of your choices has had the most positive impact on your life?
- What's your favorite way to eat eggs, if at all?
- What's the story of your name?
- If you could communicate with any type of animal, which would you pick?
- What would constitute a perfect day for you?
- Would you want to be famous and, if so, in what way?
- If you could wake up tomorrow having gained any one ability or power, which would you choose and why?
- What's your favorite holiday and why?

---

[9] While honoring boundaries from a 2nd Circle stance, of course.

- What are the most important qualities in a friendship?
- What's a talent that you have that most people don't know about?
- If you were granted a sabbatical year to study any subject, which subject would you choose?
- What's the nicest gift you've ever received?
- Who was your favorite teacher?
- What have been your best and worst travel experiences?

See Evelyn McFarlane and James Saywell, *If: (Questions for the Game of Life)* (Villard: New York, 1995) and *If²...: 500 Questions for the Game of Life* (Villard: New York, 1996) for many similar questions.

## Chapter 12
### Isn't That Curious? *Exploring the World with Eager Eyes*

### GEMS from the JOURNEY

- *If you're curious about the world around you, you've always got entertainment. Even seemingly dull or boring experiences take on new interest when you investigate them eagerly.*

- *Curiosity leads us to see more of the world around us. That increased awareness tends to develop both acceptance and affection for whatever you've decided to explore.*

### PARADOX

- *It's hard to know which comes first: the curiosity or the noticing. No matter, once you start in with one, you're likely to trigger a virtuous cycle of both. The more you see, the more you want to see. The more you want to see, the more you will see.*

### GOING DEEPER

- *Consider a loved one in your life, someone you think you know really well. Then write down 20 things you don't know about this person that you'd like to know. If you have the courage, take on the adventure of asking them those questions!*

- *If you meet someone new, try one of the icebreaker questions included just above at the end of this chapter. Notice if the question creates a "lean-in" and, if so, ask another.*

- *Find a friend to share stories with and play "Advance-Color-Emotion" as described more fully in the Glossary of Games. See if you discover new side trips, nooks and crannies within the stories you tell most often.*

# attitude of gratitude
## *giving thanks for the many gifts*

IF I PAUSE FOR A MOMENT—this moment—to take stock of what I could give thanks for, the list could go on forever. A gorgeous sunny day with clear blue skies. Breakfast in my belly. Echoes from great laughter and conversation with a new friend. Working fingers that can type these words. The stunning ease and magic of a computer that converts keystrokes to images on a screen and saves them for your eventual reading.[1] And on and on. I imagine you could generate a similar list—and you'd likely feel a similar surge of joy if you did. Gratitude feels good.

Such gratitude shows up pretty naturally in happy times. It can also arise in the face of frustration or difficulty. I might sag at news that I've got to replace my hot water heater but bounce back when I remember I've got a home to call my own. My boss might ignore my successes, but I can appreciate that I've got colleagues who see them and celebrate them. My car might need repair, but my legs continue to carry me through the world. In other words, to paraphrase mindfulness teacher Jon Kabat-Zinn, "If you're still breathing, you've got reason to be thankful."

Tons of well-supported research suggests that a gratitude practice improves your life, lifts your mood, eases your interactions with

---

[1] Thank **you** for reading this chapter. I so appreciate it. ☺

others and bolsters your chances for success. Give thanks and life gets better. Easier, too.

Dig deeper into the practice of gratitude and you'll see even more clearly how mindfulness and improvisation make for a life well-lived.[2]

## gratitude vs. affirmation

On first take, some think of gratitude as simply noticing and giving voice to the things they like. You want to affirm so you say, "I really like this song." Or, "That veggie burger smells great."[3] As we discussed in the Power of Positivity chapter, you look for what's good and focus your gaze in that direction. But in the effort to stay positive, you might unintentionally participate in a bit of a misdirect. While *nice,* this kind of affirmation still keeps (at least part of) the focus on yourself. "This experience pleases *me,*" you say. "You're doing something that *I* like." The expression of preference has an evaluative, almost mental or judgmental quality to it. It's in the same *family* as positivity, the same ballpark, but it's somehow not quite as strong as it could be. It doesn't move you or connect you to others in the same way that deeper appreciation does.

Gratitude, on the other hand, places the focus on the one being thanked. When we say, "Thank you," we acknowledge that the

---

[2] See Leah R. Dickens (2017) Using Gratitude to Promote Positive Change: A Series of Meta-Analyses Investigating the Effectiveness of Gratitude Interventions, Basic and Applied Social Psychology, 39:4, 193-208, DOI. Also, Davis, et al, "Thankful for the little things: A meta-analysis of gratitude interventions. J Couns Psychol. 2016 Jan;63(1):20-31. Epub 2015 Nov 16. Also, "The Science of Gratitude: More Benefits than Expected; 26 Studies and Counting, site visited Nov 10, 2018, https://www.happierhuman.com/the-science-of-gratitude/.

[3] I realize my carnivorous readers might never say that last one. They (you?) can imagine a beef burger instead.

other person has affected us. We have been changed in some way. And we feel the better for it. It's deeper. It's more personal.

## the vulnerability in gratitude

It might seem like giving thanks would be easy. In the Mindfulness in Schools Project's ".b Mindfulness for Teens" course, however, the lesson on gratitude comes last—because it's actually the most challenging. As it turns out, students need to have weeks of preliminary work in order to be able to handle the intensity of practicing deeper gratitude. In the course's initial lessons, the kids work on shaping and holding their attention. They develop attitudes of curiosity and kindness. They learn to work with their thoughts, savor pleasant experiences, and make space for challenging ones. They explore mindfulness in movement (as in a walking meditation) and then practice working with difficult emotions. Only after having done all that does the course ask them to open their hearts to gratitude, to claim what has moved them or mattered to them—and then to share that with others. The vulnerability is real. And it always takes the kids off guard.

In that lesson, we use a little online video from a group called Soul Pancake. In the clip, the makers invite participants one at a time into a studio and ask them to write a description of someone who has been a positive influence in their lives, someone who has made a difference to them. Each of the participants goes off and writes those thoughts down. When they return with what they've written, the organizers have each of them call the person they have written about and read their words out loud.

As you can imagine, it's powerful. It's beautiful. And every time I watch it—probably over two dozen times now—I cry because it's so moving.[4] Because the participants don't know that they are writing

---

[4] You can watch the Soul Pancake video here:
https://www.youtube.com/watch?v=oHv6vTKD6lg.

to their person, they are more effusive and more open. Then, when they get to share their words with their loved one, you can see they're visibly moved to bring their feelings out into the open. As soon as students return from watching that video, they're also feeling opened up, ready to move into the depth and poignancy of a formal gratitude meditation.

The lesson within the ".b" course always feels incredibly healing, probably as a direct result of the vulnerability it generates. Like, simply stating and sharing what's true on a deeper level makes a difference. You step up and claim, "This is what I care about," and in doing so, claim more of who you are. And, as you do that, you recognize the ways you're stitched into the rest of the world. You're not alone.

### realizing our dependence on other beings

Stopping to notice how much you're tied into and have received from others can also prove profoundly humbling. You see people who cleaned your messes, gave you encouragement, or opened a previously closed door. Parents. Teachers. Friends. Doctors. Farmers. Coaches. Civil service workers. They've all played a role in shaping who you've become.

Maybe you notice ancestors who overcame incredible odds and rose from intolerable suffering just to make it through. Or enemies and nemeses who gave you something to push against. Maybe you move beyond the human realm to notice all the forces of nature that also make your existence possible. Sunshine, rain, and wind. Food and water. Millions of years of stored energy released from within the earth to power your body and the machines you rely on. As the Taoists say, the "ten thousand things" have all contributed.[5]

---

[5] Going back to Chapter 9, "Ch-ch-ch-changes: Learning to Go with the Flow," you might remember that it's not only that these things have helped shape you. They've also *become* you. Or you have become them.

Taking stock in this way likely disabuses you of the idea that you only have what you have because you deserve it. Or because you earned it. It's not that your efforts don't matter or that you can't help yourself out. For sure, what you do makes a difference in your own existence. Rather, you come to recognize that so much of what you enjoy has come your way through the grace of others. When you stand in that place, it can actually seem impossible to express the depth of gratitude that arises.

In my early 20s, I had a memorable moment that opened me to that level of gratitude. I had been vegetarian for a few years, partly for environmental reasons but mostly for ethical ones. I didn't want to be contributing to the death and suffering of fellow animals. At some point, though, I started struggling with my health, and my doctor recommended that animal protein might help settle my issues. When I visited my college roommate in San Francisco shortly after that, we ordered Chinese takeout and included a chicken and broccoli dish. When the food arrived, I served myself some chicken, just staring for a while. As I sat frozen, two questions kept circling in my mind—and then down into my heart: *How could I possibly thank this bird enough for giving its life for me? Why is my life more important than its life?* In that moment, I felt no end to my gratitude. I actually had to pause from the meal to let myself cry for a bit.

Granted, I was not a typical 22-year-old. And it might look histrionic to my tablemates if I fell into tears over every meat-including meal now. But it's also important to recognize that I—and you—could do so if we chose to notice what's really going on. We're *that* dependent on the grace of other lives. Vegetarian or not, things die in order for us to live. The least we can do is say thanks.[6]

---

[6] I now eat meat occasionally, but I also still feel a commitment to remember to say a specific thank you. If I'm going to take an animal's life, I damn well better stop, notice and give thanks for its life-giving quality rather than slamming into autopilot and shoving its gift down my gullet.

In that example, you can see that expressing gratitude depends directly on mindful awareness. I paused to notice the makeup of my meal before diving in. I then registered my emotions and took stock of my thoughts. In any moment, you can do the same. Pause, breathe and look around. Shift off autopilot and come back to fuller consciousness—from there you'll start seeing more of the helpful pieces that make up your life and how you're living it.

## building the gratitude muscle

Once mindful curiosity brings a wider range into focus, you can also start to register—among other things—more of what's working and what needs to come next.[7]

For this reason, many religious traditions start their ceremonies with gratitude. That's especially true among indigenous traditions, which often catalog all the things and beings to be thankful for. *Grandfather Sun, Grandmother Moon, we appreciate you. We thank you for what you are for us. The spirit of the north, east, south and west, we thank you for being present. Animal people, bird people, fish people—we thank you.* There's a whole litany of right-now, right-here beings to appreciate. The Christian mystic Meister Eckhart also spoke to and echoed this tendency when he wrote "If the only prayer you say in your life is 'thank you,' it would suffice."

The simplest way to build this muscle comes by offering gratitude where and when it's easiest. Here's a two-minute practice to do when you won't have other distractions pulling you away: just before you go to sleep, look back on your day and write down three things you're thankful for. Maybe they're events of the day or people who crossed your mind. Maybe you notice three gifts from the past. It's all good. This practice alone will start to create new neural patterns and generate tangible happiness. By remembering

---

[7] Much like we did in the Chapter 6, "The Power of Positivity: Creating a Delightful Default."

what's gone well, the world will seem to change for the better without your having to *do* anything in particular.

With this practice, you also counteract that overactive and overreactive evolutionary default that would trigger a SWAT-mode defensiveness at the slightest threat or difficulty. Usually, if you get in a traffic jam, forget a document at home, or receive a cryptic text from the boss, your amygdala might crank all the way up, leaving you swimming in a tide of fight, flight or freeze hormones. Under that intense level of stress, it feels right to clench up or get protective. In olden days, back when we were lizards or monkeys, such alarm bells probably paid off by saving our lives. In today's world, however, those seeming threats are actually quite tame. The boss might be a jerk but he's not literally going to bite your head off. In our world, launching fully and instantly into that extreme-opposition mode just burns us out. Practicing gratitude, you can interrupt that auto-pilot ramp-up. You can notice which things are fine—not necessarily perfect, but fine—and which things demand more concern. You can relax a bit. You can loosen up. And you can stay open.

Notice that this gratitude practice, while positive, is no Pollyanna lightweight. It holds its own even when more challenging situations do eventually show up. For example, Patricia Ryan Madson, author of *Improv Wisdom*, shared a story about how on one Christmas Day, she and her husband, Ron, were in a car crash.[8] Another driver rear-ended their vehicle, which made them slam into the car in front of them. As all the drivers got out of their cars to point fingers, she and Ron paused, took a deep breath, and looked at what they could be grateful for. By focusing on what was right about the situation— they'd been spared injury, help was already at hand, and so on— instead of ramping up what was wrong, they together managed to avoid the shouting and blaming that could easily have made the

---

[8] Yeah, Christmas Day. Total bummer.

situation worse. Rather than grouse or grumble, they chose to see the gifts in the moment. *You've been in a crash. OK. There is no going back and fixing that. You can choose to stay angry about it or choose to find what's worthy of gratitude in the situation. Either way, here we are. We might as well go for the good.*

## not 'everything happens for a reason'

Sometimes you'll hear well-meaning folks swoop in to provide comfort in such difficult situations, offering the saccharine bromide, "Everything happens for a reason." Please note: what I'm saying here is not that. Sometimes stuff just happens. And it sucks. In those cases, we'd really prefer a different outcome, and we just wish it hadn't happened. Or when things go well, sometimes we're just lucky without any grand plan or design behind it. It just happens. (Good) stuff happens.

That said, we *can* still proactively look for whatever gifts might be present in a difficult situation. Ron and Patricia needn't have given thanks for the accident itself. But there were still things going right. And, maybe someday, something even better will come out of it. There need not be a *reason* for the negative event ever happening. We can always find an *opportunity* coming out of it.

A classic type of improvisation scenes relies on this notion. In such scenes, one character sits alone on a bench in a park. They might be reading a newspaper. They might be looking around, taking in the scenery. All is well or at least neutral. There's no trouble or discord. Eventually, a second character—a stranger to the first—comes on and encounters the first. Somehow, one of them (or both of them) has something the other needs: a perspective, a piece of information, a life lesson. Maybe they will someday team up for some endeavor. The conversation doesn't have to lead anywhere in particular, but they do affect each other. Their fates change as a result of their meeting.

In improv, you often hear the mantra "Let yourself be changed." And it's another example of a healthy approach to meeting others. If we go out into the world ready to be changed and inspired by the people around us—our senses open to the gifts they might offer—we'll start to see that everything and everyone can help us. Everything is an offer. In the gratitude mindset, we're always seeing, hearing, smelling and sensing possibilities that can change, can inform and enlighten us.[9]

## our belief may just make It so

Some people believe that, in many ways, we create our own reality. Said another way, believing something to be true starts to make it so. Through that lens, there may be no ultimate truth to the idea that a random person on a bench has a preordained purpose in meeting you—that there's a "reason" you've met—but if you **believe** they've got some crucial information, maybe you'll discover some way that they do. You'll get something from being with them. Believing—and even better, practicing—that you've got something to be thankful for will lead you to notice more things to be thankful for.

Richard Wiseman, a British psychology professor at the University of Hertfordshire, conducted a study on how luck plays a role in our lives. In one experiment, he had folks read through a newspaper and asked them to count the number of photographs inside. The self-professed lucky people took just seconds to finish the task; the self-professed unlucky people took about two minutes. The reason why? The lucky folks saw the message in bold on page two that said, "Stop counting. There are 43 photographs in this newspaper." Those who considered themselves unlucky didn't see it. It just didn't register.[10]

---

[9] Notice that the tone here is one of curiosity and humility rather than one of consumption or objectification. We're not looking to rip an insight out of someone we meet the way we might extract oil from the ground. We're looking for a mutually beneficial exchange.

[10] Richard Wiseman, *The Luck Factor* (Talk Books: United Kingdom, 2003). Wiseman also conducted a "Luck School" to see if people could learn to

Again, if you believe that opportunities are everywhere, you keep your eyes open and then see opportunities everywhere. If you believe that every stranger you encounter has something to offer you, they do.

One of my favorite improv pre-show exercises makes use of this type of proactive gratitude. Instead of just making eye contact with the other players or saying, "I got your back"—both tried and true improv troupe rituals—each player says out loud something they enjoyed or appreciated during the show, *as if it had already actually happened.* So, one player might say, "Marlene, I loved the way you jumped on stage with boldness." Another might offer, "It was so great the way we really tuned into each other's needs without having to say much at all." A third could share, "I really loved how we took the time to let our scenes unfold." Again, it's as if you were at the end of the show, looking back on what happened, and expressing your appreciations. You're just doing it before the show. More often than not, whatever great dynamics get mentioned do tend to show up during the show. Whether troupe mates "create their reality," prime their brains or crystallize their purpose and intention with these exercises, they're changing the outcome with pre-emptive gratitude.

One could take this same approach to develop a more refined or turbocharged gratitude practice in daily life. Rather than needing to wait until the end of the day or until something "good" comes and finds you, you could try waking each morning and giving thanks for something you imagine is on its way to you. Some stranger will pleasantly surprise. Some natural vista will open up. Some idea will finally arrive. In other words, you're priming the pump to get a gift

---

become luckier. Turns out they could, if they followed four guidelines: 1) Maximize your chance possibilities by keeping an open mind (and pair of eyes), 2) Listen to your lucky hunches (which meditation helps you cultivate), 3) Expect good fortune, and 4) Turn bad luck into good (as in, seeing the positive side of failure or misfortune). Sound familiar?

from an unexpected place. With that frame, each day becomes like a little scavenger hunt. You're looking for the positive possibilities, and just like "lucky" folks, you start to find them.

---

### Café Gratitude

In the spirit of affirmations...

During the early 2000s, Northern California had a group of organic vegan restaurants that went by the name of Café Gratitude. All of those restaurants either closed or got sold in the process of a legal dispute in the early 2010s, but while they operated, they had a charmingly quirky—and stereotypically Californian—practice. When your server first came to your table, he or she would ask if you wanted the question of the day. Maybe it would be, "What's something you love?" Or "Who's a teacher who shaped your life?" Something to get you in the gratitude mindset.

In addition, every item on the menu—rather than having a typical name like garden salad or hummus sandwich—had an affirmation for its name. Something like, "I am beloved." Or "I am enlightened." "I am cherished." "I am forever radiant." "I am brilliant." Then, whenever the server brought the food out, instead of asking "Who ordered the chips and guacamole?" they'd ask "Who is beloved? Who is cherished?" And each person who ordered would get to (*have to?*) say their affirmation. "I'm beloved."

Perhaps a little over the top, but it's still a sweet notion.

(Contrarian that she can be, Monster Baby co-host Lisa Rowland considered putting together a rival restaurant called Café Passive Aggressive. There, the dishes could be called "Not that you care." Or "I'm perfectly fine on my own, thank you for asking." Or "If you want to." Depending on my mood in any given moment, I honestly might prefer that one. Could we call it Café Attitude instead? )

---

## what's not wrong?

Vietnamese Zen monk and mindfulness teacher Thich Nhat Hanh offers another great gratitude practice that he calls the Toothache Meditation. He starts by acknowledging that we rarely ever notice that that we don't have a toothache. We only notice when there is a problem. We don't notice the absence of the problem. Well, this practice chooses to do just that: register the places in our lives where things are not wrong.

In it, one person asks the other, over and over, "What's not wrong in your life?" Partner A keeps asking and Partner B keeps responding. Here's an example:

**A:** *What's not wrong in your life?*

**B:** *My hard drive has not crashed.*

**A:** *Mm-hmm. What's not wrong in your life?*

**B:** *I didn't lose my wallet.*

**A:** *What's not wrong in your life?*

**B:** *I have not been given a 30-day eviction notice.*

**A:** *What's not wrong in your life?*

**B:** *My animals are healthy.*

**A:** *Mm-hmm. What's not wrong in your life?*

**B:** *I am healthy. I am not in pain.*

**A:** *Very nice. What's not wrong in your life?*

**B:** *I have money in the bank.*

**A:** *What else is not wrong in your life?*

**B:** *So much is not wrong in my life. I don't have cancer.*

**A:** *Yeah. What else is not wrong in your life?*

**B:** *I don't even have a sunburn right now.*

Noticing what's not wrong, of course, usually leads quite naturally into noticing what's right. Astrologer Rob Brezsny has coined a term to describe that kind of attitude. Instead of "paranoia," which suggests a belief that the world is out to get us, Brezsny offers "pronoia," the belief that the universe conspires on our behalf. His practice flips to the other side of the Toothache Meditation coin. Rather than considering *What isn't going wrong?* he asks *What's going right?* Before you ever leave your home in the morning, so many miracles appear before you to help you on your way. Your roof has held strong during the night. Your sheets that kings and queens of yore would have been lucky to have slept beneath have kept you warm. The magic of electricity has lit your way to the bathroom where the miracle of running water carries away your human waste. Your refrigerator has kept eggs fresh for you, and your stove heats them in mere minutes. And so on.[11]

Again, when we pause to register—and given that you're reading this, you're likely included in that "we"—we can see that we're completely surrounded by gifts to be thankful for. The question isn't whether they're there. It's whether we'll notice.

---

**Chapter 13**

**Attitude of Gratitude: *Giving Thanks for the Many Gifts***

**GEMS from the JOURNEY**

- *Though they're similar, gratitude and affirmation are different things. Affirmation simply means noticing— and maybe vocalizing—what pleases you. Gratitude comes from the heart. It expresses an active appreciation for having received or experienced that which pleases you.*

---

[11] Rob Brezsny, *Pronoia is the Antidote for Paranoia* (Televisionary: San Rafael, CA), 2005, pp. 2-6.

- Because gratitude reveals what you care about—and that you actually do care—it can generate feelings of vulnerability.
- Your well-being depends on the kindness and generosity of others.
- In order to express gratitude, you first need to notice what you're thankful for. In this way, it calls on the skills of mindfulness and curiosity you've developed.

## PARADOX

- You can offer gratitude for both good times and bad times. Potential lessons and blessings lurk in every experience. That said, giving thanks for the lessons from the challenges you have faced need not suggest that "everything happens for a reason." Maybe there's no reason something bad happened—but you can still look for the gifts that might arrive as a result of that event.

## GOING DEEPER

- Find a partner to do Thich Nhat Hanh's "Toothache Meditation," as described in this chapter. Make sure to include enough repetitions of the question "What's not wrong in your life?" so that your answers begin to surprise you.
- Consider Rob Brezsny's "Pronoia," the notion that the world conspires on your behalf. Open your journal and write down 40 to 50 little things that made your life easier today through no effort of your own.
- The next time something does go wrong—even if it's a big going-wrong—ask yourself, What gifts might arise from this situation? And then be open for the answers that arrive in response.

# a cup of courage
## *taking action in the face of fear*

THEY SAY THAT MORE PEOPLE fear public speaking than fear death. Put those same people in a position where they have to speak *spontaneously* in front of others—as in improvisational theatre—and it feels like the rising fear might actually cause their death.

This fear represents a stumbling block for the clients of applied improvisors, people like me who bring the tools and techniques from the world of improvisation into other arenas: health care, business, teaching, personal growth, and the like. Often, when I first mention the word "improv" in a workshop, jaws and sphincters tighten. Breath gets shallow. Arms cross and participants steel themselves in advance against self-exposure. *I'm not funny. I'm not fast or clever or insightful. They'll think I'm stupid. Or boring. Or embarrassing.* Folks get so caught up in their anxious anticipation that they never imagine that most such exercises actually won't ask them to get in front of others or to make anyone laugh. It takes a while to demonstrate that, with the right teacher, improv principles and practices actually move in the *opposite* direction. In fact, they generate the very courage we need in order to move through that kind of fear.

Those who regularly practice mindfulness know its tools and techniques do the very same thing.

## courage from the heart

The word courage has a poetic power all its own. Its root, "cor-" traces back to the old French *corage*, which meant "heart or innermost feelings" and the Latin *cor*, more simply just "heart." In other words, courage contains the power and muscular strength of the heart as well as its tenderness and exposure. Having courage, then, involves a willingness to be seen, to remain present and active in the face of fear or vulnerability. *Yes, I'm going to acknowledge this fear in my heart. And I'm going to keep going anyway.*

Some of us might feel courageous physically. We'll jump off a cliff or lean a motorcycle through a hairpin turn at crazy speeds. Others find that strength for performing, singing in front of large groups, teaching in high-stakes settings, or launching a championship-winning shot with millions of fans on the edge of their seats. And others have the courage for emotional revelation, entering into conversations that others would shrink from. Again, wherever you find that courage, it seems to come down to *a willingness to move forward in the face of fear, uncertainty or anticipatory discomfort.* You feel the feels and still make your move.

I've never had the physical courage I've seen in others. I've never gotten into fights.[1] Contact sports like hockey or football or extreme sports like skiing, skateboarding, or speed racing never made sense to me. The potential risk of injury just seemed too high—as my lone experience getting tackled by brother's friend apparently confirmed. If someone were attacking me physically, I imagine—or at least I hope—I'd muster up some active response, but I'm not sure. I know I'd try to use all my communication and connection skills first to make sure the encounter never rose to that level of danger in the first place.

---

[1] OK, one with my brother and two in sixth grade when I was defending Sarah Tuttle's honor. Those were plenty.

Over the years, though, I *have* grown the strength for making presentations and demonstrating emotional vulnerability. People often admire my ability to speak without preparation, to raise an uncomfortable question, or to uncover the hidden dynamics in a relationship. They marvel at my transparency or my willingness to acknowledge what's happening. In these realms, I do have the willingness and capability to step into dangerous waters, even when I feel the threat of uncertainty or risk.

## practicing with low-stakes risks

Taking an improv class with strangers asks for this kind of openness—and ideally creates a safe space for risking it. The same is true for any mindfulness class: you might end up encountering sadness or frustration in unexplored corners of your mind. But a skillful teacher and supportive group will make safe space for all that. The risks in such settings *feel* real, but realistically, they're likely low-level.

I had a mild moment of such vulnerability a few years ago on a music cruise in the Caribbean. Our boat had stopped at Roatán, an island just off the coast of Honduras, and most of the passengers had spilled out into the little port reception area. Shops selling all sorts of doodads and knick-knacks. Outdoor bars with thatched roofs. Jewelry and artisan vendors lining the walkways. After I walked that gauntlet out to the main street, there were more than 20 tour vendors aggressively hawking their wares: *"Hey, you! Sir! Sir! Come ride with us! We'll take you anywhere!"* The noise, urgency and feeling of desperation were overwhelming. And the situation seemed ripe for rip-off: wealthy (or at least comparatively wealthy) Americans jumping off ship and brimming with dollars to spend in a community that depended directly upon those dollars being actually spent. Though we'd received assurances that this island was safe, I knew that the mainland coast—not so far away—did not merit the same confidence.

I took a deep breath, looked around and found one vendor who seemed quiet and centered, grounded outside that fray. I made eye contact and he smiled, so I walked up to him. Like most of the people on the island, he was clearly of African descent and I, like most of the cruisers, was clearly white. Despite our differences, I struck up a conversation, going back and forth between Spanish and English. I was enjoying the interaction, so, without comparing or talking to other vendors to negotiate prices, I decided to go with him.

I knew it was a bit of a risk from the beginning. I could be getting fleeced. Though he seemed trustworthy to my internal sensors, I couldn't be 100% sure. That uncertainty only grew when he took me out from the staging area into the parking lot and told me he was going to be sending me with his "brother" so he could stay and continue making sales. *So now the guy I've established some intuitive level of connection with is going to pass me off to a total stranger?* After he chatted a bit more with the security guards at the gate to the parking lot, he came back to say, "My brother's not available, so I'll just take you." While I was glad to be back in his hands, we now seemed to be going even further outside whatever regulated system might exist. The question marks kept growing. Eventually, I had to take a deep breath and trust my intuition.

In this instance, my intuition panned out, and the trip turned out awesome. Mike Dilbert[2] took me on a one-of-a-kind, 5-hour behind-the-scenes tour of the island. He showed me the kinds of places that cruisers almost never see: the tiny village where he grew up and the sand-floored school where he attended second grade (we met his teacher as well!), the up-on-stilts houses along the water where his brothers were struggling to raise their daughters without much available work, and the tiny backwoods office where he needed to stop in to pay his electric bill. We paused at a hilltop vista that

---

[2] Yup, Mike Dilbert. Perhaps the whitest name imaginable for such a dark-skinned guy.

afforded a panorama of all the lands his father used to own, and he told me stories of how his father had tragically been killed by Nicaraguan soldiers while fishing off the coast in disputed waters. I heard about how Mike had almost gone pro in a big-city Honduran soccer league but never made it because he missed his island community too much. He just couldn't stand being away from home. Everywhere we went, people smiled at his (and our) arrival and he smiled back—"They all know me! I'm the only Mike on the island!" We ended up sharing a late afternoon ceviche lunch on the beach just before he dropped me back off at the boat. Everything was fine—and more than fine.

Admittedly, going off with Mike had only been a measured risk. I had had some safety nets in place. The dude was an official vendor serving the cruise ships, and I knew it wouldn't serve him well to mess up that income-reliable relationship. And we could speak two shared languages so I could express what I needed to. Still, you don't have to take risks to be courageous. I could have been paralyzed by the (even reasonable) fears and hesitations I did have. Instead, by acknowledging and moving through those fears, I got to meet a delightful man and got a personal tour of the island. And the best tour I could have had, apparently.

As my day with Mike illustrates, courage can take you to cool places. Adventures await in all shapes and sizes. Maybe it's working up the courage to go on a date after a long time out of circulation. Or maybe it means speaking up in a meeting when your boss is present, and you decide to trust that, even if you "mess up," you'll at least get a good story out of it, not to mention an opportunity to learn something.

### courage and nervousness

Sometimes the feeling that you need to move through is just a simple, even undefined, nervousness. It doesn't have to come from a world class event with gold-medal stakes on the line. Your nervousness might make no rational sense—like, here you are, raising a toast in front of people you know and love, people who adore you and would completely accept you even if you messed up—but the jitters still show up. It's not the rational brain doing the nervous-making. It's a more primitive limbic system firing into play. As Cara Alter, founder of the Bay Area coaching firm Speech Skills, says, "Nervousness is a human response. This is not about your character or preparedness or talent level. Olympic athletes get nervous and they're more prepared than anyone. Presidents and Prime Ministers get nervous and they outrank you. Tony Award winners get nervous and their talent is through the roof. You're gonna get nervous too." More simply, it's a natural thing.

This is one of the ways that improv can prove so helpful. You get to practice building the neural muscles of feeling vulnerability and nervousness—and stepping in to perform anyway. Any spontaneity game where you have to discover things in the moment will do the trick. In the game "Three Things" for example, you get an outside stimulus that could cause you to feel nervous—*They gave me the name of a category, how am I going to name three things that belong to it off the cuff?*—and you respond. You let yourself be seen. Boom. Here we go.[3]

In "I Am a Tree," you go even further because there's no specific turn to take. One person starts the short scene, stepping to the center of the circle to say, "I am a tree." Then anybody else in the circle can go in and add to the story. Maybe someone says, "I am a wrapped present under the tree," and another enters the game, saying, "I am a star on top of the tree," and the game is off and running. In this game, though, nothing says you have to jump in at a given point. You have to *choose* to make the leap to get yourself into the game. It's really easy to remain in the background until you have a good idea. So, it takes a different kind of courage to move into

---

[3] See the Glossary of Games for a complete description of "Three Things."

uncertainty *of your own accord*, maybe even moving your body physically into the circle before you know what to do. Can you step in? Can you move into that void voluntarily, knowing you're taking a risk by getting in there? In the end, you simply make yourself go. Not because you have to or because it's your designated turn, but because you can sense that it's simply the right time.

Once you've played "I Am a Tree" enough times, you come to see that, even if you step into the circle before any idea has occurred to you, an idea will show up once you get in there. The courage muscle grows stronger and more flexible. The pattern becomes more reliable. And your nervousness morphs into excitement and eagerness.

Eventually, you can transfer that improvisational courage into your daily life. You keep building those muscles, getting better and better at sharing vulnerability and trusting the moment. When someone asks, "How are you?" (and they mean it), rather than filtering or taming your response, you can say honestly, "Today I'm feeling sad about my heartbreak from six months ago. And I'm excited about a new client who wants to work with me. And I'm angry about what's happening politically in the country." Or whatever it is that you're really feeling. Each question becomes an opportunity for honest self-inventory and willing self-expression. Bringing "Three Things" into ordinary life like this demands courage. And builds it.

Said another way, improv trains you that you have what you need for life. *Oh, I wasn't totally ready, and I had no clue what was coming, but things worked out OK.* Your practice then becomes less about preparing for life's uncertainties, and more about honing, strengthening and living this belief that when you get to an uncertain place, you're going to have what you need. Eventually, that tide of confidence will rise and reach the shores of your life where you've been less courageous, due to traditions you've inherited or habits you've developed. *I have attention and resourcefulness and the willingness to say what's there. I have the willingness to be obvious. I have the willingness to ask good questions and notice what's around me.* And always, you've got curiosity and kindness.

## the courage of mindfulness

As we discussed in Chapter 9, "Meta-tation: The Benefits of a Bigger Picture," mindfulness also has the power to defang the discomfort of dread. You feel your fear, and then choose not to fight it or flee from it. Instead, you witness it. *OK, I'm uncomfortable. I don't have to do anything about that. I don't have to fix it. I can breathe with it.* When you can remain still in a seated meditation through little pains and distractions, like itches or tensions, you learn to ease your reactive fear of discomfort. You realize you've been uncomfortable before, and you can make it through the unpleasantness. It's not gonna end you. The big-toothed fiend has had its incisors pulled by sheer familiarity. It's just a gummy monster now.

So often, people think of mindfulness as escaping from life's problems, soothing away all our worries. It's quite the reverse. It's being willing to face what is. It's turning toward your challenges and hanging out with them. Unflinchingly facing them. It's saying *This is what's true. This is what's real. I'm taking away the illusions I've been holding onto in order to protect myself. When I strip them away, this is what I'm left with. This is who I am. This is how I've been. These are the ways that I've hurt the people I love, or these are the ways I'm not being who I want to be. Now what?* Even to acknowledge, *Oh, this is what I'm feeling,* is an important step. It takes an engagement. It takes a risk. You put down your distraction or hesitation and get in there to wrestle with—or at least sit with—what's really going on. That's a kind of intrapersonal courage that few have developed.

As with improv, mindfulness also develops courage because you come to see that, when all the discomfort is said and done, you'll almost certainly end up OK. When you sit and face your demons, stripping away your illusions, you're left with the reassurance of your simple perceptions and experiences. Whatever this "I" is, I'm still feeling and sensing and connecting and breathing. I'm still here. Maybe now I can face this bigger challenge. Maybe I can create more and more spaciousness around what's hard—or even make space for what's good (which is sometimes even harder).

Having a partner, friend or colleague who is also a mindfulness practitioner can amplify the benefits of this kind of courage. One time, a woman friend and I were exploring whether we wanted to be romantically involved. We considered the risk of going on that music cruise together: the entertainment and sunshine looked both fun and exciting, but we knew we'd be on board a boat in tight quarters. For seven days. Without knowing each other that well. In years prior, I might have passed on the opportunity because I'd have feared things exploding into an awful mess. *Oh my god, I'm stuck with this person for a week. What the heck were we thinking?* But because this woman was also a mindfulness practitioner and we had evidence in our friendship of sorting through discomforts pretty easily, I actually felt both comfortable and confident. Whatever came up on this trip, we'd be able to sort it out. Ultimately, we chose not to go the romantic route—and still had a great time. We hit a few bumps and tricky spots as we processed the dynamics, but we just kept coming back and checking in with each other. *What's true for you? What's true for me? I'm sensing this. What's your perspective?* Mindfulness gave us the courage to try something bold because we had the tools to look at our stuff. We knew we could handle it. We could take care of each other. And we did.

## enough courage to allow full intensity

Eventually, you might even develop such full reserves of courage, skill and resourcefulness that you don't need to do any defanging at all. You can confront your fears and discomforts as they are, in their full intensity. Seasoned improv teachers will give their experienced students an explicit instruction: **don't** defang the cobra. Meaning, if characters come upon a dramatic tension and resolve it right away, they've sapped their story of its dramatic potential or purpose. In that case, you don't want to defang the cobra; you want to re-fang it or extra-fang it. Let the cobra get even scarier so you have to develop the resources to handle it. Don't take the stakes away by taking the snakes away. Face the menace.

As I mentioned in Chapter 11, "Adventure Time: Seeking the Joy of New Experience," you'll also often hear the improv instruction "Go into the cave!" Too often, two onstage characters stand at the mouth of a risky cave and find all sorts of reasons not to go in. They'll talk about what's in there. They'll discuss their fears. They'll decide they should go home instead. And their waffling defuses or diminishes the dramatic tension. In that scenario, the audience will feel cheated: they've been robbed of an opportunity for excitement. "Go into the cave!" asks us to brave the uncertainty. Follow the intensity even though you're not sure what you might find. Even though your character may get hurt, die, or—*gasp!*—be changed in some way, you can get in there and give it a go. Take your courage in your hands and make the adventure happen.

On a more metaphorical level, you can ask "What's *my* cave?" You can stand outside dithering and dallying, avoiding confrontation with some uncertainty that will move your life forward. Or you can walk away and leave it for another time. But you might be cheating yourself out of the story of your life. Maybe you owe it to yourself as your own improv partner in life to go into the cave. In fact, fear may serve as an indicator of just where you ought to be going.

Again, as with the "Nope!" option when creating adventures with another, it's important to check in with yourself before diving into any risk. Your fear may offer a healthy warning about honoring personal boundaries or maintaining physical safety. But if you've checked in and realized your hesitation doesn't come from deep, instinctual self-preservation—if you see it's just nervousness or a default reaction—then you can challenge yourself to step out of your comfort zone. Sure, it may be hard or awkward or strange. You may not impress everyone you want to impress. But you're going to learn and grow and connect and experience. The fear becomes a positive indicator, a little flashing light to activate our courage: *Oh, yes. Interesting. Find out what the heck that light is. Go into the cave.* The courage brings a juice and vitality to the rest of your life.

## get to it

Improv has a bias towards action. Instead of talking about the cave, you dive in. Don't imagine what you're going to learn. Just go, get in there, and learn. Take a step toward your idea—or your fear. See what happens.

Engaging that action orientation need not mean something huge, just as taking on adventure didn't have to mean scaling a crazy-dangerous mountain peak. Sometimes, when I teach an applied improvisation game, the group will suggest a variation on the game, and I have to challenge myself to try it out. A group of health care professionals, for example, wanted to play "Sound Ball," a game where participants send and receive random sounds around the circle.[4] This time, instead of passing sounds, they wanted to send words related to the work we'd been doing on relationship to failure. In years past, I might have resisted. *That's not something we can do. We don't have time for that. I don't think that will work. That's not how the game's played.* This time, though, I decided to challenge myself: *Am I saying no because I don't want to lose control? Am I afraid I'll be uncomfortable?* We went ahead and tried out their suggestion, and it turned out to make for a super poignant variation on the game that deepened the work we'd done all week. Now I get excited for such opportunities to mix it up with the unpredictable. *Let's try it*

---

[4] You'll find a more complete discussion of Sound Ball in the next chapter and more complete directions in the Glossary of Games.

out. The worst that can happen is it's not fun. Even when it goes "bad," we learn. Woo-hoo!

To be sure, there are good reasons to say no to some risks and to pass on confronting some fears: personal safety, appropriate emotional boundaries, financial pressure, and the like. That said, simply avoiding mild discomfort isn't one of those. It's just not a compelling reason.[5]

In the end, you'll come to see that the more chances we take, the more even more chances show up. Our courage opens doors of opportunity. Both externally and internally, our gaze expands and the world of possibility grows wider. We see more. We experience more. And we grow stronger. Courage begets courageousness.

---

### Chapter 14
### A Cup of Courage: *Taking Action in the Face of Fear*

#### GEMS from the JOURNEY

- *The word courage comes from the root "cor-", or 'heart.' Similar to the heart, courage includes both great muscular strength and tender vulnerability. Courage calls for noticing your raw emotions and taking action anyway.*

- *Choosing to regularly take low-level risks—like on an adventure or in an improvisation exercise—can build courage muscles for life's greater challenges. You're putting money in the courage bank to help get you through tougher times in the future.*

- *Nervousness is a natural human response to stressful situations. It need not shut you down or block you from taking action.*

---

[5] If I were overly cautious, my gravestone might read: *Here lies Ted. He lived a comfortable life.* Bleh. Let me deserve something more adventurous in the end. Please.

- Mindfulness both develops and demands courage: you learn to look your fears squarely in the eye and sit with them as they are. No rejection or resistance, just curiosity.
- Improvisation gives us the inspiration to "go into the cave" of our fears, to take bold action that gets us into life's mix. You can trust that you'll have what you need when you get there.

## PARADOX

- It can prove helpful to defang our fears. It can also prove helpful to head straight into the fear so our courage gets even stronger. Knowing which approach to take in any fearful moment takes time, discernment and sometimes the perspective of reliable loved ones.

## GOING DEEPER

- Do a little research about the anatomy and function of the heart. What do those facts show you or suggest to you about courage as it shows up in your life?
- Identify what scary "caves" you might be waffling outside of in your life. What step can you take today to move more into that cave, to begin to confront that fear, take on that risk?
- Sneak in a few rounds of "Three Things"—or any other spontaneity exercises—throughout the day so you face the mild fear of having to come up with ideas on the spot. See the Glossary of Games for full details and super-fun variations.

# it's not about you
## *finding the ease of wider concern*

FOR THIS FINAL CHAPTER, I invite you to get your favorite slippers on, make a cup of tea, curl up with a nice warm blanket, and shut out the rest of the world. You're the boss. You deserve it. It's all about you.

Once you've gotten into this comfy state, though, I'll need you to notice it's not actually all about you. That may come as a shock. But it's true. Maybe it's about *us*. About all beings. Or about something even larger.[1]

I suggest we all get over ourselves. Thankfully, we can support each other along the way.

### self-care matters, narcissism can go

It's fair to say: living a healthy life requires an intermittent focus on yourself. Whether you're keeping the tires on your car rotated so you stay safer on the road or maintaining a stable blood sugar level so you can handle your kid's temper tantrum, you have to take care of your own literal or metaphorical vehicle. Self-care is good.

That said, narcissism is not. Living with a focus on me-me-me—*How did I look? Did I do OK? Do they like me? Will they keep liking me?*—can whip up the winds of a mental vortex. You compare yourself to others and usually can't measure up. You fret about when you'll get

---

[1] Can you feel it? You're right: we're about to step straight into another paradox!

what you need or want. You stoke the fires of apparent "identity" until you get burned by your attachment to it.[2]

## turning toward others

Shifting your attention onto other people—especially toward serving or helping them—distracts that soul-sucking self-absorption and pulls you out of it. In such moments, you then have more traction to start moving forward in your life.

Patricia Ryan Madson taught the Stanford Improvisors this lesson over and over in stark fashion. Any time she saw a performer in class or in rehearsal freeze up or lock up, she'd call out, "Get out of your head. Get out of your concern. It's not about you." As she wisely noted, any scene isn't about your self-concerns. And the answer you need for guiding your next step doesn't have to come as a referendum on your cleverness or ability as an improvisor. Be with your partners. Concentrate on making them look good. Make eye contact. Notice what else surrounds you. Do those things, and your next step will emerge. Naturally. Gracefully.

It's a simple directive—and a profound one. Let's explore it in more detail.

## staying low to the ground

Humility recognizes that none of us has all the answers. When you're humble, you don't need to have the most status in the room. You don't need to know the most or show the most. You can be simple and live simply. Humility also has a touch of agnosticism to it: you don't know for sure, you can't know for sure, and you can come to peace with—even get happy with—exploring that uncertainty. There's mystery in any given moment, and you remain open to

---

[2] Even just considering all this, you may notice tension in your chest or a quickening of your breath.

learning from others. Everything's a mess—including you (and me!)—and we're all doing our best to work through it all.

It might surprise you to know that humility comes from the same root, hum--, as do the words "human" and "humor." *Hum*—as in *humus*, the thick, dark and rich soil that proves so fertile for supporting life.[3] When we *exhume* someone or something, for example, we dig them up from underground. So, humble means "of the earth" or grounded, literally. Nothing high-falutin'. Nothing celestial. Humility's made of dirt and detritus, things lost or discarded, shells and rinds and leaves that have composted. Humus decomposes and then makes sense—and even treasure—of what has gone before. It works from the roots up, right here, right now. It serves growth in others, from seedlings to sequoias.

With a humble mindset, we don't have to be excellent at everything. We don't all have to be leaders. Some can choose to make excellent followers. Role players, behind-the-scenes peacekeepers, everyday facilitators, stagehands. You need not travel out in front to have influence. You need not serve as banner-carrier in order to serve the banner.

### whom do we serve?
OK. Let's say that you accept this notion of humility. If it's not all about you, then who is it all about?

On an improv stage, one could argue that the primary focus belongs on your teammates, helping them perform their best, taking care to support their ideas. That keeps players free from the kinds of self-judgment or censorship that can stifle creativity. Others suggest the proper focus lies on the audience, making sure they're having a great

---

[3] Notice that *humus* is not the same as *hummus*, the Middle Eastern chickpea-based superfood. That said, if you've accepted that it's not all about you and you find yourself in a Mediterranean restaurant, you might find it actually *is* all about the hummus.

time. The company plays together to provide a transformative experience for those who have gathered.

Still others might say the story itself takes precedence. All players stand on stage to serve that end. The unfolding tale has its own agenda (as we have seen). In that case, you just do what the story needs you to do. Maybe that means stepping into a heroic lead role when you'd rather hang out on the edges. Maybe it means waiting in the wings and leaving the stage open for a poignant monologue. You could have family or friends in the audience eager to see you on stage or to hear you belt out a spontaneous musical number, but it might not be the right time. You choose to serve the story first.

Of course, you **could** always shoehorn your way in. You could leave others in the dust. Get louder or go for the joke. Keep stealing the scene. In the long run, of course, though such maneuvers do gain attention, they don't serve you well. You just end up looking like a jerk.[4]

The takeaway here: whether you're focusing on teammates, audience or the larger improv story, it's not about you.

In leadership circles, maybe it's about the larger organization. If you direct a hospital—or even if you just work in it—you're serving the people who come for care or you're serving the health of the institution. Or even the larger field of health care. If you're on a high-performance team in sports, in the arts, or in the corporate world, the same holds. It's not about you. It's about a larger mission and vision getting expressed through the group. You play a part and others do too. Something larger is going on.

---

[4] Even if you're as electric in your upstaging as Robin Williams was, other folks won't feel uplifted by playing with you.

## ego self vs. eco self

This whole topic brings to mind the question of how you think about who you are. What are the boundaries of "you"? Most of us—and I include myself in this— tend to think in strict ego boundaries: I exist within the space of my body, my thoughts and my emotions. I can tell what I want, whether I'm hungry or healthy, whether I'm meeting my professional goals. I've got my financial situation, whatever love or sex or romance is going on in any moment, and whatever entertainment I choose to bring into my world. My friendships, my pets, my family. *My, my, my.*

That sense of boundary changes, though, when I (and you) not only shift *attention* to a wider scale, but also shift *identification*. "Me" doesn't just end at the boundary of my skin or the total of my bank account or the bottom of my resume. "Me" extends elsewhere. Further. As the Buddhist term *anatta* showed us in Chapter 9, "Ch-ch-ch-Changes: Learning to Go with the Flow," your seeming self includes all sorts of "non-self" elements. Along those lines, Joanna Macy—whom we've also mentioned before—makes a distinction between the "ego-self" and the "eco-self." We can choose to see ourselves as one link in a long lineage, a chain of evolution, and recognize that we are a single part of the larger whole, Earth. That vision generates a different kind of motivation, courage, belonging and patience.

Joanna's colleague John Seed worked for years on behalf of the rainforest in Australia. One time he was questioned about his efforts and how he summoned the courage to face off against the lawyers, politicians and mega-corporations who opposed him at every turn. He responded by saying (and I paraphrase), "When I remembered that I was the voice of the rainforest coming through me, I had no fear." In that moment, Seed wasn't speaking up to further his ego self. He was extending and experiencing his boundaries beyond his skin, his bank account. He was the rainforest and it was him. In that sense, his speaking up was no self-aggrandizement. It was one of the rainforest's acts of eco-self-preservation.

This kind of simultaneous loss of self and self-expansion can happen at many levels. Am I an improvisor in a group, or am I part of an improvisational theater group that speaks through me? Am I a boyfriend/spouse/partner, or am I one component of a larger relationship that has its own momentum? Am I an American, and what does that mean in these turbulent times? What "America" might speak through me? Am I an advocate for animal rights, for beings who cannot speak for themselves? Perhaps it not just that I'm intellectually upset about the cruelty of factory farming. Maybe it's that I'm connected with these beings and I'm resisting the unnecessary suffering that they—that this larger "I"—must endure.

The notion of interconnectedness is a big, big idea, one that changes your life if you truly take it on. If you operate from that place, so much of your limiting fear and self-doubt melts away. You gain the courage of centuries of genetic ancestry and the certainty of longevity beyond your own limited lifetime. When you have no separate identity to defend, the slings and arrows of comparison and competition land harmlessly at your feet. You just don't get hooked the same way.

That said, expanding your context like this can also mean that you feel more. When you focus on interconnectedness, joy anywhere becomes your joy. A friend's triumph or recovery evokes a rush of endorphins and real elation in you. Witnessing a random act of kindness triggers a deep sense of reassurance that we'll all be OK in the end. Likewise, pain anywhere becomes your pain. Seeing a freshly clear-cut mountain feels like having your hair ripped out. The loss of an anonymous refugee child trying to cross a sea to safety halfway around the globe leaves you aching with grief. While, in the big picture, it may be healthier or wiser to notice and live from an awareness of interconnectedness, it may simply hurt too much at times. So, in those times, you might choose to put your walls and boundaries back up for a while. To kindly and simply say, "Nope!" to taking it all in.

As I mentioned at the beginning of this chapter, a more traditional focus on "self" helps sometimes. You have to understand your own boundaries, how much energy you have, and how much you have to give. For some, it feels easy to focus on always making other people happy—at the expense of their own happiness—but this orientation proves unsustainable over time. The rent comes due eventually. And that rent needs to be paid in the currency of self-care.[5]

## patterns of privilege

In Western culture at least, there's also a gender component to this whole ego-eco dynamic. Though the dynamic is changing, women still get trained to please other people. So, many women come to find a sense of self in serving others. In contrast, most men are trained to do what they want. They learn to be decisive, to step up, claim the stage, do the thing. It's the rugged, bootstrapping legend of the hero. *Just do it.*

In many ways, I got some alternative training as a man—growing up in a single-mom, feminist household will do that—but even there, my default focus definitely still fell on myself. As a result, I got pretty good at advocating for my opinions and making sure my needs got met. And as a white, heterosexual educated man, the world reinforced that I had permission to do that. More than permission, really. It was expected. Even now, I can consciously work to recognize that I'm actually *interdependent* with those around

---

[5] The classic airline directive about putting on your own oxygen mask before helping others applies here. You have to make sure your system still functions before you can work to keep others up and running. Otherwise, you're no good to anyone else anyway.

me... and I still usually think of myself first. However it got formed, it remains a strong default.

Given all that privilege, I might not be the best person to tell other folks (that is, to tell *you*) "Hey, it's not about you." If your voice has been excluded from conversations of power, maybe it does need to be more about you. And I shouldn't be the one to tell you to back off from stepping up. We actually need more of you.

In other words, this "It's not about you" lesson might remain a valuable one, but it's important where and when it gets offered and in what words and ways it gets communicated.

## the language of mindfulness (instruction)

Those who teach mindfulness have another way of loosening our identification with the self—and it's a subtle one. If you listen to the most skilled instructors when they lead a meditation, you'll notice they more often use '-ing' words rather than commands. Instead of directing you to "Feel your feet," as if they were giving orders—even soothingly voiced, compassionately intending ones—they'll say, "Feel**ing** your feet...," indicating that the desired action is already happening. By avoiding a directive tone and thus the potential impulse of rebellion that might rise against it, the instructor more gently leads the participant into the practice.

Taking it even further, the meditation leader might opt out of pronouns like "you," "your" and "I" altogether, avoiding any suggestion of identity at play in the process. Rather than "feeling *your* feet," then, she suggests "feeling *the* feet." Instead of "noticing *your* breath," it becomes "noticing *the* breath." Using pronouns actually activates a social interaction—*you and I*—and all the status and desire for approval that goes along with it. In this case, the practice isn't about *YOU* doing anything. It's about focusing the phenomenon of attention—happening in and through "you."

We may have no conscious idea that those leader and follower roles get enlisted, but they do. So, though it may sound a bit odd, wishy-washy or mealy-mouthed at first, this neutral language actually allows for a better meditative experience. In the same way that a sensory deprivation chamber lets you experience your thoughts in a different way, this approach creates a kind of *social* deprivation chamber. For a few moments anyway, you can rest your attention on what's true in the moment rather than jumping into personal or relational concerns, even minor ones: how you look, what others might be thinking of you or how well you are doing. You can stay more fully present to what is.

## leave it at the door

Some of the best improv teachers also have little tricks to support this notion of softening the ego. Games like Word-at-a-Time Stories demonstrate pretty quickly that any grandstanding or trying to be funny will derail the process. When any would-be-witty player makes it about them and pulls focus away from the unfolding moment, they actually throw up clear roadblocks to a successful exercise or show. They betray the process and the group. Sometimes in the Word-at-a-Time game, you, the player, will get an opportunity to offer a big, juicy noun or verb. Or you might get the chance for a colorful adjective. Just as likely, your turn will ask for the humility of an article or simple conjunction. In each instance, it's not about what you want. It's about what's happening.

This should be clear by now: any unfolding improv work—whether in a show or in a rehearsal—can't be about your agenda. Your job is to show up in the moment, respond honestly to what's happening, and stay in connection with your stage mates. If you've got something going on in your life, as these teachers say, leave it at the door. Imagine dropping a little suitcase by the threshold as you come in. (You can pick it up on your way back out if you like.) Whatever turmoil you have going on personally, you need to set it aside.

This might sound harsh at first. *Where's the compassion?* But there's an underlying kindness behind it as well. It's to say, your ego stuff doesn't matter. If you show up late, we don't need to hear the thousand reasons why. You can apologize and we can get on with the show. No need to give you any hassle. No blaming, shaming or shunning. If it's a chronic problem, we can address what it means to work as a professional. Absent that pattern, we're glad you're here. We love and trust you. Let's play.

Another improv game that I use often in trainings for spontaneity and group presence is called "Sound Ball."[6] In it, the participants stand in a circle. One person makes an underhand gesture, as if tossing an imaginary ball, and makes a sound—any sound—as they "throw." The sound need not be funny, interesting or clever. It's just a sound. The person to whom they tossed the ball then makes a gesture of receiving while repeating the sent sound as best they can. Then they pass a new or different sound to someone else who receives it and passes another new sound along.

Usually, when folks first learn the game, you'll see great hesitation. People want to be "right" or "good," so they slow down and try to *generate* a good sound. They'll plan ahead before the ball gets to them so they won't get stuck. And the game kind of plods along. Again, that fear of failure or concern for what others will think creates a tension and the tension constricts possibility. The "ball" moves more slowly and the sounds stay within a narrow band of expression. All that self-concern shuts it down.

But here's the rub—and the cool part. You can pause the game at that point, with folks working so hard and struggling a bit, and suggest a tweak. Rather than focusing on *making* the sound, turn your attention to *receiving* what's sent to you. Honor *that*. Mimic it

---

[6] See the Glossary of Games for a full description.

lovingly. Do right by the person who sent it to you. And then send your new sound out.

Almost always, the game instantly transforms. Suddenly, folks get more connected. They're more relaxed and freer. The sounds start ranging farther afield and, as a result, get more surprising and a heck of a lot more delightful. Rather than worrying about looking good, participants turn their attention to helping *others* look good. Nobody cares how well you play "Sound Ball" except you. No one's on that page with you. Or, even if they do care, they'll probably like you better if you play with greater freedom, ease and spontaneity. And that happens when your self-concern gets out of the way.

### learning to yield

In her 2$^{nd}$ Circle work,[7] Patsy Rodenburg uses another exercise to help ensembles develop this quality of yielding. She asks the group to mill about the studio space, walking naturally though not in any particular pattern. Just moving about. Then she asks, "Are you a group yet?"

At first, the group looks to her in consternation, as if to say, "What do you even mean, Patsy?" And she'll just repeat, "Are you a group yet? Are you moving as a group?" When I took part in the exercise, we knew right away that, no, we were not yet in synch. So, some of us adjusted, changed rhythm or pace or style, and we got a bit closer. But a few holdouts still couldn't drop into the larger flow. They couldn't yield their own preference to the pattern moving through the group.

Then she had us step back out into a circle and asked a single person to step into the center and mill about. After a bit of time, she invited a second person in—who needed to honor and match the walking style of the first person. So the second needed to yield to the first's leadership. With that one-at-a-time spotlight, it became clear who

---

[7] See Chapter 10, "Got Presence: Moving into Second Circle."

kept resisting letting go into the whole. And whenever that would happen, Patsy would ask a beautiful question: "Do you want to be part of the ensemble?" And the follow up comment: "If you do, you're going to need to yield sometimes."

Then that person would step back out to the edge of the circle and reenter until they got it down. (Sometimes it took several tries!) Eventually, having stretched and developed those muscles of releasing control, the feel for the group would emerge and a tangible unison would snap into place.

In our me-me-me culture, this act of choosing followership actually represents a radical act of leadership. It's making a choice to influence the group by joining the group. Not by dominating but by participating. You can leave the ego stuff at the door, notice what's already happening, and step into the stream. It's more relaxing than gripping and constructing and wrestling for control. Like a ballroom dancer following a lead, you're still dancing. You're still moving beautifully. And you're still in rhythm with the music. You're just doing so through response rather than initiation.[8]

## again, the paradox

So, there may be times when you *do* need to make it about you. Times when you need to draw the line, claim your space and defend your interests. You need to speak up for yourself. But there are also times when it's most definitely *not* about you. And it's better to yield.

In the end, it's about taking up your fair share of space, but not more than your fair share. And perhaps adjusting your sense of the "you" that gets included in determining "your" fair share. If you're speaking for the rainforest or on behalf of a marginalized group, maybe you get more space. Otherwise, try yielding.

---

[8] Remember, as a ballroom dance follower, you get to wear the prettiest costume. Heck, you might even get to wear sequins.

## Chapter 15
### It's Not About You: *Finding the Ease of Wider Concern*

### GEMS from the JOURNEY

- A healthy focus on self-care helps you stay balanced and resilient, and have a vibrant life. A narcissistic focus on self-aggrandizement does not.

- Humility keeps us grounded, of the earth. From there, we can serve growth from the roots up.

- Shifting self-identification from a separate "ego-self" to an interconnected "eco-self" that stretches across time and species boundaries engenders far greater courage, strength and resilience for facing life's challenges.

- The precise language of mindfulness instruction offers a helpful method for loosening up the stickiness of self and identity.

- The seemingly urgent agenda of your personal concerns—will I be OK? Do they like me? But I'm hurting!—may not rank as urgent to the groups you're a part of. Can you acknowledge what's going on for you and then put it to the side, if just for a few moments?

- Learned cultural patterns shape who among us feels we have the right to speak up and assert ourselves. In other words, who gets permission to say, "It's all about me." When challenging any focus on ego-attachment, it makes sense for those in positions of privilege to speak carefully and respectfully to make room for those whose self-assertion has been long-denied.

## PARADOX

- There are times where it is (or should be) all about you. And there are times, maybe far more than you would like to admit, where it really isn't. Learning to yield with grace and humility can, paradoxically, be a noble act of leadership.

## GOING DEEPER

- *Make a list of at least 30 non-self elements that make up who "you" are and have become. Here's five to kick off your list: Water, sunshine, the fossil fuel that has powered all the places you've been, the words in this book, the favorite city you traveled to when you were younger. How many more can you list?*

- *As you walk through the day, try yielding to others in terms of space. Open doors for others. Let another car enter your lane, even if it wasn't fair that they cut in front. Move over on the sidewalk. Then notice what thoughts and feelings arise in response. Do you feel generous or taken advantage of—or both? How do your choices affect your mood and your energy levels? Does it matter that you're choosing to yield rather than being forced to do so?*

- *Play the classic improvisation warm-up "Sound Ball" with a special focus on paying attention to your partners throwing you the "ball." See if you can let go of any concern you have for looking good or sounding clever. Just zoom in on honoring those around you and see what that does for your anxiety about playing the game.*

# epilogue
## *wrapping up the journey*

And so, my friends, we come to the end of this joyful journey. I hope these pages have helped you feel more acutely alive and connected to yourself, to those around you and to the world at large.

I hope you have begun to greet the "photograph" you see each day with wonder, anticipation and engagement. And that you now act with more boldness—and make ample space for others to do the same.

If you've taken these words to heart and begun to rewire old patterns, you may have discovered that societal or familial forces would rather you keep your wild and joyful "monster baby" under wraps. I sincerely hope that you've chosen instead to find, feed, and befriend this part of you so it becomes a great ally. This part has tremendous power and deep wisdom. It will help you reconnect with the amazing gift of being alive.

Most of all, I hope that you have *experienced* the many, many ways that mindfulness and improvisation can make life better: how they refine your capacity to pay attention, build your confidence, deepen your calm, and enrich your ability to collaborate. Both practices encourage you to get more engaged with whatever's *actually* happening (as opposed to what's happening in your mind), to stay humbly curious and to bring your full awareness to bear on each unfolding moment. In different and complementary ways, they show you how to cultivate the skill of quality presence, a universal key that unlocks uncountable doors.

On this journey, you've learned to change your attitude toward failure by developing a growth mindset (and the ability to shout, Woo-Hoo!). You have stretched yourself by puzzling over the conflicts that appear to arise at the intersection of mindfulness and improv: *Is it better to follow our impulses or to pause before we act? How do we include other's voices without surrendering our own? What's the best way to balance our desire for something better with an acceptance of how things actually are?*

You've also learned about other wisdom that emerges from mindfulness and improvisation: why starting with positive choices makes for better life "stories," how to handle the chaos that can consume our lives, how to find the peace of a wider perspective, and how to make sense of the inevitable march of change. In addition to all this learning, you joined me on an exploration of four qualities that make life far more fun and a heck of a lot healthier: adventurousness, curiosity, gratitude and courage.

Finally, you've looked in the face of one last paradox: finding out that it's not all about you makes for *good* news, not bad.

Truly, it has been an honor to travel on this romp with you. Going forward, please know and believe that you are OK. You are enough. Know, too, that failure can actually help. It's fun to share control. Taking a playful approach and making others look good both help heal everyone.

My last encouragements to you? Get present. Stay present. Keep experimenting. Go on adventures. Open up. Connect. Relax into change and start over when necessary. Say thank you. Take a mindfulness course or an improv class. If you get knocked down, get back up. And keep going. For God's sake, keep going.

Consistently weave these ideas and practices into your life—reset to a mindful improvisor's default of freedom, ease, spontaneity and joy—and I guarantee you will see more, feel more, and love more. Inevitably, you will then inspire others to do the same.

For the hope of an ever more joyful, creative and generous world, may it be so.

# glossary of games

Each of these exercises illustrates or reinforces a principle discussed in the book. Taken together, they make a great way to embody and expand the insights you've learned. They also offer a perfect avenue for bringing others with you on your curious romp. Families, classrooms, work teams: purposeful play creates genuine connection for more cohesive groups.

Please note: these games appear in alphabetical order. In an effort to honor the gifts of those who came before me, I have mentioned where I first learned them.

Enjoy!

## 1-2-3 or Clap-Snap-Stomp

*From Chapter 2: "Take a Circus Bow: Changing Your Relationship to Failure"*

(From Lisa Rowland)

This exercise serves as our go-to for opening a class or workshop: good laughs, healthy challenge, and reliable insight into our relationship to failure.

Have folks break into pairs, one partner facing the other. Their joint task is to count to three again and again, as fast as they can, alternating numbers. Partner A says "One," Partner B says "Two," and A finishes by saying "Three." As soon as they've finished, they start again, this time B leading with "One," so the counting loops around in continuous fashion. After a minute or so, check in with players to see how that went. You'll likely find folks surprised by how difficult the task proved.

After Round #1, offer directions for Round #2: with the same partners as before, count back and forth again, but instead of saying "One," participants should clap. Now, the sequence goes Clap-"Two"-"Three," Clap-"Two"-"Three." Invite players to register their reactions if they "fail" or make a mistake. What happens, specifically, in their bodies, faces, or thoughts? After this round, you'll often find that your pairs struggled even more—the toggling between verbal and kinesthetic processing requires a bit more brain time for most.

Round #3 ups the ante even further: instead of saying "Two," players now snap their fingers so the rhythm goes Clap-Snap-"Three." Same partners, same task: alternate back and forth, going as quickly as possible. Before starting folks off on this version, however, offer one other instruction. If a player makes a mistake—saying the wrong number, making the wrong gesture, taking too long, or just getting generally flummoxed—they should raise both their hands above their head with a joyous release of "Woo Hoo!!!" (Yes, this is a simplified version of the classic improvisor tribe's Failure Bow or Circus Bow.) In a short debrief after the round, make sure to ask what it was like to inject the "Woo Hoo!" into the proceedings. Most likely, you'll find that it lightens the mood, adds laughter, and makes the mistakes kind of fun.

Round #4 makes the entire pattern kinesthetic, shifting all the way from "One-Two-Three" to Clap-Snap-Stomp. Here, the task becomes like a step routine, a rhythm to sink into. After giving directions but before sending the troupe off to try it, ask them to tweak their "Woo Hoo!" practice as well. This time, when either partner messes up, both should break into the enthusiastic "Woo Hoo!" After giving a good bit of time for the practice, again check in with the group. "How was that? What did you notice?" Usually—though not always—your pairs will find this easier than the previous two rounds. And the shared "Woo Hoo!" builds the feeling of partnership. Interesting stuff!

As a final challenge, invite your pairs to go all the way back to the beginning to try their original "One-Two-Three" verbal sequence. Almost inevitably, folks find that they're faster, more comfortable, and more connected—and they make fewer errors. This makes a great teaching moment: in just a few minutes, they have put themselves through an honest challenge and they've achieved real growth without even realizing it. The metaphors for teaching and learning are plenty here. Feel free to dive in explicitly or just to nod in their direction. Either way, the exercise will hold its own.

*Insider Tips:*

- In each round, encourage folks to go even faster. We tend to slow down to keep ourselves safe and do the task "right." The point of this game is to get to that dangerous (and fun!) edge of imminent "failure."
- Pay attention to posture and stance. As is almost always true, an athletic, engaged, and ready position should help a pair's performance.
- When folks reveal that they've discovered a helpful pattern—I noticed early on that I could concentrate on my part alone and just say "1-3-2" in order and I wouldn't have to even pay attention to my partner!—you can note how

cleverly the mind looks for solutions to keep us safe. Honor that impulse and then encourage folks to put such "tricks" on hold for the time being. Let them sink into the uncertainty.

- When you first introduce the "Woo Hoo!" practice it a few times with everyone together so they can work through any hesitation for the goofiness of it. *Oh, everyone else is participating? I guess I can go there too.*

- Invite participants to make eye contact with their partners and see if that changes the experience at all.

## Advance-Color-Emotion

*From Chapter 12: Isn't That Curious? Exploring the World with Eager Eyes*
(From Dan O'Connor of L.A.'s Impro Theatre)

This exercise provides a great mechanism for enlivening conversation and storytelling—both speaker and listener get to explore new dynamics of stories they may have told or heard before.

The structure goes like this: Partner A listens to a meaningful true story from Partner B's life—preferably one that they have told many times—and can pause Partner B at any time that Partner A wants to move the story in one of three directions.

If Partner A wants the plot to move forward, they say, "Advance," and Partner B speaks about what actions actually came in consequence of earlier actions.

Should Partner A want more specifics—what someone looks like, what setting the story's in, what sounds and smells were present—they can say, "Color." Partner B then pauses the story's movement to describe the details of that given moment.

Lastly, if Partner A wants to understand what the characters in the story were feeling, she says, "Emotion," and Partner B steers the story toward describing the emotions involved with that moment: how are the characters moved or changed by their experience?

If A asks for Color, B might share what the people in his story were wearing, what the landscape looked like, what aroma was in the air, and so on. If A calls for Emotion, B recalls how they were feeling at the time or how they imagined others were feeling. When A swings back to "Advance!" B moves the story along in time or logical consequence.

The story "director"—in this case, Partner A—should do their best to make sure the storyteller is given all three directions as the story progresses.

Then, of course, the partners switch roles so Partner B gets to choose Advance-Color-Emotion for Partner A's story.

*Insider Tips:*

- In this game, the storyteller often comes to see parts of their story in a new light. It can turn that new light into valuable insight if you give the partners time to debrief for a minute or two after each round: "What did you learn from telling the story in this way?"
- Make sure the "director" of each round makes the switches in a spirit of curiosity rather than manipulation or control. They choose which angles to focus on based on what might delight their storytelling partner, for example.
- When asking for "Color" or "Emotion," watch so the storyteller doesn't slip into moving the plot forward. That's most people's pattern in sharing personal stories. What happened next? A gentle reminder encourages the speaker to snap out of that default and luxuriate a little longer in the realm that's been requested.

**Ball**

*From Chapter 1: "A Word About Words: Defining Mindfulness and Improvisation"*
(BATS Improv in San Francisco)

Whereas Sound Ball[1]—another classic improv warm-up—relies on an imaginary sphere, this game uses a real-life ball (thus the name of the game!). The rules of Ball resemble those of volleyball—minus a court, a net, and any sense of opposing teams. In this case, the group works as one unit to keep the ball up in the air, counting aloud each time the ball gets hit. As in volleyball, no player can hit the ball twice in a row. If that happens or if the ball hits the floor, the count starts back at one.

Every so often, take time to pause and discuss whatever insights the group can generate about what's working to keep the ball alive. You'll likely hear, "Hit the ball higher!" or "Be bold about moving into the center!" Try giving the cue to "Pass the ball to someone else rather than just hitting it!"—which will transform the quality of the game-playing.

For sure, the joy of a good round of Ball lasts far longer than the time it's played. Tim Orr, a superlative improvisor and instructor, suggests that an improv workshop that contained nothing but the game of Ball would still teach those attending most of what they need to know about the art.

*Insider tips:*

- Make sure to keep everyone counting aloud. It makes for a great vocal warm-up and builds cohesion that's valuable for whatever learning activity comes next.
- Switch people's positions in the circle every now and then— new spot, new neighbors—to generate different permutations and possibilities.
- The ideal size for the ball is somewhere between a volleyball and a soccer ball. You want one that's light enough not to

---

[1] See later in the glossary for a description of Sound Ball.

damage your room or your players but sturdy enough to be bounced around without much effort. A Gertie brand ball works well. Even better for the fully dedicated, find a fabric Boingo brand ball as well and pull its bladder out. Then, put the Gertie ball inside the Boingo, stitch the whole thing back up, and re-inflate. The ball's just the right weight—and you've got the pride of having crafted your own!

## Camera Game

*From the Prologue: "Welcome to 'A Curious Romp': An Orientation to the Adventure"*

This activity comes from the world of environmental education but fosters the qualities—curiosity, kindness, awareness, transience, trust—that make mindfulness and improvisation so powerful.

The game is played in pairs; it's helpful for the facilitator (you!) to demonstrate with a volunteer before sending the pairs afield. In this demo, you act as the photographer and the volunteer acts as the camera—and a super-precious one at that. The photographer's first and most important job is to take great care of the "camera."

Before starting in earnest, the photographer should ask permission to guide the camera. ("Is it OK if I place my hands on your shoulder?" works well.) If the camera approves, you can move forward. If not, you can find another solution, maybe a hand on her elbow or guiding hand-to-hand.

From there, the camera closes her eyes and the photographer leads her slowly through the space to find a "photo" to share. Though the pair should avoid chit chat or joke-making to preserve the camera's experience of the vulnerability of moving without seeing, the photographer can (and even should) coach the camera on upcoming terrain: *We're about to take a small step up*. Or, *we're just about to switch to a gravel road but it's all good*. Do take good care—it can be particularly jarring for the camera to stumble when their eyes are closed.

Once in place, the photographer then frames the shot by gently positioning the camera's head. He might ask the camera to squat down, look up, or bend slightly at the waist to align with the shot. If the pair feels bold, maybe they'll lie down and look up. With that specific positioning set, the photographer gently squeezes the camera's earlobe, signaling the camera to open her the "shutter" of her eyes. A steady squeeze makes a longer exposure. A quick pinch means a shorter one. Once the photographer releases the ear lobe, the camera's eyes return to closed.

Each photographer takes five photos and then the camera and photographer switch roles to find new locations and take five more. When finished, invite everyone to join up again for a short—or extended if there's energy for it—debrief.

*Insider tips:*

- If you can get folks outside for the game, it usually offers a wider variety of interesting shapes, colors and textures for the photographers to share with their cameras. Alternately, finding an interesting indoor space can work well too.

- When you ask for a volunteer to serve as your demonstration "camera," promise that you'll take good care of that person. When they're done demonstrating, offer them public thanks or get the group to applaud. It's a vulnerable position and their courage deserves acknowledgment.

- Encourage creativity and boldness. Maybe the photographer wants a panorama—hold the earlobe while slowly turning the camera's head. Or maybe the photographer takes a "selfie" by pointing the camera at himself. The options are endless!

- Ask pairs who finish before others to remain silent as they return to the group, both to maintain their own subtle reflections and to preserve the focused experience for other pairs they might pass on their way by.

- During the debrief, it can help to ask separately for participants' experiences as photographer and as camera. It also helps to frame your questions to draw out the qualities you're trying to cultivate. Were there any particularly delightful images that stood out? Did their partner do anything to help them feel safe?

## Clover

*From Chapter 5: "Want Without Need: Balancing Aspiration and Acceptance"*
(from Pam Victor, Happier Valley Comedy School in Hadley, MA)

This word association exercise has a Zen-like meditative quality and breeds so much of what makes improv great: relaxed readiness, simple contribution, and an ongoing faith in the game's unfolding.

With the group in a circle, get a suggestion for a noun. When someone responds (let's say with "camera"), the whole group repeats that word in unison: "Camera!" The person to the left or right of the originator then generates a second word based on the first, like "snapshot." The next person in the circle word-associates with that new word ("snapshot"), doing their best to let go of any echo from the original word. For example, here one could say, "Moment," and that would clearly be independent from "camera." "Instagram" might still have some trace of it but be OK. And that's fine. "GoPro," on the other hand, would be relating to "camera" rather than responding to "snapshot." One way to help is to prompt a person to silently start with "When I hear 'snapshot' it makes me think of…."

Eventually, the goal—though it remains loosely held—is to circle back around to the original word, like a clover leaf. It can take a while but it will happen. Ideally, the momentum becomes obvious enough that the whole group could say the original word in unison. Once the word association returns to "camera," for example, start a second round with that same word and then, eventually, a third. The game finishes after the third round—when the "three-leaf clover" is complete.

As the game continues, it becomes a playful *experience* of the paradox we discussed in Chapter 6. The group returns to the origin word without *trying* to return to the origin word. They just word associate. Play the moment. Say what comes next. The endpoint emerges of its own accord.

*Insider Tips:*

- Help folks see that the word association need not be clever, provocative, or funny. It's simply what comes logically and naturally to mind in response to the immediately previous word.

- Though there are no wrong answers to offer, less-right answers might include a crafted joke, a non-sequitur, or a forced lurch toward the original word. Go for the natural extension of the word that came before.

- See if you can model the unhurried, effortless discovery that the game's going for and coach folks away from lurching too quickly back toward the first word. Admittedly, there's a paradox here: you're returning to the origin without trying to return to the origin. Pam Victor, the friend who introduced the game to me, calls it "skating the razor's edge of non-doing," going for "that eye-brightening sensation of recognition and natural association, which is quite different [from] an external, exerted force."

- Encourage participants to notice if they start judging their own (or others') words as "good" or "bad." Oftentimes, the words that seem like missteps or misdirections can take the game on a delightful side jaunt or can bring it back home in an unpredictable way. It's all good. Or, more accurately, it's all what it is.

## I Am A Tree

*From Chapter 3, "Stop and Go: Dancing with the Tension of Impulse vs. Pause"*

(From the Stanford Improvisors, for whom it serves as a "home" game [the Stanford mascot is The Tree, a Palo Alto redwood].)

You'll need three or more people to start. With the group in a circle, one person starts the scene by stepping into the center and taking the static pose of a tree, any tree. That person then declares, "I am a tree." A second person joins in, choosing something that would go with the tree. They might say, "I am the blue jay calling from the tree branch," and they clasp the tree person's arm. Or maybe they say, "I am the water running beneath the roots of the tree," and they lie down on the floor to wriggle at the tree person's feet. A third person then joins the first two, choosing their own identity and a pose that connects with the first two—"I am the lovers' carving in the bark on the tree" —while forming a heart with their hands near the tree person's torso.

At this point, the person who started the scene—here, the tree—chooses one of the others to take with her off stage ("I'll take the lovers' carving") and they leave the third person to remain in the center. That person repeats their identity ("I am the blue jay calling from the tree branch") and another two players add to the pose with identities connected to the jay. The person who started this round on stage alone—here, the jay—chooses one of them to come off stage, leaving another behind, and the cycle begins again. Rinse and repeat as needed.

*Insider Tips:*

- If you find folks trying to be funny by being random or creative, encourage players to connect their addition to what's on stage already.
- Each subsequent trio need not relate to the full image that came before it. In the example above, the blue jay is now in a completely new scene. The next person might say "I'm a Toronto Blue Jays baseball fan" and now there's no tree nearby.

- Encourage players to have the third person in any group link with the two that are already there—rather than just responding to the original and ignoring the second person who has come in.

- Once your group gets familiar with the game, it can make for a sweet conclusion to find a way for the last person to say, "I am a tree."

- For another fun alternative ending, let everyone in the group add a component to the final image.

## I Am Playing 'I Am A Tree'

*From Chapter 8: Meta-tation: The Benefits of a Bigger Picture*
(A version first iterated by Ted DesMaisons and Lisa Rowland)

This game reconfigures the improv standby introduced in Chapter 4, "I Am a Tree," by adding the notion of meta-perspective. In this version, you play by the same rules but encourage participants to find a meta-perspective (see what Lisa Rowland and I did with the title there?). Once the first element in a particular tableau has been established, can folks find a viewpoint that moves either further out or further into that first prompt? For example, in the normal version of the game, if someone started with "I am a soldier," another might say "I am the soldier's gun" or "I am a tear running down the soldier's face." Both those responses are there in the soldier's direct vicinity. They're both in the immediate circle of possibility.

A meta-perspective would pull out further: "I am a general assessing troop movements at command headquarters." Or, "I am the director setting up his Oscar-winning shot."

A reverse meta-perspective would dive further in: "I am the soldier's nervously beating heart." Or, "I am the soldier's memory of his son back home."

A horizontal meta-perspective would take us away from the immediate environment: "I am the horrors of war." Or, "I am the gunsmith who made the soldier's gun."

Whichever meta-direction participants take, encourage them to look for opportunities to jump, whether playfully or poignantly, to a new angle.

*Insider Tips:*

- Stay aware that this version of the game can get a bit heady with folks losing the playfulness, whimsy and devil-may-care enthusiasm they have for the simpler "I Am a Tree" game. Should that happen, remind folks that they don't have to be clever, interesting, or perfect. They are still using the same bold improv attitude they've been developing. As with the game Clover, they are holding an intention but they're holding it lightly.

- The game might go to some challenging or painful places as players get into and out of meta-perspectives. That's part of the design. Be ready for that amplified emotional field before it happens so you can stay calm and grounded.

### Line-at-a-Time Drawing (or Muse or Deity)

*From Chapter 4: "You, Then Me. Me, Then You: Finding the Delight in Shared Control"*
(from Cort Worthington, Haas School of Business, UC Berkeley)

This exercise takes the word-at-a-time structure (see "Word at a Time Exercises later in the Glossary of Games) and translates its wisdom to a visual form.

Two partners start with a blank piece of paper and a pen or marker, or maybe two markers of different colors. If they're drawing a character, they begin by putting two dots on the page about a third of the way down, evenly spaced horizontally. Maybe those dots will become eyes, maybe not. In any case, one person then makes a a line, a circle, or some other written "gesture" on the page. Then they put the pen down. The other person picks it up and makes another line or mark which may or may not connect with what's already there. Go back and forth, one line at a time. Eventually, an image or some new being emerges.

When one partner feels the time is right, they start writing the character's name or a title for the image, one *letter* at a time. In the end, they have a name or title for whatever has come into being through the process.

*Insider Tips:*

- In the spirit of shared control, discourage folks from striving to exercise more than their fair share of control—or from keeping their pen on the page for a super-long time.
- Each subsequent set of characters need not relate to the one(s) that came before. Also, you could call them "deities," "muses," or "notorious criminals." Whatever serves the group's needs.
- For an optional add-on, have partners introduce their newly created character to the rest of the room. Just as they created the drawing one line at a time, they can make the introduction and description one characteristic at a time. Their partner should enthusiastically "Yes/and" them, thus making each additional characteristic 100% right as it emerges.

## Metamorphic Circle

*From Chapter 9: Ch-ch-ch-changes: Learning to Go with the Flow*
(From William Hall, BATS Improv and Fratelli Bologna)

Begin with a group of players standing in a circle. Player A starts by passing a simple sound and movement combination to the next person, Player B. Player B then turns to Player C and passes that same sound and movement combo as best they can. Player C does the same, sending it along to Player D. And so on.

Note: however imperfect a reproduction of what was received, whatever gets passed along represents a new "perfect." Players should not try to "correct" or "undo" any seeming mistakes in interpretation. Instead, they should note what has come to them and pass that along as carefully as they possibly can. There's nothing to revert to. The world has changed.

*Insider Tips:*

- The more acute the observation and the more genuine the re-presentation, the more delightful the game becomes. There's something magical about effective imitation.
- Encourage participants to tune carefully into all the elements they could pass along: physical gestures, left-right orientation, facial expression, tone of voice, and the like. Can they widen their perception to include and pass along ALL of what they receive.
- Almost inevitably, folks will start to have laughs, coughs or confused gestures around the original task (or its subsequent translations). Those seemingly extraneous sounds and movements should also be included. They're part of what's gotten passed along. They're part of the new normal!
- Occasionally, you'll get an aspiring comic who introduces changes on purpose. If that happens, gently remind the group that the intention is *not* to do that but instead to convey the "message" as faithfully as possible.
- In a similar way, sometimes you'll catch players taking on a bit of a mocking tone for the movement they received. Coach them instead to *honor* what they've received. That will help preserve the group's cohesion—and manifests a healthy relationship to change.

## Positivity/Negativity Spectrum

*From Chapter 6: "The Power of Positivity: Creating a Different Default"* (created by Ted DesMaisons and Lisa Rowland)

This game illustrates how we might develop range in our typical responses (either on stage or in regular life), challenging our usual default of criticism or negativity.

Start by establishing a line of five people facing the rest of the group or "audience." Each of the five who have stepped up get a number, 1 to 5. A sixth player—or you as facilitator—goes up to person number 1 and offers a neutral line of dialogue. It works best if it's just a factual statement, nothing fancy or intriguing. The examples I used in the chapter were, "The guests will be here at six o'clock." And, "I decided to sign up for ballroom dance class."

Each of the five players will get the chance to respond to the same neutral prompt, making sure to proceed as if that given line of dialogue were real and true. (In improv jargon, not "blocking" the offer.) In other words, the player responding won't deny the reality of what's been presented.

But here's the angle that makes the game instructive: Person Number 1 responds super negatively. Person Number 2 responds with mild negativity. Number 3 responds neutrally. Number 4 comes back with something mildly positive. And Number 5 rejoices with wild positivity.

As we mentioned in the chapter, an exchange might go something like this:

**Neutral offer:** "Francine, it looks like we're going to have to go to the market today."

*Person #1:* "Uggh! I hate the market! It's always so crowded, and all the produce is always rotten already."

*Person #2:* "Oh did you forget to go on your way home from work? Again?"

*Person #3:* "OK."

*Person #4:* "Oh good. We just ran out of potatoes, so we can get some more."

*Person #5:* "Perfect! We can bring our reusable bags and walk home along the coast afterwards. How does that sound?"

Or perhaps like this:

**Neutral offer:** "I brought another log in to help make a great fire."

*Person #1:* "Dammit, I just cleaned up the fireplace and finally got rid of all the old ashes! Arrrrgggghhh!!"

*Person #2:* "Oh, did you forget to call to fill the oil company to have them refill the furnace? Again?"

*Person #3:* "That sounds reasonable."

*Person #4:* "Thank you. That was very sweet of you."

*Person #5:* "Yeeeeaahhhh, baby!!!!! Buuuurrrrrnnnnn!!!!"

Once a round is finished, rotate everyone so that the intiator slides into position #1. Position #1 slides to Position #2, and so on. If you have more than six people in your group—the five responders and the one initiator—include your "audience members" in the rotation so the audience member becomes the next initiator and responder #5 re-joins the audience.

## Sound Ball

*From Chapter 15: It's Not About You: Finding the Ease of Wider Concern*
(First learned with the Stanford Improvisors)

This exercise can serve as a foundatoin for moving past self-judgment, fear of failure and restrictions on spontaneity. It's also a great way to play with the theme of Chapter 15—"It's Not About You"—by encouraging a focus on any part of the game *other than* paralyzing self concern.

To start, have the group stand in a circle. One person makes a sound—any sound—while also making a throwing gesture towards another person in the group. That second person then "receives" the sound with a physical motion, as if catching a ball or a sack or a ray of light and—importantly—repeats the sound sent to them as best they can. Then, without hesitation, the receiver sends a new sound with a new tossing motion to another person in the circle. Keep the sound moving quickly and boldly to get everyone involved.

*Insider Tips:*

- Make sure to get the body involved and not just the voice. An active, athletic stance—as you would need if you were prepared to catch a real ball—helps loosen up the mind.
- Encourage participants *not* to predict or plan what sound they'll make if the ball comes their way. Better to receive the one sent and then send a new one that emerges of its own accord.
- Coach folks to actively *receive* the sound sent to them before sending one out. It's a great affirmation to the sender and helps build a spirit of generosity.
- Add your own variations as your group gets better with Sound Ball. We've played City Ball, Vegetable Ball, Names that Start with M Ball, and so on. Keep encouraging folks not to have their responses teed up or waiting in the wings to use. Or, even better, let them have a response in the wings—but then choose another one in the moment.

## Three Things

*From Chapter 14: A Cup of Courage: Taking Action in the Face of Fear*
(Learned from BATS Improv in San Francisco)

This energy-builder works in any setting where you've got a few minutes between other activities, but it's also awesome as a standalone.

The whole group forms a circle and chants in unison, "Three things!" while bouncing their fists as if pounding a table. One person initiates the play by turning to an immediate neighbor and asking that person to name three things that fit a particular category. *"Three brands of cars!" "Three things you'd find at the back of your closet!"* or *"Three terrible excuses for showing up late!"* would all work, for example. As quickly as possible, the person giving the responses declares them with authority. When they have finished, the group again chants, "Three things!" and the person who just responded gives a category to another person in the circle. Play continues until everyone has had a chance to provide and respond to a category.

Maybe the answers will end up fitting the category "appropriately"; maybe they won't. Or maybe the same answer will come out twice in one round. It's all good. The crucial key: generate and celebrate the quick response. You're trying to access a type of wisdom that comes before cognitive planning. We're going for speed over "quality."

*Insider tips:*

- Some folks will lessen the tension of the challenge by adding a little preamble before each response. Maybe they repeat the category or toss another time-staller in: "For military vehicles, I would choose a tank. I would choose a jeep. And I'd go with a Navy Destroyer." Much better—and more rewarding to just say "Tank! Jeep! Destroyer!"
- Responders can build their own confidence by counting with authority on their fingers. Other players can help out by nodding or making small affirmative sounds: "Mm-hmm;

yes; right, of course," though they don't want to get so loud as to upstage the person on the spot.

- While you don't want to get stuck on "accuracy"—it doesn't really matter if a response fits the category— players should at least *try* to have the responses fit. Throwing out completely random words misses the point here.

- More abstract categories can stimulate a little more creativity—and a lot more laughs. "Three vegetables you'd find at the grocery store!" will work fine. "Three unpublished Harry Potter titles" might be even more fun.

- Unlike most of the other spontaneity exercises where you're trying to keep players' minds fresh, it's OK for players to "plan" a delightful category before their turn.

- Feel free to get creative with variations. Western Massachusetts improv maven Pam Victor introduced me to "Seven Things," a more intense version of the game where folks have to name seven things in each category—Whoa, I bet you wouldn't have guessed that!—and the other members of the group count out loud with an urgent chant as the responses emerge. For example, if someone suggested "Seven toppings you wouldn't expect for a hot dog..." you might hear responses like:

Marshmallow. *One!*
Chocolate sauce. *Two!*
Crushed glass. *Three!*
Sand. Four!
Earthworms. *Five!*
Semen. *Six!*
Angst. Seven!
Seven Things!

This version does a great job of short-circuiting the usual censors in the brain and thus grants access to a different level of creativity.

## Three-Words-at-a-Time Poems

*From Chapter 7: Chaos Theory: Balancing Preparation and Pandemonium*
(Adapted by Ted DesMaisons from similar exercises)

Here's another variation on the Word-at-a-Time game described in detail a little later in this Glossary: Three-Words-at-a-Time Poems.

Participants start by sitting in a circle, each with a blank sheet of paper and a pen or pencil in front of them. After a bit of instruction, every person writes the first three words of a poem—maybe it's a two-word title and the first word of the rest of the poem or maybe it's the first three words of what will end up as a seven-word title. It's up to the writer. Once finished with those three words, each author passes their incomplete poem clockwise, and the next person adds the next three words of the poem, looking to justify, support and build on what's already there. Then each poem gets passed again, until it makes its way around the circle once or twice. Each author who started a poem gets to finish it—with only three additional words.

*Insider Tips:*

- As mentioned in the chapter, one could choose to play the game with the direction, "Pass the poem on when you're done with your three words." Or one could use the instruction "Hold your poem and we'll pass them together." Choose the directions to match—or mitigate—the mood and personality of the group as needed.
- As with other word-at-a-time exercises, emphasize that the point isn't to be clever or funny. It's to honor and continue what's come before.
- Depending on the size of your group, maybe it makes sense

to have the poems go around two or even three times before each finishes up in the hands of its first author, who then adds the concluding three words.

- Assuming you've got time, conduct a spoken-out-loud poetry slam where each participant recites "their" poem. This makes for a crowd-pleasing and hugely fulfilling wrap-up. Often, it's uncanny how the creations actually sound like... poetry.

## What Comes Next?

*From Chapter 11: Adventure Time: Seeking the Joy of New Experience*
(A classic learned from Barbara Scott, BATS Improv)

This game offers a great way to engage with spontaneity—to trust one's impulses—AND to honor one's own limits and preferences. It's a great way to learn what delights each player and their partner.

To start, Partner A invites a story opening from Partner B by asking, "What comes first?" Partner B responds with a short sentence. Partner A then asks, "What comes next?" Partner B continues to respond until Partner A hears something she's not delighted by, in which case she responds with a wide-eyed smile and a high-pitched voice, cheerily declaring "Nope!" Partner B then asks, "What comes next?" and Partner A now gets to continue the story.

They continue until Partner A makes a contribution that doesn't delight Partner B, and B says "Nope!" The questions and responses continue until the story comes to a natural conclusion, switching asker and responder only when there's been a cheery "Nope!"

*Insider Tips:*

- Remember that a player doesn't need to know why they're not delighted by what came before. No justification or explanation is needed. Their hesitation doesn't even need to make sense to them. They just have to track the previous answer, and if they don't light up at the suggestion, they get to say: "Nope!"[2]

- Though the "Nope!" can be given freely, make sure that it doesn't get hostile, angry or dismissive. The player need not insult or berate the person who offered the suggestion. They're expressing a preference, and they're still in the game together. It's just a light-hearted "Nope," one that rebuffs the offer but keeps them connected to their partner.

- Encourage players in a pair to start a new story if their first one finishes before others in the larger group are done. Sometimes, some pairs will get a couple complete stories in before others have finished one.

### Word-at-a-Time Exercises

*From Chapter 4, "You, Then Me. Me, Then You: Finding the Delight in Shared Control"*
(Also from the Stanford Improvisors)

Word-at-a-Time represents shared control at its most raw. You need at least two people but can play with a group of any size. Directions are straightforward: each person offers one word toward a sentence or paragraph or story that's being built. And everyone continues until the sentence, etc. comes to a natural conclusion.

Though it's not necessary, it can help to offer some minimal structure. Maybe the players are crafting a letter to a customer service department. Maybe they're making up an ancient proverb, a bit of valuable wisdom to carry forward. Or maybe they get the title of a story that's never been told. (If they're making up a fairy tale, it might start with "Once... upon... a... time...." Feel free to experiment!

*Insider Tips:*

---

[2] In this way, the game becomes a great mindfulness practice too. Players are repeatedly asking themselves, *Am I excited by what I'm hearing right now?*

- Encourage players to just say what comes next. They don't need to be funny or clever. Their role at any given moment may be just to offer an "a" or "the." Whatever is needed. Whatever serves the whole.

- The more animated and natural-sounding folks can be, the easier the game becomes. Hesitant, monotone Gregorian chant-like utterances tend to slow things down and lower the creative energy.

- Getting specific with names of characters can snap a story into life.

- Reincorporation of elements that have already been mentioned usually proves immensely satisfying for audience and performer alike. For example, if an early character likes to play marbles, maybe that hobby somehow helps her solve a problem later. It can help to look for such opportunities.

# bibliography

Alter, Cara Hale, *The Credibility Code: How to Project Confidence and Competence When It Matters Most* (Meritus Books: USA, 2012).

Brezsny, Rob, *Pronoia is the Antidote for Paranoia* (Televisionary: San Rafael, CA, 2005).

Cuddy, Amy, *Presence: Bringing Your Boldest Self to Your Biggest Challenges* (Orion Books: London, 2016).

Da Vinci's Notebook, "Title of the Song" from *The Life and Times of Mike Fanning*, Uncle Buford Records, 2000.

Davis, et al, "Thankful for the little things: A meta-analysis of gratitude interventions. J Couns Psychol. 2016 Jan;63(1):20-31. doi: 10.1037/cou0000107. Epub 2015 Nov 16.

Dickens, Leah R. (2017) Using Gratitude to Promote Positive Change: A Series of Meta-Analyses Investigating the Effectiveness of Gratitude Interventions, Basic and Applied Social Psychology, 39:4, 193-208, DOI: 10.1080/01973533.2017.1323638.

Dweck, Carol, *Mindset: The New Psychology of Success* (Ballantine Books: New York, 2006).

Jagodowski, TJ and Pasquesi, David, with Pam Victor, *Improvisation at the Speed of Life: The TJ and Dave Book* (Solo Roma: Chicago, IL, 2015).

Johnstone, Keith, *Impro: Improvisation and the Theatre* (Methuen: New York, 1981).

Kabat-Zinn, Jon, *Coming to Our Senses: Healing Ourselves and the World Through Mindfulness* (Hyperion: New York, NY, 2005).

-------------- *Wherever You Go, There You Are* (Hyperion: New York, NY, 1994).

Kelly, Kraft-Todd, Schapira, Kossowsky, and Reiss, "The Influence of Patient-Clinician Relationship on Healthcare Outcomes: A Systematic Review and Meta-Analysis of Randomized Controlled Trials," PLOS One. 2014; 9(6): e101191

Macy, Joanna, *Active Hope: How to Face the Mess We're In Without Going Crazy* (New World Library: Novato, CA, 2012),

Evelyn McFarlane and James Saywell, *If (Questions for the Game of Life)* (Villard: New York, 1995).

------------ *If²...: 500 Questions for the Game of Life* (Villard: New York, 1996).

Nachmanovitch, Stephen, *Free Play: The Power of Improvisation in Life and the Arts* (Jeremy Tarcher: New York, NY, 1990).

Palmer, Parker, *A Hidden Wholeness: The Journey Toward an Undivided Life* (Jossey-Bass: San Francisco, CA, 2004).

Perel, Esther, *Mating in Captivity* (Harper: New York, 2006).

Rodenburg, Patsy, *The Second Circle: How to Use Positive Energy for Success in Every Situation* (WW Norton: New York, NY, 2008).

Ryan Madson, Patricia, *Improv Wisdom: Don't Prepare, Just Show Up* (Random House: New York, 2005).

Stillgoe, John, *Outside Lies Magic* (Walker Publishing: USA, 1998).

Tarrant, John, *Bring Me the Rhinoceros* (Shambhala: Boston, 2008).

Wilcox, David, "Leave it Like it Is," from How Did You Find Me Here, A & M Records, 1989.

------------ "Show the Way," from *Big Horizon*, A & M Records, 1994.

Wiseman, Richard, *The Luck Factor* (Talk Books: United Kingdom, 2003).

Zweig, Connie and Adams, Jeremiah, *Meeting the Shadow: The Hidden Power of the Dark Side of Human Nature* (Jeremy Tarcher: Los Angeles, CA, 1991).

**FROM THE INTERNET**

Sandee LaMotte, CNN, "Jazz Improv and your brain: the key to creativity?", Updated 7:58 pm ET, Sunday April 29, 2018. https://www.cnn.com/2018/04/29/health/brain-on-jazz-improvisation-improv/index.html

Mandy Len Catron, "To Fall in Love With Anyone, Do This" from "Modern Love" in *The New York Times*, January 9, 2015. https://www.nytimes.com/2015/01/11/fashion/modern-love-to-fall-in-love-with-anyone-do-this.html

Claire Lew, "The 25 most popular icebreaker questions based on four years of data," https://m.signalvnoise.com/the-25-most-popular-icebreaker-questions-based-on-four-years-of-data-893df9b27531, accessed October 15, 2018.

"Pat Kelly, 'Thought Leader,' gives talk that will inspire your thoughts," CBC Radio, https://www.youtube.com/watch?time_continue=241&v=_ZBKX-6Gz6A. Published June 8, 2016.

"The Science of Gratitude: More Benefits than Expected; 26 Studies and Counting," https://www.happierhuman.com/the-science-of-gratitude/, site visited Nov 10, 2018.

# acknowledgments

In the same way that we all owe our existence to the generosity and sword-forging of uncountable influences, so does this book. The cover may display my name, but many others have contributed. (Except for any errors, regrets or egregious omissions—those all belong to me.)

My Mom, Kathleen, encouraged and refined my creative powers from my very first days and she has improved the lives of thousands through her written words. I will consider myself lucky to have a similar influence. My Dad, Bob, and my stepmom, Patty, have provided a consistent love that has carried me (and sometimes it feels like I mean that literally) through the ups and downs of my life. I will be eternally grateful. My elder brother, David, and my younger sister, Jennifer, have been my dear friends and biggest fans along the way. I haven't told them often enough how much I appreciate the kindness and steadiness of our three-way bond. My nephews, Andrew and Tyler, and my niece, Madison, are kind, playful, and observant young adults. They give me hope and reason to keep bringing positivity to the world.

Some family members come through circumstance rather than through blood. Carol Glover helped raise me and took good care during great challenges. Her story of a mystical experience opened me up to the mysteries of the world. David and Tina Treadwell and their whole clan—Andy, David, Ed, and Jon—have always welcomed, encouraged and inspired me. I love them dearly and feel their love in return.

I have had the great fortune of learning from many brilliant women who opened my mind, softened my heart and catalyzed my love for teaching. Joanna Macy demonstrated a full-spectrum courage for facing the immense suffering of our planet and taught me with humor, wisdom, and insight. More than anyone I have ever met, she is a *bodhisattva*. Rachael Kessler showed me how to ground learning in the beauty of life's mysteries. I and the world of education miss her dearly. Karen Pryor reinforced the power of kind and clear instruction. Carol Dweck's book *Mindset* planted a seed of growth in me that continues to bloom. And, of course, Patricia Ryan Madson, my improvisation instructor at Stanford, now-mentor and dear friend, has always demonstrated this playful, mindful approach to life that I share with you here. She lives this path every day and gives as gorgeously and generously as a fountain does water. I pray that even a touch of her grace comes through these pages.

Many kind men deepened my insight, opened my heart, and forged my leadership skills during my time at Stanford University and beyond. Dr. Doug Daher first connected me to the goodness and greatness of being a man. Harrison Simms, Hugh Vazquez, and Michael Taller stood with generous power to show me the range and responsibility of my societal privilege. Jim Thompson demonstrated the same kindness, humility, curiosity and passion in his teaching that he asked us to develop as leaders. Professor Michael Ray cleared space and took heat for alternative thinkers like me at the business school. I remember his gift often. Luca Canever combined precision and heart with an ability to look for life's clues below the surface. And Dr. Jim Sharp helped me develop a kind of resilience, hope and self-care that I didn't know was possible.

I taught Religious Studies and Philosophy for twelve years at Northfield Mount Hermon School in western Massachusetts and that institution, that land and those colleagues had a huge impact. I had wide-ranging freedom, ample opportunity for development, and generous support for becoming a better teacher. Thank you,

Gary Partenheimer, Meg Donnelly, Martha Neubert, John Christiansen, Sarah White Albertyn, Peter Vearling, Tami James, Bryan Dunphy, Betty Stookey, Lara Freeman, TJ Skulstad-Brown, Tom Pratt, John Adams, Chris Edler, Nicole Durr, Bea Garcia, Roberto Irurueta, Jim Burstein, Sarah Warren, Jonathan Crowley, John Carroll, and so so many others.

The world of improvisation has given me unending joy and a time-honored method for living life as an adventure. Of course, that world is made up of specific people. Scott Allen invited me to that first dorm-based class when I was a freshman and forever altered my future. The Stanford Improvisors showed me the delight of belonging to a legacy that stretches over years and gave me a chance to recharge my love for performance. Shawn Kinley and the Loose Moose Theatre in Calgary, Alberta, sharpened my skills and sparked intellectual connections that became a fire of investigation. The good people of BATS Improv in San Francisco have become the dearest of colleagues and playmates. They regularly set a jaw-dropping standard for delightful collaboration and unmitigated joy. The Improv Playhouse of San Francisco—Tim Orr, Regina Saisi, Ben Johnson, Rafe Chase, Kat Zdan, and Remi Frazier—introduced me to depths in these waters I hadn't known existed. Dave Dennison demonstrates the genius in patient, detailed calm on stage. William Hall taught me the wisdom within the literal and figurative masks we wear. And, as she has for so many others, Rebecca Stockley generously offered her hard-earned insight and ebullient enthusiasm for my first efforts to bring improv wisdom to other arenas.

My associates—and friends—in the Applied Improvisation Network have time and again proven themselves the greatest of collaborators and inspirations. Cort Worthington helped me articulate the connections between improvisation and spirituality and our first retreat will last as a highlight in my life. Kat Koppett has offered both structure and sass to my thinking. Paul Z. Jackson has given me healthy challenge and deep respect, both of which I greatly appreciate. Drew Tarvin made me laugh—often—as he eased my entry into the logistics of writing a book. Pam Victor taught me about irreverence, trusting the improv gods, and getting back up off the mat. Joel and Ellen Veenstra showed me how much impact giving hearts can have. Jeanne Lambin and Elin Fredrikson gave me keys that opened new doors of adventure—and I don't think I'll ever reach the end of that hallway. Andy Middleton treated me to the joy of connecting improvisation with the wild coastland of Wales. Embodiment never felt better. I regret that I cannot thank every Applied Improv colleague by name.

So many mindfulness teachers—both those I have met and those I have not—have influenced my life and deepened my teaching. Thich Nhat Hanh introduced me to meditation and has served as a role model for gentle grace for close to thirty years. Jakusho Kwong demonstrated the infectious joy of a mindful heart. And Issho Fujita shaped my lessons and reshaped my practice in ways he'll never know. The good teachers of the Center for Mindfulness at the University of Massachusetts—Jon Kabat-Zinn, Saki Santorelli, Florence Meleo-Meyer, Lynn Koerbel, Paul Galvin, Bob Stahl, and Carolyn West—established a valuable benchmark of high-quality, high-integrity instruction. I do my best to live up to the gifts they shared with me. Chris Cullen and James Gibbs (and through them, Richard Burnett) of the Mindfulness in Schools Project showed me what playful mindfulness can look like. The way they walked their talk spoke volumes. Doug Worthen and Jessica Morey introduced me to worlds of possibility in bringing mindfulness to young people. Their dedication, heartfulness, and partnership improve the world. My .b teaching colleagues Charise Minerva Spencer, Peter Franklin and Lisa Wellstead have delighted and supported me along the path. Together, we've done good work. Gregory Kramer and Gil Fronsdahl have blessed me with their gentle-man-ly wisdom, insight and instruction. The Dharma shines brightly in them.

Margot Silk Forrest offered her skillful editor's eye to shorten and sharpen my expression in these pages. Jelena Mirkovic brought a keen eye and an artful touch—as well as a boatload of patience with my endless tweaking—to the cover design. It's good to work with people who know what they're doing. My cats, Luna and Marley, have kept me good company throughout the writing process.

And lastly, I have two souls to thank more than any others. Melissa Stevens offered me love, friendship, and laughter—more than I'd ever known—as we made our multi-creature home and developed a resilient, joyful partnership during my final five years in Massachusetts. She fed my intellectual curiosities and built foundations of affirmation, both external and internal, that let me launch into this bigger vision. I am a better man because of this woman and our continued connection means more than words can say.

From our very first fortune-guided moments on stage together, Lisa Rowland—my co-conspirator on the "Monster Baby" podcast that spawned this book—has been the kind of friend I dreamed of all my life. Her huge heart, powerhouse mind, relentless curiosity, and knee-buckling humor all make their presence known when she walks in a room. Lisa lives big—and inspires me to follow her lead—at the same time that she leaves plenty of room for vulnerability, her own and that of others. If you've listened to the podcast, you know that her wisdom runs throughout these pages and that many of the words here first sprung from her mouth. I remain ever grateful for her willingness to share that wisdom so generously.

To the uncountable places, people and experiences that have shaped this book, I offer my sincerest gratitude. May my efforts pay those great gifts fully forward.

# PLAYFUL
## MINDFULNESS

**For more Playful Mindfulness resources, please visit:**

## www.playfulmindfulness.info

To listen to the Monster Baby Podcast (A Curious Romp through the Worlds of Mindfulness and Improvisation") with author Ted DesMaisons and improvisor Lisa Rowland, search on iTunes and other podcast platforms or please visit:

## www.monsterbabypodcast.com

# about the author

Ted DesMaisons has been synthesizing innovative approaches to collaborative learning and personal development for over 30 years.

After earning degrees from Stanford's Graduate School of Business and Harvard Divinity School, Ted taught religious studies and philosophy for twelve years at Northfield Mount Hermon, a private boarding school in western Massachusetts.

He trained to teach Mindfulness Based Stress Reduction (MBSR) with Jon Kabat-Zinn, Saki Santorelli, Florence Meleo-Meyers and a host of others at the University of Massachusetts Medical School and has since served as the exclusive US Partner for the UK-based Mindfulness in Schools Project.

He has studied, taught and performed improvisation internationally, including at the Loose Moose Theater in Calgary, Alberta and BATS Improv in San Francisco where he serves as Board Vice President. He has also trained intensively with renowned UK acting, voice and presence coach Patsy Rodenburg.

Currently, Ted teaches Playful Mindfulness and voice and presence courses through Stanford University's Continuing Studies program. He also co-hosts the Monster Baby Podcast ("A Curious Romp through the Worlds of Mindfulness and Improvisation") which reaches listeners in more than 63 countries. www.monsterbabypodcast.com

He lives a 10-minute walk from the stunning coastline of Daly City, California, and shares his home with Luna and Marley, two quirky and charismatic spotted Ocicats.

CPSIA information can be obtained
at www.ICGtesting.com
Printed in the USA
BVHW042140120319
542472BV00003B/3/P